# The Making of a Jewel

## Lisa Denny

PUBLISHED by PARABLES
*Earthly Stories with a Heavenly Meaning*

Title: The Making Of A Jewel
　　　The Diaries: A testimony of one rescued from the Pit.

All Rights Reserved
Copyright: September, 2017
ISBN 978-1-945698-29-3

*Most scripture references are from the New King James Version. Copyright 1982 by Thomas Nelson, Inc. Used by permission. All rights reserved.*

Published By Parables
www.PublishedByParables.com

# The Making of a Jewel

## Lisa Denny

**PUBLISHED by PARABLES**
*Earthly Stories with a Heavenly Meaning*

# *Jewels*
Rev. W. O. Cushing    Malachi 3:17[1]

   *1. When He cometh, when He cometh*
*To make up His jewels*
*All His jewels, precious jewels*
*His loved and His own.*
*2.   He will gather He will gather*
*The gems for His Kingdom*
*All the pure ones, all the bright ones*
*His loved and His own.*
 *3. Little children, little children*
    *Who love their Redeemer*
    *Are the jewels, precious jewels*
    *His loved and His own.*
*Chorus    Like the stars of the morning*
        *His bright crown adorning*
        *They shall shine in their beauty*
        *Bright gems for His crown.*

'....those who fear the LORD and who meditate on His name. "They shall be Mine....on the day that I make them My jewels".....'         Malachi 3:16

---

1    Alexander's Hymns No. 3. Edited by Charles M. Alexander. Marshall, Morgan & Scott, Ltd. Jewels. No. 321.

# Table Of Contents

| | |
|---|---|
| Preface | p. 2 |
| Introduction | p. 3 |
| Part 1   Little Lisa   Lost Innocence | p. 6 |
| Chapter 1 | p. 7 |
| 2 | p. 10 |
| 3 | p. 15 |
| 4 | p. 28 |
| | |
| Part 2   Search for selfhood | |
| Bruised reed to Beautiful woman | p. 41 |
| Chapter 1 | p. 44 |
| 2 | p. 63 |
| 3 | p. 75 |
| 4 | p. 114 |
| 5 | p. 141 |
| | |
| Part 3   Facets of Being.  Is it worth it? | p. 187 |
| Chapter 1 | p. 188 |
| 2 | p. 237 |
| 3 | p. 272 |
| 4 | p. 296 |
| Epilogue | p. 329 |
| Additional Bits and Pieces | p. 332 |

# THE MAKING OF A JEWEL

##  Preface

Dear Reader,

The bulk of this book is dated diary entries belonging to a woman of middle age who is looking back over her life. From a time of thinking, 'yea right, as if that works, is reality', to the now when she knows the truth of Scripture, that God is reality, that His way works best and that He is unchangingly trustworthy.

But how to explain, or show this to others?

And so the need to put this book together was born.

It is not about correct doctrine or theology. It is about her journey towards and maintaining a relationship with the biblical triune God. May it make you consider your own need for relationship with Him.

This is her truth, no one else's. And though at times she may sound to be harbouring bitterness and the unforgiveness of a victim, feeling very misunderstood and wrongly judged, she does no longer. In her Father's world there are no victims. There are many others who have a life far worse, who have and are experiencing unimaginable horror because of abuse. However this was God's way to break her and to remake her as He wanted and needed.

Being a mostly content nobody in the eyes of the world, she prays you will come to see God and worship Him for what He eagerly does to and for repentant 'nobodies' still.

In Christ,
Lisa Denny.

Whatever makes us more and more able to enjoy making much of God is a mercy. For there is no greater joy than joy in the greatness of God. And if we must suffer to see this and savor it most deeply, then suffering is a mercy. And Christ's call to take up our cross and join him on the Calvary road is love.[2]

---

2   John Piper Don't waste your life. Crossway Books 2003 p. 62

# Introduction

It is September. Spring. I am forty-four years old. The blue skies are dotted with white puffy clouds; the land is green, the air fragrant and filled with morning bird song.

I am inside.

Facing Martin.

We have met often over the last couple of years. This is the third room I have sat in. He now knows that for me the door has to be left slightly open. I have to be seated so I can see out the window, to focus on the blue sky beyond the gently swaying branches, to escape. He cannot position himself between me and these places of safety. And he must not come too close!

He tried once. Watching my face intently, rolling his chair across the carpet, inching closer, closer still, never taking his eyes from my face.

I lurch my chair violently backwards.

He stopped.

He had come close enough.

The painting that had been leaning against a wall in the previous room was now hanging on this soft creamy, wall. Those big roughened, hardened hands, scarred, emerging from a swirling, misty darkness, so gently cradling and protecting the tiny sparrow, which had taken refuge in one palm, and was now settled, sleeping, covered and hedged by the other hand, mindless of the storm without.

But today was different.

As much as I was desperate to blindly soar out of the window or lose myself in that painting, my sight, my attention was riveted on those heavy red lines. So red. So angry. And they were all aimed at and hitting her.

Martin had drawn up my family tree on a big piece of white paper, pinned up on his board. A couple of generations before and the one after me, including my exhusband, his family and our children, were identified there.

Then Martin used a red marker to draw lines showing in stark reality, those not-so-nice-a relationships between her and certain family members.

All those red lines around her; pinning her, trapping her in a net of angry physical and verbal lashings. A tightening net of fear, of darkening suffocating hopelessness, lostness, selfhate and guilt. I sat there immobilised by sadness for her.

**But I am Her!**

Martin had been shaking his balding, grandfatherly head with each new line he drew, muttering how it 'explained a lot' and how he was 'amazed I'd survived'. I was momentarily startled. Why the amazement? This had been my life. I had thought it was normal. I had lived it as such – everyone has problems don't they? And yet.......

Seated on that soft sofa in that quiet safe room, with my loving supportive husband of nearly six years, gripping my hand, I gazed at that 'little girl'. She hurt so much. Her throat was tight and sore from trying to get someone to see. Her eyes hot and dry. She had struggled for so long, against so much, never accepting, wanting to hope that there was something better, something more, needing to believe this. But after each crushing blow the struggle to rise and move, to continue became a little harder, till she began to wonder if this time it would be the last, or even if it was worthwhile at all....

And the guilt! For all that was around her now was so much better, she was living the impossible, God had given so much, icing as well as the chocolate cake....yet the weight of all that, that which was past, the seemingly continual consequences and the pain, that never ending pain and then new pain, pain she could have never imagined possible that just would not end was becoming too much... again...

NO!

This time I have Him.

I pulled myself upright, feeling my husband shift his attention from those lines back to my face. I glanced out at the sky. It was still blue. Still that blue. I took a deep, shaky breath...

No more, by God's grace no more.

So my Lord God, help me and others like me to stand, wait, to be still. To be one of those who stands in the midst of personal chaos

and uncertainty and declares faith in You despite what is around them – that You will hold them and will take them through the shadowy valleys and into the warm clean sunshine.
So that I will not be ashamed and that all shall know that You, the LORD are my Saviour and Redeemer, the Mighty One of Jacob.

> *Will not the End explain?*
> *The crossed endeavour;*
> *Earnest purpose foiled?*
> *The clinging weariness,*
> *The inward strain;*
> *Will not the End explain?*
> *Amy Carmichael.*

# Part One

## Little Lisa. Lost Innocence.

Jeremiah 2:32 *Can a young virgin forget her ornaments or a bride her attire? Yet my people have forgotten Me days without number.*

'Get me out of this and I'll come back to Church.'

I don't know if those words were cried out aloud or not but suddenly I was alive as never before in recent memory.

The smouldering candle struggling to be, that was inside – that was me -- roared into glorious warmth, a brilliant steady flame.

Everything was abruptly deafeningly still and quiet.

Hope and joy swirled around and settled in me.

I became aware I could dream. I had not for so long.

There was a tomorrow. I, yes I could have a tomorrow.

'All the way no matter what, just don't leave me Yahweh', became my mantra.

So my dear Reader I hope you have settled back, cuppa within comfortable reach and that you are encouraged by your reading of my journey, my moulding. Or as a dear friend once put it – 'the making of a life marred by sin into something beautiful by God's loving care'. (Philippians 1:6)

## Chapter 1

Other counsellors had introduced me to 'little Lisa' in the past. One, a middle-aged female, had encouraged me as an adult to consider how I could help her.

I was challenged to consider what I do if I could come face to face with 'little Lisa'. Days later I wrote – I'd hold her tightly but gently. I'd swing her up high, round and round till she squealed with gleeful delight and abandonment. I'd joyfully smell her soft curly hair and cuddle her warm wriggly body and I would tell her how beautiful she is and how much I love her, no matter what...

After considering my scribblings she asked me to write 'little Lisa' a letter. So some days later, taking up a pen I wrote --

Dearest little Lisa,

I know Mother and Father tried to do their best, in the only way they knew how, in their circumstances to love you but you don't and cannot understand this. All you knew was the confusion you felt at not being cuddled and loved as you wanted. As you grew this became worse as you realised you were not heard or understood and the feelings of not belonging became so big you wondered out loud if you were adopted. At that time you could not understand why your cheek wore Mother's handprint or why you had to wait for Father to come home from the paddocks.

Then the guilt started, for you must love your parents. But do they love you? You were not sure. If they could not, who could, who would? Me, of course little one, I love you. You are so full of love and so loving, how could I not! And you, just because you are, deserve someone who will love you for you and not for what you can do for them...

This particular counsellor had also encouraged Lisa to go back through her diaries, to sit and think and feel and write out the memories that came. Some of these memories are what, you my dear Reader will be considering along with her diary entries.

# THE MAKING OF A JEWEL

But none of these counsellors had made me consider 'little Lisa' as forcibly or as vividly as Martin had that September morning.

Little Lisa had grown up in a world alien to most now. A carefree world though perhaps a hard isolated one. Any town of reasonable size was around one to two hours away by car, where groceries were purchased monthly, usually when our cattle or sheep were taken to market.

By the time she was thirteen she could bake bread, tarts, roasts, throw a fleece bigger than herself, endlessly fill metal buckets with stones and stride across ploughed ground, turn over five hundred bales of hay in a day, drive tractors and bulldozers as well as ordinary vehicles, milk cows, churn butter, inject, ring, draft and drench lambs and sheep, help slaughter sheep and cut up, and though she could skin a rabbit her fists were a little small to do a sheep (mind you the 'big Lisa' would feel a tad green doing this now!), chop wood and keep all her fingers and toes, shoot a 22rifle which she preferred to the shotgun that kicked against her shoulder leaving it bruised, preserve fruit and vegetables, plunge sheep into the dip, make sauces, jams and jellies, and the boring household stuff like dusting, washing, ironing but with the ones you heated on the wood stove hob, play the piano, crochet, sew, waltz, etc. Then there was the fishing, swimming in dams and creeks, horse riding, bonfires, crackers, rockets, Catherine wheels, tadpoling, yabbying, tree climbing and cliff climbing (shoeless of course), bottle feeding and playing with lambs and calves, warm sunshine, big open skies, long green grass. Quiet. And time.

Time to think, to wonder....

And God.

Lisa actually cannot remember a time when she thought there was no God, noone up there, watching and doing things. She used to get away, go walkabout, to have time alone. Lying down in the grassy paddock, watching clouds changing shapes and dissolve into the blue, and talking to this God.

This God who made all she could see and feel, as laughingly she would gently stop the hungry lambs from nibbling her ears. How amazing it was that you could put a dried, wrinkled, dead looking seed – well actually lots and lots of seeds -- into warm, moist, dark soil, wait a bit and the land would become a moving sea of green. Lisa could not understand or accept because of all that was around her that there was nothing after you died. This seemed to make life, the effort of making, sustaining and living it rather pointless.

Why bother?

Why did her father say, 'There is no God, you just die like a dog'? Whatever that was supposed to mean!

Sometime between the age of six and ten, before Lisa went to school but after the Fire, there is a memory of being transfixed by a human 'crow' one Sunday in a tiny, wooden country Church.

A tall, skinny man, with a wide, white collar tightly encircling his throat in a strange black 'dress' that had wide flappy sleeves which became like wings when he waved his arms excitedly about – which he did frequently -- banging his fists on the box he stood in, as his words painted pictures. He spoke of a lake, not of cool clear water but of a Fire that never went out. Lisa was not sure what 'Brimstone' was but if it was as he said, 'raining fire on our heads' and of a place called Hell which also seemed to have a lot of flames and fire, they were not good things to happen to one or good places to be sent to.

She knew what 'burnt' smelt like, looked like and sounded like. Lisa knew fire did this. She would do anything not to go there, and that anything was to say she believed in this God he spoke of, and this Jesus. Jesus, God's Son, that she cut out from Christmas cards during Sunday School, who shone in rainbow hues from sunlit windows, smiling gently at children and carried lambs in His arms, who gave us a reason for Christmas cake, pudding and gifts.

And so Lisa believed....

Would not any child do the same?

## Chapter 2

Little Lisa was a child of the early sixties; deliberately conceived so her parents of legal age but on different rungs of the social ladder would be given parental permission to marry.

And she was a girl.

Girls did not stay, they did not carry on the family name, they just got married, becoming someone else's responsibility and got pregnant. Despite her paternal Grandmother being a school teacher and home schooling her till her senior primary years, Father's view was that education for girls was a waste of money and effort. So Lisa became a recipient of a bursary that would pay for the books she would need to finish her secondary schooling and begin training as a nurse.

She loved the freedom of open spaces. The land, dry and scorched or waving lush and green, hills and valleys, streams (but not the leeches), cliffs, rocks, the endless blue of day or the diamond studded deep black of night, the roaring heaving seas and windswept lonely beaches or the shimmering mirror flatness that beckoned curious eyes and fingers to search for treasures under rocks.

She grew up on her paternal Grandfather's knee, head filling, imagination racing on stories and poetry of Biblical, Greek, Aboriginal origins, fairies, dragons and highly exaggerated yarns of his bygone youthful adventures and dreams. Then there was the music. Grandfather, bow in hand, fiddle tucked under firm square chin. Grandmother upright on her stool, her fingers running surely over the aging ivory as Lisa turned pages at her nod and the three voices lifted, united in song – *'Granny's Highland Hame', 'Irish Eyes are Smiling', 'It's no Secret what God can do', 'Jewels', 'Beyond the Sunset', 'Sunbeam', 'Trust and Obey',* waltzes, preludes, sonata's, *'Grandfather's Clock', 'Greensleeves'* and so, so many more.

She ran free.

But then came 'real' school, her Grandfather's death and innocence lost...

She was not quite fourteen when he died, woken by her Grandmother's scream one night. Denied that last look at his beloved face by her Father. Pushed aside. A 'Go to bed' barked at her by Father. Alone. Empty. Forgotten.

She was told not to cry. There was enough to deal with without a scene from her. And so two days later she helped her Nan make sandwiches and answered the phone. She sat in her Grandmother's lounge room, the coffin in front of the heater.

It was far too small for her Grandfather surely!

She wanted to see but the lid was on tight.

Years later she was to write of her memories – Too many people, too little space. Then standing around the grave site, Murray blubbering. Loudly. Father must not have told him. Everyone looking, comforting him. I'm alone. Nan stands close, some warmth. I want to snuggle into that big bosom but I can't. Why can't someone hold me?

Everyone eating. Talking loudly. Why can't they be quiet? Someone laughs. Murray's in the centre. I'm on the outside. Polite. Serving tea. Carrying plates of yet more food. I want to scream and scream. How could people be enjoying themselves, did they not understand that my Grandfather was dead, that my whole world was forever changed? Escape outside. On the back lawn. Still. Trying to breath. A small thin very old man appears. Not touching but I feel warm. He's not eating either. He talks quietly, soothingly. Calling me by name, yet telling me he has not seen me since I was a baby. I do not know who he was. Grandmother goes away, I go back to school. I hear how Grandmother was trying to do CPR, how Father had to pull her off, how stupid and irrational she was. Why does Father show nothing but irritation and impatience? I am invisible.

The fire had come several years before this and there was no escape. Lisa had to be brave and look after her brother while the grownups were somewhere outside. They sat in the darkened sleepout, her bedroom and her Grandparent's, blinds pulled, windows shut, eating Smarties. Then they were out in the laundry under the shower fully dressed in jumpers and sitting on all the new pink woollen blankets – strange going ons!

Though the fire came close Lisa has no memories of flames, just noise and smoke. Smoke that was so dense you could taste it.

Years later she was to write – Father with a neighbour flying on their motor bikes to get the last mob...Grandfather sagging, shrunken, shaking his head, that last paddock was in flames... Mother screaming, flailing at his chest, cursing him and his farm, Grandmother silent, straight, hands clasped, knuckles white... eons later two blackened silhouettes with big mouths and eyes appeared, there had been a patch of Lucerne over the fence... the stench of burnt wool, sheep that looked like grotesque balloons ready to pop, legs stretched skywards dotting the slopes till the men with dead eyes finished shooting and burying...building fences, hands and legs sore and sooty...little brother with a box of matches behind the outside toilet, making fires...

Lisa tries to put them out, but she gets the strap. She's older, she should have known better. How could she do such a thing, look at what her Father is going through, what is she thinking!

More recollections – A family fight...doors off hinges...holes in walls...Mother and Grandmother, ankles crossed, seated in the 'guest only' lounge either end of the sofa, smothering each other in bitter cutting words... hate red hot rolled around the house that day..

Maternal Grandparents who had never travelled the dusty road to Lisa's knowledge came and took Lisa and Murray away. They had been cowered between Grandfather's bed and the wall under a blanket in the sleepout which was next to the lounge. Lisa was terrified but focused on stopping the words getting into her brother's tiny ears and muffling his sobs. She looked back through the rising dust, clutching her Ted, wondering if she would ever see that road, or hills or Grandfather alive again. Or would it be Father?

A new brick house, small and brown rose up in the paddock between the stockyards and the old blue and white weatherboard family home. A long bus trip to the primary school began where the lessons were easy but the children, her peers too frightening and strange. The quiet soothing darkness of the artroom storage cupboard was safety at playtimes, till she was found out. The nickname, 'Bullfrog' given that first day followed her through her school years till a new one was given when she moved surefooted in uniform through the sterile wards – 'Smiler'. As her body matured and still desperate to have acceptance and approval she submissively gave two girls on the school bus as well as two younger female cousins' liberties that should not have occurred.

The little brother, was just slightly younger, the son, the last true son in a family line that stretched back into English history. Her brother, Murray, the only one who could share childhood memories, who grew to be a stranger, silent, cold and distant, one to fear, one who threatened, one who hurt, who would hurl haybales down from the stack onto her back as she stacked them on the trailer, who would attempt to run her down with the tractor one morning that she was home from the hospital, because she questioned if they had put out the right number of bales in the last paddock, one whom she would have given her life for, one who was envied when she knew for certain she was a girl, never to be a son, never able to please Father.

He started and finished schooling when Lisa did. He was the clown, surrounded by friends, everyone's favourite except perhaps the teacher's.

When Lisa went nursing, he started a farm apprentice course. He was given a wage. She paid board. She strived to have parental praise, for them to be proud of her, to no avail.

Lisa learnt the unfairness and shame of necessary discipline. She was apparently a difficult, naughty child, unloving, disobedient, always wanting more, always asking and looking for answers, searching for the elusive something better, thinking that she was better than her old Mother.

Her Father's belt that he always wore, was a leather strap joined at intervals by silver rings that bit deep into soft thighs and buttocks.

The last strapping, ten cuts in total, was the most shameful. She received them because she had gone walking with a neighbour who was also a school friend, without permission; though she was sure Mother had known. The school physical educator insisted on her donning the uniform, short red shorts, or be sent to the principal's office. The just healed scars were to be on public display.

    She was fourteen.

    Lisa never felt the kiss of Father's belt again.

## Chapter 3

Lisa received her first diary on the Christmas she was ten. It came in the big yearly cardboard box, covered with stamps, from her paternal great-grandparents in the city. There were always lots of exciting, differently shaped and sized brightly wrapped gifts for all. Her diary with a lock was covered in a silky fabric with big blue daisies, a grownup diary. She has kept one ever since.

You, my dear Reader, are going to journey through these diaries, all the way to the present, into Lisa's memories, feelings and thoughts, as she struggled to make sense of life and live. But perhaps a cuppa first?

January 19. Aunty visited Should she not be wearing a bra by now, look at her. So shopping we went. I hated it. I'm topless, with an aloof Chignon and Mother, discussing me as if I had no ears. The Chignon pinching, poking with cold hard fingers and tape measure, Big girl but no breasts. So I come home wearing it. Mother pointing and seeking Father's input.

September 8. Uncle won't stop calling me 'Fatty'. When he leaves Mother and Father just tell me to ignore him, 'sticks and stones break bones but words will never hurt you.'

This uncle was still calling Lisa 'Fatty' rather than by name some thirty years later. The last time she just looked at him sitting there, bulging slit eyes in a round puffy face with a triple chin and buttons straining dangerously, as he greeted her with 'Hello there Fatty.' 'Look who's talking', she replied. He opened his mouth but then shut it.

July 10. Mother lies, and then thrashes you with the frying pan when you tell her off.

December 5. Holiday. Turned bales. Baked.

That is all that is written, but Lisa remembers an incredibly hot day just before her twelfth Christmas. She was about an hour's walk from home, rolling about five hundred bales of hay, moving three rows into one. Her first thought when she saw the blood, was that it was coming from her blistered fingers, but it was not. Stuffing grass into her pants she walked home to find rags to tear up and use like Mother did and then walk back to finish the bales.

Lisa hated herself even more. She was now a girl. Father would notice her even less. Being a girl was no fun. Washing scraps of cloth out, hanging them on the line to dry for all to see, or asking Father and a smirking Murray to 'Please move', so she could throw them – the soiled rags not her brother or father -- into the kitchen fire. What a reprieve when the physical educational teacher, (yes, the same one as mentioned earlier), refusing to excuse Lisa from swimming, told Mother to provide tampons for her daughter.

January 20. Form 2 begins. Mother has a job in town. She has only just got her license.

March. I come home from school. Prepare tea. Clean up the day's dishes, do the washing etc. Homework. Music practice. Have tea when she gets home. Dishes again. Father and Murray sit and watch T.V. No fun.

My dear Reader that was about all from that year other than schooling issues and farm and weather reports so we will move on to the next year.

February 9. Form 3 begins. Very upset about school work. Don't think I will pass this year.

March 2. Grandfather died. Cut sandwiches. Answered phone.

March 22. Nanna's funeral. I go to school.

Nanna was one of Lisa's maternal great-grand parents. Lisa got to sleep in her room when the family went there on holidays. Nanna liked reading late into the night, snuggled in bed, sipping hot chocolate. Lisa was allowed hot chocolate, if she promised not to tell, and she even got marshmallows!

April 4. Murray and I have both misbehaved so we might be sent to boarding school. Mum says she is speaking to Dad tonight.

April 5. Threat seems to have gone.

April 19. Homework and headaches crying at night.

April 20. Lazy.

May 3. I am very lazy.

Lazy.

This word is a frequent entry from now on in the diaries over many years. Just this word, perhaps Lisa was reading books instead of doing work, perhaps she was told she was being this, perhaps...

May 7. I know I am mad even to think Michael could love me but how I wish...

May 23. Working in the sheep yards.

This may have been drafting sheep. That is separating lambs from ewes, or selecting wethers for sale, taking rams out of the flock, drenching or marking. Mostly Lisa chased, herded and penned, trying to avoid hooves, being squished against walls or slipping in poo and going down among all those legs. Sometimes she got to do the gate, but you had to be fast, strong and alert for the 'jumpers' who were not concerned about young arms in their way.

Sometimes it was working with cattle. Lisa would wave her arms around and yell a bit, but mostly she would try to stay close to the high timber fence so she could quickly scale it if those big bodies got close, hoping Father was not noticing her fear.

May 29. Youth Club.

This was run by the local church, about thirty minutes away by car. The Good News Bible was read and used for studying and discussions. But about what Lisa does not remember. She does have vague memories of games played in moonlit paddocks, bonfires, dances and films though.

June 25. Murray told parents about Michael. Not happy as with that name he'd be a Catholic.

Lisa is not sure what Murray would have told because as with this student and the others, (and there seems to be a lot so I won't be boring you, my dear Reader with all the entries on this subject!), she 'fell in love' with during her secondary school years, she rarely spoke to them or interacted. Like the senior who caught her in his arms, as she fell yet again while racing up the stairs. She instantly forgot all the others. He had such lovely eyes that lit up with his wide smile when they would pass in the corridors. Lisa always managed to blame their lack of returned 'love' on to her shyness and inability to make the first move.

June 30. I cry at any stupid incident. Just want to sleep.

July 9. Doctor says I'm mentally depressed. Have to take tablets.

Having to take tablets was seen as a weakness. Later Lisa wrote of this time – I'm so tired. So tired. Like a robot. I get through school. Walk home. For some reason there is a mattress on the lounge floor. I curl up and sleep. Nothing but warmth and the crackle of the burning fire. Peace. Stillness. Go away, No, I don't want tea, let me be, I just want to sleep. Sleep felt so good. I don't know how long this went on for, how many days or weeks. I don't remember hearing but rather felt the words... 'she's crazy... needs help'...mentally depressed Doctor says, this means I am mad in 'family language'. The little white tablets make me feel so confident at school despite being teased by class mates; they are saying the biology teacher fancies me as he is always helping, leaning close over that microscope, showing interest, I thought it was because I was a good student, eager to learn, hungry, fascinated. Outside I'm better but deep, deep inside the monster lurks – keep the lid shut tight. Let no one see.

July 11. Marked lambs.

This was an all morning, or depending on the amount of frost or lambs to get through, an all day job. Portable pens were taken to the paddock and set up. The mob was rounded up and penned. All helped in grabbing and lifting the lambs up and away from their mums, placing them into another pen. The lambs were then caught again after the ewes had been released into the paddock and lifted into a cradle, lying on their backs with back legs locked into stirrups.

Lisa usually got the injecting job (maybe that is why her needles as a nurse never seemed to hurt) and ringing. Ringing was how rams became weathers as well as removing all those wriggly tails. Using a gadget called an elastractor, a thick green rubber ring was stretched over their tails and 'purses' (scrotums), ensuring these were 'full' first. She was glad not to be back in 'the good old days' where one's teeth were used to remove the lamb's testicles!

Sometimes Lisa would have to earmark and drench as well. She rarely did the mulesing job though, where the skin around the lambs buttocks was cut away to reduce risk of fly strike. It was hard, noisy and bloody work.

July 16. Saw a film by Josh McDowell, The Secret of Loving. God is in me.

August 20. The usual, going to school, hoping Michael might like me, hoping that my maths and science will improve. Should do more music practice but never find the time or energy.

September 27. Picking up stones, house and farm work.

Picking up stones was done to prevent machinery damage when ploughing, seeding, or harvesting. Lisa would carry a metal milking bucket in each hand, fill these up with stones and carry them across the paddock to the growing mound. This was usually a day long task for the whole family, several times a season every year.

October 2. Shearing.

Shearing lasted several weeks. Sometimes there were two paid shearers and sometimes just one plus Father. That is till Murray was able to take over this backbreaking task. Lisa was taught how to rouse, throw a fleece and skirt – which was removing the unwanted bits – and press the fleeces into bales. She did not like the job of removing the 'dags' (dried faeces) from the crutchings, but this was usually her job after tea before bed while the others pressed the fleeces into bales. It was not so bad if the dags were dry; but wet well that was a different matter!

October 9. Made our Christmas cake.

December 24. I had prayed for rain. God answered. I woke to its sound.

December 28. To church with family.

January 2. I had one of my bad fits today. I cannot really understand what happens. Everything seems to mount up inside and I get so mad I just feel like ripping everything to shreds or sometimes I have hit my knees so hard that they bruise. I feel as though I have to do something violent with my hands. Last year at school I would feel like hitting the lockers or wall – sometimes I did. Walked up cutting and posted letters of introduction and application to four hospitals.

Around this time Lisa began to be aware of the world powers voicing concern of possible nuclear threats to life, to the Planet.

January 4. Sometimes I wonder if we have any right to bring children into a world that could be hell. What kind of world will it be when I am fifty? My only good thought is that God will save those that believe.

January 5. Saw the most beautiful miracle – the setting of the sun. The hills were bathed in gold, the sky was more golden than gold. If everyone stopped and watched and was thankful what a beautiful world it would be. But noone has time to watch something that happens each day and yet is never the same. 'All wondrous things are free if man hath found time to repent', so say I, Lisa.

January 6. Last night I signed a statement saying that through God I have eternal life. As long as my faith grows I know I will do well in this land so that I will be ready to go home to the Kingdom of God. I will have His strength to help me over the problems that seem so bad and unpassable.

January 11. Unloading trailer load of wood.

For most of Lisa's life on the farm they had wood fuelled cooking, water and home heating. As a result there was always wood to be collected from the paddocks and brought to the house to be chopped and stacked.

January 25. Holiday with the city relations. I sleep better here but miss the stars and milkyway.

February 8. Sometimes I think I will never have a boyfriend like May. I will have to lose some weight, stomach, hips, 60kg at present. Still making own clothes. Picked up a trailer load of stones.

February 11. Put up new curtains, they had taken the day to make.

February 12. Watched a TV program with Pat Boone and the actor who played Dean in Herbie, the Lovebug films preaching about God, it was beautiful.

February 19. Disagreeing with parents all day. I got upset because Mum tells me to do something this way then Dad tells me to do it that way. When I get upset they just laugh at me. Yet if I tell them that they laugh at me, they deny it. Now I understand why kids turn to drugs. We want understanding, love and help, not beltings, scoldings and disrespect towards our adult ideas and actions. Most of all we want help because we are losing our innocence and childhood and beginning to hate. I want to feel love, to be loved soon.

So the year Lisa completed her Year 10 education or as it was called then, Form 5 began with her crying herself to sleep – Not really knowing why, but that I felt really sad and lonely.

Yet Lisa ended this year silently cursing the man who was attempting to court her with her parent's encouragement and approval!

Lisa's family was a family that did and still does keep secrets. You just don't ask questions or talk about personal stuff. With almost forty years hindsight and Nan loaning her diaries to Lisa some questions found answers. This year may have been a difficult time for Lisa's parents personally for early in the year her mother, Irene, was in hospital for over a week. Their father, Bill, took the children to visit once. Almost two months later, Irene was still needing Lisa to do most of the housework and helping Bill with the crutching and stock feeding, as a result of 'bad pains'. This may have been when Irene experienced her miscarriage.

Not long after this event the family had a holiday at a granduncle's. One son, who was close to Lisa's age, had been having treatment for leukaemia. She writes of the evening that he had to be rushed back to hospital -- I will never forget the look of dumb misery in his eyes as he looked at me. I could see and feel in those few minutes all the pain, regrets and hopes he was feeling. He was very close to tears as we hugged.

He never came home.

Besides the usual 'farm job' entries throughout this and the following years such as unloading super (where truckloads of super phosphate, a fertilizer, from a city waterfront terminal were shovelled into wheat bags and stacked till needed), hoeing thistles, marking lambs, picking up stones, and fumigating rabbits (this was throwing a tablet into the burrows as you held your breath which was much easier than cutting up bags and bags of carrots for the poison 1080); household chores including dress and curtain making, homework, and music practice BOYS became a bigger than usual focus of her entries.

There is Jack, a fellow class student – I hope he loves me; he is in my mind continually. Makes me feel peaceful. Every day holds something new and beautiful.

And, yes, this time they talked. It would have been interesting, working on chemistry and biology projects together, if they had not!

Then there is Jake. Yep, Jack vs. Jake!

Lisa met Jake at the country dances the family went to most Saturday evenings.

Then, just to make things more interesting a girlfriend's older brother, Andrew, starts to come to the dances. Father does not approve, muttering about 'knowing what men like him are after, like a dog on heat'. But there were also other eager dance partners, like the policeman, and a dairy farmer who wore his steel caps. Oh Lisa's poor toes! She fell in love with them all and hoped and prayed that this one would be the one.

My dear Reader, please indulge me here for a brief interruption. When I started writing this book I shared these entries about boys along with others that have since been edited out, with a visually challenged, gentle, whitehaired lady of grace and wisdom, Ann, by name. Ann's response while listening, to these bits was ...well, one of laughter! Laughter that began with a few muffled giggles that ended up exploding! I was a bit confused... 'Oh, Lisa, you are putting beautifully into words what most girls around that age go thru'. 'I am? Really?' I had thought all these years that there had been something seriously flawed in me. Ann continued, 'Oh no, my dear. (Another giggle) Please continue I can hardly wait to hear who next...'

Now where were we? Oh, yes diary entries --

September 13. I like/love both. Can I do that?! I pray to God that I will have the strength of mind to allow things to carry on naturally, to see what happens.

September 22. Somebody ought to congratulate me. Jack is no longer a 'temptation' this week. It is Jake that makes me feel so good and full of life and laughter and love. I thank him for that. Cried tonight over Grandfather, began to realize I will never see him, won't be able to talk to him about Jake.

October 1. Jake visits. Oh Lord/diary help! I lost my tongue I cannot find words or anything. Please HELP. I felt AWFUL. A big knot is in the pit of my stomach making me feel SICK. I was GLAD when he left after tea. He brought Mum and me chocolates.

October 2. Still not right. Damn and blast and curse the Lisa Thomas that will not allow me to be like other girls but makes me clam up like a shell and hate Jake.

October 7. Andrew danced with me. Jake upset about this. I had told him I just wanted to be friends after he gave me a bluebird pendant on a gold chain the other day. He was very hurt but would not take it back. Wish he had. I feel guilty.

October 8. Jake visited and decided to visit relatives with us. Mum's cross. She said I 'acted angrily towards him.' I did not mean to but I had not asked or wanted him to come, Mum had.

October 15. Jake visiting Sundays. Says he is teaching me how to drive. He 'doubts that I feel the same about him as Andrew.' Both just friends I tell him.

October 21. I did not go to dance, too tired. Jake is getting on my nerves.

October 22. He visits. Takes me driving.

October 27. I'm in hospital. Emergency appendectomy.

October 28. Jake visits with flowers and lollies. I feel like screaming and slapping that stupid smile off his face.

October 29. He came again today. I had a hard time not to yell at him.

Poor Jake rings a couple of times over the next few days. Lisa wishes he would leave her alone. She tries to explain her feelings, but Jake will not listen. He informs Lisa that he is going to give up going to the dances and instead will visit every Sunday

-- He will not take my no for an answer or listen to me. I am not heard.

November 7. I came home. I was not keen to do so. Mum and I seem to let sparks fly.

November 14. Andrew makes me laugh, lets me be ME. With Jake I have to be stiff cannot relax. Sometimes I think I will explode I get so tensed up.

November 15. Jake is all wrong. I feel trapped and I shouldn't. I just want to study.

December 20. Why can't Dad stand Andrew? Andrew and his sisters come to take Murray and I to the dances when Dad can't, spending time chatting to Dad before we go. Dad however says nasty things when he is gone. They can't understand me, 'Jake is such a nice young man, so well mannered, bringing gifts, flowers, he comes to visit you – you should be grateful'...but I'm not!

December 23. Nan and Pop to tea. Jake comes, Mum invited him.

December 25. The feeling of Christmas for most people vanished today for me. All it means is presents, lollies and food, far too much food. Is this it?

December 30. Mum and I had a serious row. If there was an easy way given to me today to die I think I might have taken it. As it is, I feel as though I am slowly dying, drowning in a black pit of evil and hatred. Chewing my nails again, fat, sucking my thumb again, hatred of Jake, and hatred of the person I have become since knowing him, being a failure where Mum and Dad are concerned – is enough to kill any person. What a way to end a year in a bullfrog's life.

December 31. Made to go to the New Year's dance. He was there I refused twice and accepted twice He can go to hell as far as I'm concerned....

January 24. Can see self as an old-maid Andrew is engaged.

February 13. I love HSC (Higher School Certificate = Year 12) biology, chemistry, maths and books. I want to learn what makes all things 'tick'.

February 17. Never thought I could be so tired and yet keep going. I have not done enough music and I can't do all the chemistry homework. Family problems, especially between parents and Grandmother. I can't cope with their emotional problems as well as everything else and there is this continual tug of war between school work and music each year. My strength has lessened this year; I have hardly enough to fight back. Failure is forever laughing in my face.

March 6. Today the barrier was broken. Paul and Garrick sat next to me put their arms around me, said 'go' and then squeezed my breasts.

Later Lisa was to write more on memories of not fitting in, of barriers -- I was tired of not being accepted, of feeling that I did not belong. One evening I was allowed to stay overnight in town and as a class we went out for tea. Most were smoking and drinking. 'Don't bother the bookworm'. 'Right, hand them over!' I smoked a few with no effects, no coughing, going green, whatever...eyes watching...I then sculled several drinks. Nothing. Next morning, at school, I was dared to finish the remaining half bottle of Drops on the Rocks before we sat an exam. I got the highest mark I'd ever got! For some reason I seemed accepted and respected, even though I never did a repeat performance.

March 19. Back to the slog....I slog but the teachers complain it's not enough.

March 21. Carol's sitting on Jack's knee, comfortable, loving. Why not me? Why am I always the odd one out? I try to be cheerful but inside I am crying....

March 31. Mum 'mentioned' in a conversation today that I was conceived before she was married. Am I illegitimate...a bastard??

August 31. Perhaps I am only capable of one night stands.

I feel that clarification may be required here. Lisa had meet Tom, another young man at a dance, where there were no parents or little brother, who spent the entire time by her side, talking, holding, dancing, watching, laughing, then kissing her very thoroughly at the conclusion of the last dance; Lisa's first 'real' kiss. He arranged to meet her at the next dance, but Lisa became shy and felt awkward. They danced and talked but it was different. There was a promise of meeting again, but Lisa never saw him.

October 12. My grandaunty and her friend are matchmaking me with a nephew of hers, only slightly older than me, so Mum says, and this is why they have invited me on a holiday.

October 29. My piano teacher says she 'is disgusted' with my playing. That hurt. I've been struggling to get in enough practice, even missing school to do so.

December 23. Not long had colour TV. Watch film, The Greatest Story ever Told.

January. I failed HSC including music; only passed chemistry, biology and English literature. Worried about how to pay back the bursary. Ringing hospitals to see if can still be accepted. YES! Preserving fruit dress and jam making.

February 3. Start studying and working at a large country hospital.

So my little Lisa grew and flew. She found safety in her room at the nurses' home to go solo, to be, despite experiencing the shock of homesickness. And guilt that it was not for family but for dirt, trees, fragrances and the silence of wide open spaces.

Lisa emerged after the three years, feeling confident and in control, a different person who could stand her own ground and be respected – at least when that uniform was on.

She turned eighteen towards the end of that first year as a student nurse. Lisa's first pay packet was the most money she had ever seen with her name to it – a grand total of $170:95 and that for a fortnight of class room work!

If you feel like continuing to wade through Lisa's diaries of these years please keep reading the next chapter, and if not, well you can skip it you know, because I won't know...

*Do you have a shell?*
*I do.*
    *Is yours hard and impenetrable or is it soft?*
    *Mine was soft but the scars are many now.*
*Do you have a heart?*
*Mine is frozen.*
    *Is yours spontaneously warm and loving?*
    *Mine is bounded and cooled with bitterness*
    *And pain.*
*You, my envied friend were born to live a full life, one of joy and fun.*
*I was born to enjoy one of hardships and*
*Sorrows.*
*Pity me not though, for you are as you*
*Were created and I am as I was created.*
*We have no say.*

                                                *L.*

## Chapter 4

So Lisa commenced P.T.S. (Preliminary Training School for nurses). She lived in the nurses' home on the hospital grounds, for the duration of her student years. Board was very cheap. There was a shared kitchen and bathrooms on each floor. The baths were of a size that an elephant could drown in. Well not really but you get the idea! And no family to interrupt, or use the bath water before her. What bliss!

Her dream of becoming a nursing sister was beginning. In three years, after passing, she would be commencing a lifelong career in nursing.

But dreams can be shattered by other dreams that then themselves shatter, turning all into nothing but a waste land of darkness scattered with sharp splinters of regrets, 'what ifs' and guilt, ending years later with this observation that she scribbled on a scrap of torn heavily doodled on paper – The only end to this eternal misery I inflict on others and myself is my death – and I would welcome it if not for the fear that it would hurt others.

But I am getting ahead of myself aren't I?

So let's return to Lisa's diary entries and thoughts

February 14. We were presented with a white Gideon's New Testament, began to read it when not studying.

During these eight weeks of PTS, after practicing a procedure in the class room on the dummies or each other, the students would be let loose on the wards for a try on real people, real patients.

The day came when Lisa and Bec found themselves on an all-male ward, having to do their first full body sponge, or bedbath, to a very handsome, wellbuilt male of their own age, who was strung up in traction with a broken femur and both arms in plaster.

Tricky!

They introduced themselves, pulled the curtains around and went to collect the necessary equipment, and coin toss to decide who would wash and who would dry. Lisa lost. She got the drying job which took more care and time.

All was going well, that was till it became time for Bec to wash that last frontal body region. She dropped the wet, soapy washer on his sixpacked abdomen and fled. Lisa, with a face that now felt much hotter, muttering apologies, did what had to be done, the uncovering, washing, drying, followed by washing and drying the back area and finishing with the dressing and bed making, wishing she was brave enough to run also. Lisa was so glad that first times only occur once!

February 26. Friends tell me to stop studying and start socializing.

March 31. My first full day of real work as a Nr. (nurse) on the wards.

April 10. Unloading super phosphate.

Yes, Lisa still had her farm jobs when she was home. With no driving license yet Lisa only got home when her Father was in town on farm business.

April 22. An almost mid-aged patient takes a running dive out of the ward's first floor window to the cement below; inoperable brain tumour. He died.

This was the time before airconditioning, when you could have real fresh air and sunshine enter the wards. It was also before debriefing and counselling were seen as routinely needed for staff.

May 10. A male tells me I have a 'lovely face', that I'm a spunk! Me? I wonder if he meant it.

May 20. Why do I feel as though I'm an empty shell? I do what is expected and feel nothing only emptiness.

June 8. Starting to question my belief in God. Would he, how could he be interested in me, care about my issues when parents who are meant to don't? I don't want to be responsible for murdering him. I didn't ask for him to die and not like that! I'm not worth it!

June 12. Oh God please – how can I make you see that you have to make him get in contact?

Boys! Yes still problematic. Greg, the one, who told Lisa she was a spunk, had kept in contact. They went out a couple of times. He seemed very interested, very attentive. Later Lisa reflecting about boys during this time penned – I went out with friends of friends to the drivein or pubs, once or twice then never heard from them again. I got 'picked up', sitting around in the public gardens reading one spring afternoon, while on night duty and taken out for coffee. We met again several times; he was around eight years older. For some reason I felt really safe with him, to talk and explore ideas and discuss feelings. It was a whole new experience to converse with a man on such a wide range of topics, and to know he was physically attracted to me yet cuddles and kisses were enough. He never asked for more, telling me, 'You're the sort of person who gives easier than receives. Be careful. Trust your feelings. Don't hide them.'

I was still going to the country dances when home, taking Murray with me. And yes, Jake was there, but so were several others...but nothing, yet again. During my second year of nursing, an expatient, one of those nice elderly, gentlemen types, stopped me in the street, 'How's your love life?' 'Nonexistent.' 'Well', Mr. N. replied, 'you're doing something wrong.'

Yep there was something wrong with me for that was the only possible explanation. At one stage I did wonder if I was capable of love. I felt that I was only interested because of how I felt as a result of having male attention.

June 26. Watched Miss.C. die in my arms as I helped her back into bed. She looks so much like Grandmother. Had to wash and wrap her for the morgue by myself as short staffed.

June 27. I am taking Paracetamol to sleep. If I don't think about or remember yesterday much I'm okay.

September 14. God help me to be a good nurse to the patients. Don't let my 'moods' injure my work.

October 9. Studying for exams, wonder if I will make it – what do you think God?

December 12. It was Dave, not an old man whose chest I watched and heard crack open. Oh my God WHY?

December 14. Still very numb. Very old. NOTHING can be the same again. *NOTHING.*

Among the many things included in the young nurses'

education was the viewing of an autopsy. Lisa had actually been looking forward to this. Remember this girl had enjoyed, from an early age, dissecting sheep, then frogs and rats in biology at school!

Lisa was concerned when the time came however; as she knew that an old school mate had been seriously injured in a car accident and was in intensive care. Their teacher, Mr. K. had assured her though that the autopsy was to be performed on an elderly male who had died of natural causes.

When they had been shown into the upstairs viewing cubical, Lisa and the others were busy looking around and studying the instruments and layout, as the body was still covered and they were yet to do their rounds in the operating theatres.

As they began to uncover the body on the cold stainless steel table she was still not that interested as by now she had seen and handled many dead people, but the instruments, power tools like the farm shed contained, now that was interesting!

As they started, she was still glancing around, slightly nervous now as this was after all a human not a sheep, and saw the board. Saw the name as she heard the sternum cracked open, Dave's name – NO!

Mr. K said it'd be an old man, where's the age on the board? – NO! NO! It was Dave!

Dave, naked and being ripped apart.

Lisa ran, weeping. Mr. K. caught up with her in the corridor, apologetic but firm. Lisa was sobbing, shaking, she was hysterical – I never want to feel that out of control again.

Lisa was to lose Bec and her fiancée to a car accident during the holidays. They were coming home to marry instead they were buried together on a spring afternoon.

  December 25. Because of my shifts I spent the free part of Christmas with a local friend, Sharon and her family.

  December 27. Not feeling well. Home. Family are not pleased as I refused to go boating with them.

  December 31. New Year's Eve dance with family. Got a talking to from Mum as I refused to kiss Jake, I thought she had understood....

# THE MAKING OF A JEWEL

Lisa was now a second year Nurse, more responsibilities, including the care and supervision of the new PTS's and more study. She loved it, yet...

February 9. Nightmares. Headaches.

February 23. Dad's in town because of Murray's night schooling but finding he had to fill in time wanted me to go out with him. I refused. Felt a real bitch. Miserable. Cried later.

March 10. The annual 'bed push' down the town's main street, great fun.

This was a fund raiser done by the second year students. One of them would 'dress' up in bandages, slings, traction, hospital gown etc. and slump in the old metal cot sided (if lucky) hospital bed, while the rest, carrying shiny metal pans, urinals, sputum mugs, emesis bowls, dressed in full uniform and collecting donations in these receptacles, pushed.

The first leg was easy, all downhill. It was not so easy turning around and going back, but still a day of giggles and sunshine. Of course during this journey the 'patient' would require care; oversized syringes, mock enemas (these were the days when jugs of soapy water, funnels and long rubber hoses were used!), CPR, sheet changes, toileting, were some of the procedures acted out much to the delight on the onlookers.

April 14. Feeling depressed till after I'd watched the film Jesus of Nazareth. Been reading the Gideon's New Testament a lot lately, feel a lot better for it to.

April 25. Anzac Day A day for picnics or tears, a day to make money or to remember?

July 9. Had a disagreement with Dad while doing farm jobs yesterday; he hit me across my jaw. I had to keep working and finish the job before going back to the nurses' home. Miserable and in pain most of the night. Hurt. Lonely. Not too bad on wards working, but lonely after.

*SMILER*
*Smiler, paint your face white –*
*The ghostly pallor suits your mood.*
*Smiler, paint your cheeks rosy*
*Curve your mouth,*
*Point your eyebrows and place the red ball on your nose.*
*And Smiler – dry your eyes.*
*Smiler, make the crowds laugh,*
*Make them forget their troubles*
*With the laughter you create from false gaiety.*
*Away from the spotlight*
*Allow the tears to pave their way,*
*Allow your mouth to droop,*
*For there is no one to make you laugh.*
*Ah, Smiler, you give them everything and more –*
*But, is there none who will give you the*
*Laughter and love your starved heart cries for?*

*L.*

July 12. To Lil's for tea then church. I walked up the front and proclaimed Christ as my Saviour. She and her family clapped, congratulating me. They'd been praying for this.

By second year Lisa had two close friends, Lil and Sharon. On reflection it was a curious threesome.

Sharon was very comfortable with boys, very outspoken. She had been in a relationship for quite some time, her parents did not approve, but her younger sister thought he was 'cool'. They lived together for a while before marrying during the third year of training.

Lil came from a Christian family, who not only said grace at every meal and attended church every Sunday but were also involved in church activities during the week and personal Bible reading and praying, plus family devotions and theological discussions around the table during the family evening meal.

Then there was Lisa. She sat in the middle. She agreed with Sharon that Lil was a bit pushy, a 'Biblebasher' when she got up steam and a bit weird. Weird as in she had a list of requirements that her future husband had to meet, that she expected God to fulfil, like height, hair colour age, faith. She was just going to wait till this one appeared, and absolutely nothing sexual, nothing that even hinted of such till married. Definitely not living in the real world! Despite Lil making Lisa feel a little clumsy and silly; she loved the feel of her home, her mum's demeanour, and of being involved in their church.

Sharon's first marriage ended after about twelve years. Lil received her 'order' and they are still happily married some thirty plus years later.

August 24. Somehow with God's help I have to gather enough courage to ask about getting baptised. I just don't like the idea of all the attention I may face. I do not want to be congratulated for doing something like that, that I should do.

August 30. Church film night -- *What's up Josh?* I could associate with the guy; he too was being divided in two by differing emotions.

August 31. Attended a meeting where an American Doctor of Religion spoke on the authority of the Bible, very interesting.

September 6. To church with Lil and her family, some members came back to their home for tea and singing. Lovely... *'Lamb of God I come I come.'*[3]

September 9. Christian book shopping, a bit different from my usual occult type stories!

September 15. Community nursing rounds. Met an alcoholic –ex., with childhood hangups, broken marriage etc. 'God is protecting you, helping you, I feel it', he said.

November 18. Working in midwifery, bathed a new born today – slippery eel! I nearly dropped him!

November 23. Doing night shifts. Seem to enjoy it better than most.

December 28. Sleeping at home after a night shift, there's a fire on our property, a CFA (Country Fire Authority) member got burnt slightly. I take him into Cas. He seemed interested, lots of questions, saying he will ring, I wonder. He seems too immature, nervous.

---

3  Just as I am. Charlotte Elliott. No. 265 in Alexander's Hymns No.3.

Cas. or Casualty was the name of the department in the hospitals back then that is now known as the Emergency Department.

One more year and Lisa will be in the white uniform of a Sister! No cap to worry about keeping on and straight, or starched. The three friends organise a beach holiday together and travel via the Tree Tops Christian Convention camping grounds where Lil's family are camp leaders. The McCrae's, friends of the family are also staying there. They have three boys around the girl's ages, great fun to be around, easy, carefree and safe. Lisa is asking questions about baptism after listening to some of the talks. Some months later, watching another lady, in the required white gown arise after being fully dunked in the baptismal tub, and seeing how the gown became transparent, Lisa decided that this was not, definitely not for her.

January 8. Sunset on the beach. God if it is your will, take my life into your hands.

Four days later, Joe, the CFA guy, enters Lisa's life. He rang as he had promised. He arrived on time to take her out for a 'thankyou' meal. Then rang again, the following morning as he had promised, arranging to pick Lisa up and go to the local dance at the end of the week. It was not unpleasant being taken out by him but....

Leaving the dance he kissed Lisa It was an undemanding, gentle, nothing kiss but I wished he had not. Changes everything. Emotions mixed. He's round shouldered, weak looking, no muscles, short, nervy, jumpy but I feel as though I owe him a few...

Do I hear you my dear Reader ask, 'A few what?' I'm sorry to say, but I have no idea!

After four days of not hearing from him she feels that she has to contact him, but he rings first. By the end of the month, while watching the sunset together, he asked her to 'go steady', and Lisa says yes.

Well why not? It's not as if she has other interested guys lining up, eager for her attentions. Besides, she thinks, if it does not work out, she can walk. Andrew, his sister and some of her other dance partners are engaged or married as well as a few of her old school mates and nursing peers. Some even have children. Sharon is organising her wedding. Even Lil seems to have met someone who ticks all her 'boxes'. And Mother is not too subtly suggesting Lisa is 'getting too old and will be left on the shelf if she does not get a move on.'

A couple of days later Joe tells her he loves her and her parents express concerns that his father is a Catholic. Lisa is unsure what she feels writing – I wonder if I can love him while admiring someone else's physique. I worry about hurting him. He seems so much more seriously involved than I, getting upset when I try to explain my feelings, fearing he had 'lost' me, saying he 'never wants to let me go, that he wishes he could take me home to stay.'

February 14. I took Joe out swimming and horse riding with Lil and the McCrae boys. Joe is withdrawn muttering something about 'seeing this sort of thing happen to other guys'. I did not understand so asked him to explain. He was talking about losing me to someone else. I drove home, he felt too sick. Do I feel love or pity? He continually tells me he loves me and how much, yet I don't know. Confused. I like being held tightly, feel safe but when away from him doubts enter.

February 24. I rang Joe. No mention of when I will be seeing him again. I miss him.

March 6. Can't get used to the idea that someone can love me as much as Joe, though I love him so much it hurts – but what is love?

March 15. Bad storm, sat it out so very late getting home from Joe's, my parents are very angry. I'm terrified they will stop me seeing him.

April 26. To Lil's. A heavy discussion about God and what it means to be a Christian, how to live but I have more questions than answers. Paul has never told her he loves her. I'm glad Joe has told me.

May 6. Rang Mum, she said 'Joe had rang her very upset about the other night' – I'd rang him from Lil's replying I could not go out with him when he asked as had already made other plans with Lil. 'Would have to tread carefully,' Mum said, 'or you'll lose him'. I was upset. Rang Joe, he did not sound or seem upset or worried, thanks Lord. 'I'm the daughter his Mum always wanted but never had' he says.

May 14. On Theatre rounds. I do my first minor scrub. Not enjoyable. Will not agree to assist with this procedure again!

This procedure was a surgical abortion, if memory serves me well it was called a 'suction curette'. This was the time when all medical staff, including nurses, could refuse to be involved in certain procedures if they upset or violated their personal values or beliefs, without any reprisals. Lisa writes later of this day – I am holding a flask. I can see tiny bones; we had been taught that foetuses had no recognisable structures. I had convinced myself someone had to do this, the girl on table, think of her health, wellbeing, and care for her first. This was a blob, a nothing. Oh God, those bones! I've assisted in a murder! Never again! Oh God forgive me. May that child, when I meet them in heaven forgive me. Oh Lord, enable me, strengthen me, to discern all my actions against your Word, so I may do right, not evil.

June 17. It looks as though Joe will be shifted to the city with work. Mum made me feel guilty about not seeing them over the weekend. I'd spent my 'awake' time off with Joe.

June 19. Mum and Dad angry, 'I'm a 'man-chaser'. It's a boy's privilege to break things off by not seeing the girl but how can he as you're always down there...you're courting him etc.' Really hurt. Joe said, 'I fight for what's mine,' apparently he'd come close to losing me but would not explain further.

June 29. Rang Joe from the nurse's home. When I said I was feeling lonely he replied would be over in 45min. and he was.

July 9. Joe visits. Oh God it was good to be held by him, the horror of last night watching that elderly man bleed to death from his nose, ears and eyes after falling drunk down some steps faded. But he is considering going interstate with work.

July 19. Joe's safe with the possibility of a future, but the soldier in a cas. cubical, though fun and handsome, possibly only the one-nighter type. I wish I loved Joe as much as he loves me all the time. I don't want to hurt him, but I have the unwanted power to do so.

August 7. Joe talked about his past. He 'nearly died, had nightmares for ages afterwards.' He'd been admitted to psychiatric care 'because of ongoing problems'. He is 'scared that he could lose me by telling. He would not want to live if that happened, would kill himself but too much in love not to tell me. Does not want pity.' Wish I could wipe the pain away.

September 1. Joe tells me 'he wants to make love to me, but will not.' At least he's honest.

September 12. Joe's asked me to go to the coast with him for a weekend. God should I take the gamble? Accept?

September 14. Joe is surprised I said yes. He had thought my Mum would have said no. Oh Joe, not her but me, I was going to.

Lil was vocal of her disappointment over Lisa's decision, so was her mum. Lisa's mum however, said nothing, she seemed pleased.

They had separate rooms. Other than Lisa falling asleep in his arms and Joe saying, 'Mrs. Fenn, hum, sounds nice,' absolutely nothing that shouldn't happen happened, at least that time anyway.

Around a fortnight later Joe asked Lisa if she wanted to make love – I do but I can't and I'm not sure if I should. Oh God help me please...

Before the end of October Lisa was no longer a virgin. Joe was happy. Lisa was not. Backseats of small cars are uncomfortable, embarrassing. There was no time to think or feel.

If this is what it's all about, I don't understand. I feel cold, flat and dirty.

There are now hints of marriage from Joe. Lisa seems to have settled in her mind that this behaviour is acceptable as he is who she wants to be with, who she wants to have children by, to marry.

The day she starts taking the contraceptive pill; Joe visits. He is in a very bad mood, claiming that Lisa does 'not appreciate him coming, visiting. That she does not show any feelings for him'. She is hurt and confused.

Joe rings the following day and apologises. This was the beginning of a pattern that was to last many years. Joe would get 'nasty' then one or two days later apologise and the matter would be forgotten.

Joe begins to talk to his Mum about their future, wanting Lisa to talk to hers -- If I can be sure of myself, I can wear his ring.

Joe officially proposes while tinkering under the bonnet of his car while Lisa is sitting in the driver's seat. She got home late that night, again, but before her midnight curfew. When she went into her parent's bedroom as usual to say 'goodnight' they accuse her yet again of being 'a manchaser, a slut.' So wrong, so very wrong. Really hurt.

A few evenings later Lisa gets the courage to ask her Mother what she would think if Joe and she became engaged. Bursting into sobs, Irene replies, 'I'm losing my little girl.'

November 10. Joe's not touching me. I feel as though I am being used. Sex is all he loves me for. I'm all mixed up. God please help me – this is the man I've promised to marry.

December 28. Joe finally asks and gets Dad's permission.

The following day, after considering what else they have to spend money on when married and have to set up a house, Joe allows Lisa to choose the price range and the engagement ring is purchased.

The tension at home is palpable. Lisa can't seem to stop crying. The Mums are discussing guest lists, Irene is not at all happy.

Then Lisa had to go and try on, for fun, because her Mum was not there, a wedding dress that was not her style, while in town with her future mother-in-law. Only to find it was perfect. O oh, if before was bad, now was really bad!

During all this Lisa's nursing results arrived in the mail, she had passed. Lisa was now a 'Sister'. No bursary to pay back. But there was no family joy or celebration. There was too much tension, anger, disappointment. Not even when Lisa was employed as an InCharge Registered Nurse in a local smaller Hospital, for the next few months before the wedding.

April 10. Joe up home for tea as Mum is not happy, accusing me again of 'courting' him.

April 17. Mum still upset about the amount of time I'm spending with Joe compared with home, when not working.

May 6. Why does getting married have to cause such unhappiness within a family?

May 13. Oh God why does everything I do and say upset Mum? Perhaps I should not be marrying Joe, but I want to more than anything, even though I can't stand this unhappiness in Mum.

May 14. Terrible day. Can't stand the tension any longer. Thought perhaps I should not marry Joe and had it out with Mum. Why can't she be happy for us? And to make matters worse, if possible, Joe's not in a good mood either.

And so Joseph Fenn and Lisa Thomas got married, in a local church that was 'pretty', following several meetings of instruction by the Minister. Lisa drank these in. And Joe?

Well Joe had talked about 'how to do an amicable divorce if the time came, where they would remain friends especially if there were children involved.' He declared that 'the children and their mother would remain in the family home, while he would move out, but come for visits.'

I can remember standing on sunlit, red velvet carpet next to Dad, while Mum fussed around, pulling, poking and shaking the train of my dress, just outside the doorway into the main church. It was darker in there. I could see Joe. And I did not want to start walking down that darkened aisle. This was all wrong and I knew it was far more than bridal nerves or cold feet! Was it mature and responsible to discuss 'divorce how to' in case someone better came along later, before you said, 'I do...till death do us part?' Is that the way to approach marriage – ending it before beginning? This was wrong. I tried to explain, to speak to Mum and Dad but to no avail...the shame....the money spent....the people waiting.... the presents....so I walked.

# Part Two

## Search for selfhood.
## Bruised reed to beautiful woman

*Isaiah 61:10 I will greatly rejoice in the LORD. My soul shall be joyful in my God; for he has clothed me with the garments of salvation, He has covered me with the robe of righteousness as a bridegroom decks himself with ornaments and as a bride adorns herself with her jewels.*

How common, my dear Reader do you think it is for a bride to spend that first evening with her groom, on her knees, picking up every colourful flake of confetti that covered the floor, while he snores?

Joe and Lisa's honeymoon accommodation was at least five long hours' drive away from where their wedding reception was held.

When Joe ended his shower, Lisa undressed to shower but confetti fluttered out all over the grey carpet. A lot of confetti!

After issuing the command to 'clean this mess up', as he 'did not desire the cleaning staff to see and talk', Joe climbed into their honeymoon bed, rolled over and went to sleep.

So perhaps.....After all he had done all the driving.....

And it was not as if they did not already know each other's bodies. There was no uncontainable rush of thrilling, nervous excitement or eagerness to hold and discover by exploration. Actually nothing happened. Joe slept on his side, turned away from his bride all that night.

And Lisa?

Well Lisa, after picking up all the confetti and cleaning up, lay on her side wondering...

## THE MAKING OF A JEWEL

Dr. Kevin Leman wrote in his book, *'Sheet Music'*[4] –

'...Couples rarely suffer from a lack of information as much as they suffer from a lack of innocence in the marital bed. You can make up for a lack of information after you're married; the lack of innocence will mark your relationship for life.'

Still having the need to write prose, Lisa in the month of her second wedding anniversary writes –

> *Ah, Smiler*
> *No longer needed*
> *Pots of colour*
> *Stand collecting dust.*
> *For there is*
> *One*
> *Who cares, who loves.*
> *Ah, Smiler*
> *He has given*
> *Laughter and Love*
> *And your heart is still.*
>              *L.*

During their marriage Joe and Lisa owned two cats, sixteen motor vehicles, one berretta rifle, one shotgun, one hand gun and had paid off and fully owned two homes, though not at the same time. There had been at least thirty-three times where Joe was that unhappy or unsettled with his job that he was applying for different positions, either within the company that he was already employed by or another. He considered jobs outside of his field of expertise as well as ones in different towns or states.

On paper Joe and Lisa's marriage lasted around fourteen years, till he filed for a divorce. About twelve months before this, Lisa had asked Joe to leave. Unknown to him, she was prepared to just put their two children in the car registered in her name and drive off. To run, taking nothing but hoping to find a safe place to

---

4    Dr. Kevin Leman. Sheet Music. Uncovering the Secrets of Sexual Intimacy in Marriage. Tyndale House Publishers, Inc. 2003. Pg.20

sleep. To her surprise Joe left that night without any fuss or even conversation.

In spirit their marriage had ended long ago. Perhaps when Joe first committed adultery, possibly in their second year together when he first started coming home very late and had lost interest sexually in her. Or perhaps it was when Lisa became more desperate for children than he. Both of them were too needy, too self-serving, and incapable of living out the true meaning of their vows till death parted them, unaware of what true and lasting loving really involved.

Sitting here, today, so many years later, a life time ago it seems I am unsure how to show you, my dear Reader, what it was like for Lisa. How to take you in your imagination through that door, into the hell that she knew; the fear, the confusion, doubts, feelings of insanity, the total helplessness and aloneness that she experienced. Maybe allowing you to read more of her scribbling will open that door a little.

But my dear Reader, please have a cuppa first for I am in need of one after a stretch. See you later..........

## Chapter 1

The first couple of years away from both families, Lisa remembers as good times of discovery, learning of each other as they lived out everyday life together. She enjoyed working in the new hospital and the responsibility of being incharge, running the surgical and medical wards as well as assisting with deliveries in maternity.

Reading through her diaries there are many hints that perhaps things were not as they should have been. But then hindsight is a wonderful thing! There were tensions and stresses over finances and when to start a family. Fairly normal? Maybe. Yet in her diary – I've injured my back at work. Terribly worried Joe may have to pay, as chiropractic treatment may not be covered. I have cost him too much, given him too many worries. It's not fair God, why won't things go right? Why is everything my fault? Why am I so helpless and stupid?

Due to gynaecological problems the doctor advised a lengthy cessation of medical contraception during their first year together, and again later on Lisa writes – Things stressful. Joe worried about me getting pregnant so no sex at all.

This lasted for several weeks, till Joe got around to buying some condoms as he would not permit Lisa to.

Lisa writes – Sometimes Joe does not seem interested. Most nights he is not home till around 22-2300hrs despite the business shutting to the public between 16 and 1700hrs. God forgive me, I am so scared of losing him. He is all I have now. I've lost the love of my family. Very tired, not sleeping as have to spend the nights on the sofa so Joe can sleep...

> *The futile emptiness cries out.*
> *I can hold other bundles*
> *Coo and tickle*
> *Till hunger demands*
> *Maternal bosom.*

> *And then nothing.*
> *God, I am a woman!*
> *Yet empty.*
> *Never to swell.*
> > *What use then?*
> *But emptiness remains.*
> *Joy only in patches,*
> *Of stolen cuddles and toothless grins*
> *From other's.*
>
> > > *L.*

After a few years, just long enough for Lisa to have a couple of good friends, find her way around the big city and make the house their home Joe decides they have to move back to a regional area, closer to his family.

They live with Lisa's inlaws for a period until a suitable house is found. She is not allowed to cook for, or wash and iron Joe's clothes, as his Mum takes back these tasks. She also cannot sleep with her husband as she 'disturbs' him. To be fair, she is working shifts including nights.

Joe and his Mum go house hunting while Lisa is working and find the house. Lisa gets to see it later, after the papers are signed by Joe.

The tension between Joe and Lisa over when to start a family increases. Joe, despite promising, keeps finding reasons not to – He's worried about his Mum interfering and not allowing him to be a Dad or being scared that 'they'd be loony like him'.

Lisa has raging hormones, nagging Mums wondering what's wrong with her, pregnant friends some for the second or third time and a life that she feels is empty and useless.

So she seriously considers and investigates furthering her career in nursing, perhaps midwifery, theatre, emergency or ICU (Intensive Care Unit) Joe will think about it...NO. No sex in case I get pregnant and no further study.

Being blamed for all the dints in his cars and how I ruin everything for him and cause frustration and all that is happening in our marriage. Joe is totally rejecting me. A first – holidays usually make a difference. I'm tired of fighting for him to love me as well as have our child, my child. Tense, horrible, we fought. I cried most of the day. I have never been so unhappy. I don't want to live. I can't see an end to this. No talking. No cuddles, unless I ask. No sex without protection.....

*Suspended here*
*Neither forwards*
*Nor backwards,*
*Can go I.*
    *Seasons parade*
    *Changing colours,*
    *Yet, halted*
    *Time is.*
*Suspended here*
*I may cease to be.*
*Yet,*
*Alive I am.*
*Seconds in hours*
*Pass.*
*Hope is none.*
*Yet....... L.*

It's the First of May and Lisa writes a letter

Dear God,

I'm so very afraid, for us, for our marriage. Yesterday we made love and I thought it was good, 'thought' because I'm probably deluding myself about this as well. Today we are like strangers. And this is the way it has been since we left the city. Sure we had bad times there but more good than bad. This last year however there has been more and more arguments. I only see glimpses of the man I fell in love with and married, perhaps it is the same for him.

Have I been imaging a person these last five years, a person who does not exist?

Is it the same for him? He has just told me that I'm 'a big disappointment.' What happened to me?

Once he used to cuddle and love me all the time, now I have to ask, beg, for his attention. The cars get treated more often to his attentions than I. Why do I no longer hold his attention, have I still got his love? He rarely tells me so. Yesterday happens once a month if we're lucky. Am I so undesirable now after five years? What is going to happen after 10? 20?

Perhaps it's my fault. I've been pressuring him to have a baby. The excuses have varied over the years. I was happy to wait as he suggested when we first got married as I agreed that we needed time together. Then it was, 'needed more money in the bank and to get a few things, get the house paid off and settled', now no reason just 'NO'.

Is he as uncertain about the future as I am? I never was, as thought we would be forever. Sure we would fight but not have this chasm, a chasm that is widening. God I don't know how to stop it!

I was happy to put my career on hold for a while when first married as I wanted to put all my energy into him, but now today I've found he considers my career, which before him was the most important thing in my life, 'nothing as will not be working all your life'.

Does he expect me to sit at home without children and wait?

I thought he was proud of me and my work. What does he think? He refuses to say, just goes and cleans the cars again. We used to talk so much once. I thought I knew him and I thought we felt the same.

I encourage him, or I think I do, in his work. Never trying to stop or hinder him, why does he me?

I thought he wanted children 'early so we would be young with them and then be together alone when older to explore and travel.'

Why has coming up here changed things? Is it because he is close to his Mum?

She has such a powerful influence over him, or has things always been so and I've just been 'blind with love'?

Is it me? Surely not all my fault: but perhaps so God.

He has made so many promises to me about when we can start a family, promised faithfully that we would last year, even if we had not shifted up here and I believed him, truly believed. Now the promises continue but I have trouble believing, believing anything.

The other day he forbade me to visit my Mum, because it was 'too far'. It's only 10-15min further than his Mum's! When I went, he would not speak or touch me after checking the car's speedometer when he came home from work.

It is the first time I have really gone against him. I felt as though he was punishing me like a bad child. Perhaps I am bad, irresponsible, wilful and ungrateful, for in many ways he is fantastic.

Today while I slept, as I'd worked last night, he did the ironing and packed the clothes away and did the dishes. He is great at doing the jobs around the house and has made me a lovely garden. In many ways I could not want a better husband, BUT..... So the problem is ME. Oh God please help me. I am so afraid. Where has the happiness and magic gone, have I destroyed it? Let me be free and happy again please, free to love him without the guilt.

In September she writes – The magic returns as quickly as it goes. I know not how or why. I just wish I could keep it, so we would not fight as much because it hurts. I enjoy working nights but I enjoy sleeping with him. I enjoy our childless freedom but I want his child. The problem lies with me, always has and I do not know how to solve it.

After a work promotion and opening up more about his younger years – the unstable relationship between his parents who divorced then remarried when he became seriously ill – Joe, out of the blue announces, 'I'm not sure what sort of father I'll make. Sleepless nights. I'm not looking forward to but...

At around eleven weeks into her pregnancy, while both were part of a family bridal party, Lisa starts to bleed heavily -- I am saying goodbye to my darling little one as I dance with my handsome husband. We 'have to stay, it's our duty,' he says. I want to go home. I don't want to smile for the cameras. I want to scream and scream...

Two days later I'm sitting on the toilet looking at what is left of my baby on the floor. Had to pick it up and put it down the toilet. My mind and heart screamed against this. Then I walked up to the public phone to organise a doctor appointment and ultrasound.

What else could Lisa have done with the bloody mess on the floor?

Joe would be home soon. She had to tidy up before going up to the phone box. She was not allowed to use the home phone, as it 'cost too much' according to Joe. He had told her if she kept using the house phone he would 'have it locked.'

Surgery was required.

When the consent form was worded in a way that pleased Joe, as he had wanted this child and objected to the phrase, 'surgically remove the products of conception', for he felt the wording sounded as if he was agreeing to an abortion, he left and went back to work.

Lisa never learnt how her husband felt about this loss, it was never spoken of, and she never saw him shed a tear or felt a comforting understanding hug when her sadness broke through.

Lisa woke to his Mum patting her arm and telling her that there was no need to be upset, as she could have lots more -- I wanted to punch her lights out but still too dopey, I'd miss!

One week later -- Back to work, nights. Back to normal, whatever that is....

Irene, Lisa's Mum, for the first time speaks to Lisa of how she had miscarried perfect little twins who could fit into matchboxes, and then wonders what's wrong with Lisa, 'why is she still moping?' Advising her to 'just get over it.'

Over ten years later Lisa attended a memorial service for women and families who had suffered miscarriages. She learnt for the first time about a special area in the town's cemetery that was marked by a plaque, 'Cherished, but not cradled', and is encouraged to give her child a name and writes --

Hope, though you never really became, you were my first and I loved you. Forgive me and thank you for the gift of Tyler.

# THE MAKING OF A JEWEL

Now you have a place to rest my love.

Now back to where we left off. It's now November and Joe becomes very eager to make Lisa pregnant and fast. He has decided it will be a girl and has the name already chosen, and he is also talking about moving again.

While they were looking around at houses however, he announces to Lisa that they 'won't be moving as these new homes are too expensive and good for the likes of her'.

Within a month Lisa is pregnant again and weighing sixty-one kilograms. Joe has started going to work very early and coming home very late, sometimes not till after one in the morning. He is also going into work some Saturdays and Sundays, which had never been working days before.

Towards the end of her pregnancy Lisa, at eighty kilograms, has the doctor concerned. Her face, feet, legs and hands are swelling with fluid. He threatens her with admission to hospital if she does not start lying down every afternoon. Joe though believes she is 'being lazy and that she should be exercising.' Joe says he 'knows I cannot help it at the moment but he does wish I was more feminine.' I will have to do something about this weight but it's a bit difficult at the moment.

She is sleeping on a fold out sofa on the lounge floor as Joe is unable to sleep with her due to her heavy breathing. The due date comes and goes – Doctor will decide when to induce me...shame in a way. I can't even do this right...things go wrong...emergency caesarean...it's a boy... over 10lb/5kg, yet so skinny as so long.... Mother-in-law not pleased, she also wanted a girl.... Joe's upset as I'm not walking around properly, my feet are so swollen I have no toes!...Joe decides 'since I can't stand properly or lift such a big baby easily at present and so Tyler won't be confused and will settle, while in hospital only he and I will hold him.' So now my Mum is cross. She could not buy the pram when tradition apparently says it's her privilege and now this.

One evening while still in hospital Joe brought a work colleague, Carol with him to visit. She had a big teddy for Tyler, which was to become his favourite toy. Watching them together Lisa wondered. Joe's Mum even commented on their behaviour, after Joe had left to escort Carol back to her car as it was dark. Lisa dismissed the thoughts taking form in her head, blaming hormones and lack of sleep.

A couple of months later Lisa writes – I'm scared Joe will leave me for someone prettier and smarter...collapsed had to get Joe home as could not care for Tyler, he was not pleased...very ill with severe sudden onset of acute mastitis...Joe not happy about all these doctor visits and the costs involved. I feel a failure...Joe goes driving by himself this evening for over an hour...looks and sounds sad but won't say why. I'm worried...

Sometime later, Joe rang Lisa asking her to look in his briefcase for some documents he'd left home. While fossicking through the case Lisa not only found the documents but also a card 'to big Ted from little Ted' along with what I guess you could call soft porn comics and articles.

Summoning up courage after considering all angles of response and consequences, Lisa questioned Joe that evening. His reply was not comforting but Lisa chose to believe him, knowing their marriage could not survive without trust and she also had to think of Tyler. She writes of what he said – no one would blame him if attracted and tempted by someone else while I was so fat, big and ugly during my pregnancy, but no, and not necessarily with her...

Lisa's concern was not diminished -- How do I keep his love and interest? I've never been sexy or attractive Joe says, so I suppose I can understand. I've always wondered what he saw in me anyway.

Joe had been concerned about finances so when Lisa's maternity leave ended she not only goes back to her old job on nightduty but also finds a second nursing job during the day, an oncall one.

Around Tyler's first birthday, because it was still the 'done' thing in those days, Joe agrees to have him baptised. They visit a local church and the minister visits to teach on baptism. Lisa found these visits informative but unpleasant as Joe, after the minister had left, lets her know in rather colourful language just what he really thought, both of the man and what he was saying.

It was all smiles and family photos on the day.

Into their seventh year of marriage Joe has begun to buy beautiful boxed lacy nightgowns for Lisa, ensuring that she understands they were very expensive and so are only to be worn for special occasions, yet also saying that he does not find her at all feminine or sexy.

One day, just out of the blue, there had been no problems that Lisa can recall for a while, Joe tells her to leave.

'Okay but what about Tyler?' She takes Ty and stays at her parents for a couple of nights. Nothing is talked about when she returns. A month later Joe has holidays – First day and we are already fighting. He does not think very highly of me. I am 'no longer good enough, too fat, too lazy, too ungrateful, too sloppy, why can't I wear makeup and look like his brother's wife,' on and on it goes. He seems to enjoy putting me down and dumping on me. Why is this happening? God we were so happy or was it another illusion?

A few weeks later they take Tyler to the beach. He loves it, especially the seagulls and Joe taking him down the slide but Joe is getting bored. For the first time and with Tyler listening and watching, he gets very nasty, his cruel, cutting, nonstop remarks about her deficiencies result in Lisa losing it and striking Joe across his face – I just wanted him to be quiet, to stop and my pleading was not working. Could take it no longer. Felt terrible that Tyler saw me crying and hitting his father. Think our marriage is crumbling rapidly. Don't know what to do. I am terrified. Must be mad to still love him and want another child.

By the time Tyler is nearly two, Lisa has obtained Joe's reluctant permission to pay a neighbour ten dollars to care for Tyler for a couple of hours, some mornings after working that night, so she can get a little sleep.

Joe is struggling with and becoming very angry with Tyler as he is 'not perfect or obedient, not controllable.' Nor did he 'want Tyler or any other child', and is threatening to leave again as 'sick of this shit'.

Joe and Lisa are not as careful as they should be to avoid speaking in such a manner when Tyler's present.

Now into their ninth year of marriage Lisa writes these snippets over the next few months – I am ridiculed openly by his family for the ways I feed and care for my son. I am so tired of being treated like an idiotic shadow, not to be heard or considered, not even by Joe....

Tyler starts speech therapy, lots of home exercises, but my job as he's my son. Sometimes I resent Tyler. I feel that he prevents the closeness Joe and I once shared. I always seem to be the one that has to spend the time, do the work. I get tired. Joe has his work, cars and TV, no time left for us and I cannot be bothered to make the first move...

Another rose for Valentines...

Joe still bringing in my morning coffee...

Dad's in ICU as Murray and he have been fighting. There are holes in walls at home Mum says. Joe won't allow me to visit... the farm is to be sold.....

Tyler scratches Joe's face. To paediatrician at Joe and his mum's request – Tyler's behaviour normal for age...

Joe's 'disgusted and ashamed' of us both. Said so in front of us and his family as Tyler ran naked after bath and I could not catch him without causing him to yell....

Terrible fight. Started with Joe finding a small hole in our new kitchen vinyl; ended with me handing him my wedding band. Next day he apologised and I put band back on. Following day, surprising me, he said he would not hate me if our next child turned out like Tyler and uses no protection.

There was a problem during this pregnancy; Lisa suffered a 'dirty' needle stick injury while working. The patient she had used the needle on was a known prostitute and drug user. Joe would not sleep with her or touch her till she got the all clear a few months later.

Alyssa is born, all smiles and giggles, a ray of sunshine. Bill and Irene care for Tyler despite Murray collapsing and having to spend time in ICU because of the family stresses. Lisa was in hospital nine days, another caesarean, she saw Tyler once during this time.

Two months later she writes – Joe's complaining I don't want sex. I can't remember the last time he cuddled or showed any affection towards me. Sex is usually the only time now I do get any attention or kissed, not counting the routine 'goodbye-I'm-going-to-work-peck'. It was only yesterday that he was calling Tyler and me 'stupid, dumb, slow etc.' but the last straw was when I heard him encouraging Tyler to call me 'stupid'. I'm not a robot, what does he expect? Does he think this is a turnon??

Hoping it will work as last time, Lisa starts going back to gym, to get that body perfect. Well one can dream, can't they?

Joe is rarely home of an evening before the children go to bed, sometimes not till after 2200hrs. He likes quiet, not being disturb by them after work. Perhaps that is why he has usually left before they are up. He is distant and seems cross most of the time, often spending part of, if not most of his weekends at his mother's, without his family.

Tyler has commenced primary school after going through a kinder program. Neighbours help with Alyssa as Lisa is finding night shifts difficult with hardly any sleep during the day. Sometimes, depending on them to drive Tyler to school as she feels it is too risky for her to do so.

Tyler develops asthma, occasionally severe enough to need cortisone. He is also hospitalised for pneumonia while Alyssa is only a few months old. The three of them sleep and stay on the ward. Irene visits briefly so Lisa can go home for a change of clothing and a wash. Joe does not visit.

The school speech therapist is happy with Ty's progress, despite him 'having no short term auditory memory, possibly as a result of a traumatic birth'.

Occupational therapy is recommended and exercises are prescribed. Then a podiatrist gives more exercises. All these exercises have to be supervised by Lisa, because as Joe is fond of reminding her 'he is her child'. Ty also develops a faecal problem that causes much stress for him at school and requires treatment over a period of nearly a year, not that this is something Lisa hasn't done hundreds of times before, but not as a mum It does not seem 'right'.

Alyssa gets carted around to all these appointments as well

to kinder. Then she progressed to school for reading and other class activities for her brother. Ally did this always smiling and giggling, except for a period when she suffered from croup as well as multiple ear infections, which resulted in an operation. A day procedure, no problems till they walked in the front door. Ally threw up and Joe ranted and raved then went up to the shed.

Because Ty had been Ally is allowed to be baptised but they go to a different church. The children really like the Sunday school and crèche here. Their parents are not doing well in working together to have a constant way of disciplining the children. -- Tyler is hurting Alyssa so he is sent to his room by Lisa. Now there is a hole in the wall, so Joe is telling him he will be sent to boarding school. I feel like a failure as the Infant Welfare Nurse has referred Tyler to see a psychologist and is giving me ideas to try other than smacking as I'm teaching him to do so and I must try harder not to get frustrated. IQ test by psychologist showed that in some areas he's as a two to four year old and in one area as a four to five year old (Tyler's actual age at this time is nearly five, school next year) I am told I have to change my behaviour before Tyler can be helped, including my way of disciplining but not told how and no followup. Joe is with me for this meeting.

Let's read some more of Lisa's entries, but perhaps a cuppa first my dear Reader?

March 1. Joe's promoted to manager over his area.

March 7. Kids and I walk to kinder, leave Tyler then Ally and I go on into town to get what I can carry back on the stroller. This takes about two hours. My car's speedometer is checked each evening and I have to have a good reason if it's changed.

April 29. Having to make myself do things. I would like to go into a corner and curl up. The monster is getting bigger. I am terrified of losing control. All I want to do is sleep and sleep and sleep.

July24. Joe goes to his Mum's so we get to go to church and Sunday school. Ty really enjoys it.

August 14. I'm allowed to take Ty to church if I leave Ally with Joe.

January 30. We've almost been married twelve years. Joe

decides on and organises his vasectomy.

July 4. Ty put in his room to cool off. He puts a rather large hole in his door. Instead of yelling or smacking I just quietly tell him he would have to explain to Dad and show him. Joe just shrugged and walked away.

August 23. The sofa arm rest is accidently broken. Joe states in front of the kids he 'would pay someone else to come and do my job as anyone would be better than me.' I left the evening meal and sat outside so would not retaliate in front of the kids. Joe got them cleaned up and into bed without any of my usual problems. Perhaps they would be better off without me but I need and love them so much.

August 31. Don't know what is wrong with me. I don't stop but I achieve very little. I used to be so up with everything, so sure of everything and myself. Now I am as Joe calls me, 'a stupid, useless bitch,' what happened?

September 2. Tyler and I make fudge for Joe. I started yelling at Ty to clean his teeth before Joe got home as he kept refusing to do so. He started yelling for help, I grabbed his arm and begun to pull him to the bathroom, he slipped, slid and put the back of his head thru the wall – another hole! What sort of mother am I? Oh God please help me, please someone help.

December 9. Joe's work social, our first night out for over a year. But I have to leave to take Ally to causality with uncontrollable vomiting as the babysitter was very concerned. Joe asleep by the time the kids and I home.

December 10. Ty and my turn this evening to see who uses the bucket or toilet first. Joe's not impressed as we're keeping him awake.

December 19. Visit by the school welfare guy. A joke! Joe says one thing (what is expected, the right thing) to him then another to me (truth) when he's gone.

January 30. Mammogram. Thanks God that the packed bag I was told I'd need was not required.

February 11. Joe is very angry 'you're nothing but shit so why should I listen to you or speak nicely'. Why so beastly and in front of the kids? I can't understand.

March 4. I start studying for a Certificate of Massage with Joe's permission as may be able to work from home, making and saving money, as well as nights.

March 6. Joe and I fight. He kept putting Ty down, I was sort of used to this, but then he turned on Alyssa. One look at her beautiful face wiped of its smile I knew enough was enough. I told him to stop. He replied, 'I'll never forgive you for giving me a son like Tyler'. I was holding his upper arms as he had gripped my forearms painfully vice like. I told him to 'get out', meaning him to go outside and take his nastiness with him. 'You'll never manhandle me again', and after shoving me aside stormed up into our bedroom.

Ty had taken Ally into the lounge and kept her there, his arms around her ears so she at least would not hear. Feeling unsafe and not knowing what else to do I took the children outside and across the street to our friends who were outside playing with their children. Joe came out slamming doors and aggressively reversing the car down the drive. He left. As Joe roared off at speed in the car Ty said, 'Now he can't hurt us any more Mum'. The neighbours looked a bit bemused, I felt shellshocked! I had not expected this. Now what? Where had he gone, for how long?

March 7. About 1630hrs the usual knockoff time he rings, 'Will you accept my apology?' That was it, nothing else said. I don't remember replying, but he was back and working on the cars tonight.

March 8. I went to Mum's hoping for advice or help, something, anything – 'you've made your bed...I don't want to know'.

Lisa now decided not to try and explain to anyone else, what her life was actually like, but to try and make some arrangements so that if Joe did this again she could be safe and look after the three of them. She was no longer sure what he was capable of doing. The firearms under their bed did not help.

One of the things she managed to do was get Joe to agree to her having a separate bank account, just in her name, that only her wage went into. She would not have to bother him for spending money for items like clothes for the children or stuff for the house. Before this, she had only been given a hundred and twenty dollars for the fortnightly (an increase of ten from the previous year) groceries. If more was needed for something else, underwear for an example, Joe had to be consulted and agree that it was needed before he would hand over any money.

March 14. Joe's Mum and her friend visit unexpectedly. If it were not for the bruises on my arms I would think that last week had been a nightmare of my imagination. They are experts at putting people down and burying things, hoping it will go away. I tried to talk to Joe for the first time tonight, 'stop nagging me, what is past is past'.

March 29. Our first cuddle and kiss. I felt nothing. Scary.

August 13. School welfare guy visits, this is about the fourth time. 'All okay, will ring in several weeks' Ha! He does not hear what Joe really thinks.

November 2. Envious of Joe's sisterinlaw, they are building extensions with a spa, with no jobs. I'm cutting up my old dresses to make Alyssa clothes.

November 3. Kids and I get to go to Mum's while Joe is at his – he takes her back to 'your home to clean it.' I just get put down and made feel like what he calls me: 'scum, a worthless, useless, fat slob.' My opinions or feelings do not matter. I am just something to use in bed and quickly at that.

December 8. I graduate with a High Distinction and a Credit!

January 8. Joe's verbally aggressive. It's the day after my greatgrand father's funeral. I'd been a bit weepy but I am not 'stupid or useless'!

March 19. Joe's angry again with me, because the 'house is filthy' and I 'never do any work'. I slept while Ally was in care for three hours, and then scrubbed our stove and oven. Work again tonight but organised to have carpets and curtains done tomorrow.

March 20. No sleep today. I cleaned the whole house, including the inside and outside of the windows. I can hardly move with sciatica. Joe did not seem to notice, no comment.

April 5. Doing my Diploma of Health – Clinical Massage, with Joe's permission. Study/class days are on the weekends in blocks.

August 11. I don't remember the last time Joe and I sat down and talked or touched nicely. There is this anger and impatience coming from him all the time towards me and the kids. I don't know which way is up. It's like living on eggshells.

Lisa writes – In some ways Joe had always been like this. But earlier it was like a tiny hiccough between really nice times. But somehow that changed, till there were no nice times at all, not even a hiccough during the day. I'd lie in bed for a while in the morning, after he'd get up, listening, trying to figure out how I should be for that day to survive and keep the kids safe before I get up. I rarely got it right.

August 14. A really BAD day. Kept Tyler home and went to a councillor. We both need help.

August 16. Tried to give Joe a cuddle. He just pushed me away. Payback? I partly feel relieved though.

At a Counsellor's request Lisa writes of what sex with her husband was like – Over the last couple of years Joe has changed. Sex has become like a gymnastic routine, and I'm no gymnast! Violent. I'm just something to hammer and pound, to punish. Proud of himself that he takes so long. I learnt if I made noises like in the films he liked to watch, sometimes if I was lucky, it was shorter. I had bruises on my hip bones and elsewhere, making walking painful as well as having frequent urinary infections. There was no kissing or caressing. He preferred 'doggiestyle', and anywhere. I felt used and abused and discarded. He'd go and shower as soon as he'd finished. I had to put a towel on the bed as I was 'too messy.' I dreaded it and yet it was the only 'closeness'. My 'No', especially if I had a period or was sick went unheard.

August 20. Counsellor, I 'may have to make a decision about my relationship with Joe'. I will not do this, it will get better. I will not split a family.

August 22. Joe surprises me by buying me a new car for my birthday.

September 11. I tried to cuddle him tonight and encourage

more. He tells me I'd 'better get to sleep as not been well lately.' Payback or rejection? Either way it's not pleasant.

September 12. Joe's hardly speaking to me I wonder if he has found someone else. He can hardly bear looking at me let alone speak to me. Yet he says there is nothing wrong with our marriage or him. He will not go to counselling with me but I'd better go as I am the one with the problem.

During the school holidays Lisa takes the children to the beach. Joe is to come for the weekend, arriving Friday on the bus. The children are excited and Lisa is hoping that all will go well for them. There is an incident with Tyler's behaviour, but he settles quickly. Bill and Irene visit for the day. It's a good day.

Joe is very late in arriving. Lisa's parents had long gone. He does not speak to any of his family or play with the children. He does not even come to the table or eat when the meals are ready. He sleeps on the sofa.

Lisa is confused, feeling invisible.

She takes the children for a walk the next morning, a glorious sun kissed day cooled slightly by a soft salty breeze.

Joe comes later, following them but when the children see him, he changes direction. They turn back and try to catch up with him but he changes direction again. And again, every time Lisa and the children start to follow him. She gives up and heads back her own way. The children are confused, they have no idea what is going on (neither does Lisa!) or who to follow.

Next morning after packing, they start the drive home. Lisa writes later about what occurred – Joe surprisingly sat in the passenger seat. I went the 'wrong way' home, and got a mouth full.

Then there was a huge mob of sheep on the very narrow country road, more like a sealed lane I guess but I'd grown up driving these roads. Joe was extremely enraged as you 'don't drive a new car on this sort of road in these conditions'.

He was so angry that he threatened to jump out as I was driving, undoing his seatbelt, yelling and swearing, opening the door. It was like being in a nightmare. The pain, fear and confusion on the children's faces in the revision mirror were more than I could bear.

That was when I felt an incredible calm – this craziness, this insane way of living had to stop. This was not the way loving families behaved.

Other than slowing down and telling Joe to shut the door and put his belt on, I stayed silent and kept driving. As I slowed to give way at the Tintersection between my parents' home and his, he jumped out of the car yelling, 'It's fricking finished' and he headed off at a run in the direction of his Mum's.

She brought him back that night. Tomorrow was a work day. He even slept with me. There was no conversation.

After he'd gone to work, Tyler and Alyssa helped me pack his stuff. I was uncomfortable with them doing this, not sure that they should be, but I am very sure I would not have been able to stop them. They were like little whirlwinds, going methodically through each room, thinking of things I had not even considered.

I rang Joe at work and told him his bags were packed and he could collect them. He came late in the evening, I think the children were in bed, I don't remember, 'well at least I don't have to do that, saved me the bother, thanks bitch,' he spat out and he was gone.

Lisa shut the door and lent against the wall.

The smouldering candle inside her, that she had been terrified would go out became a blazing light, its warmth spreading out through her numb body. It was so still, so quiet. In so many ways the worst was yet to come and Lisa's life, my life, as I knew and understood it was going to fall apart, yet that deep, quiet, joyful hope was never to really leave. And she kept her word, going back to church and keeping her eyes on her LORD.

Isaiah 42:3. A bruised reed He will not break, And smoking flax He will not quench.

Sound familiar?

You're right, my dear Reader. We have arrived back to the introduction of Part One. Lisa is only thirtyfive years old at this time. There is almost another nine years before she is facing Martin.

# THE MAKING OF A JEWEL

I'm going to keep writing. Do you want to keep reading? Go on, turn the page...

## Chapter 2

The Diploma of Health – Clinical Massage course was held blocks of weekends, so though I went back to church it was not every Sunday at this time. I did though, unearth my white Gideon Bible and started to revisit an old forgotten friend. Amazed at the underlining and comments I had done in those years, I again saw myself and God's love but in the 'now'.

Why had I forgotten? Why do I still?

Psalm 51 – '...behold, I was brought forth in iniquity, and in sin my mother conceived me...'

Did she what!

Psalm 55 –'...my heart is severely pained...terrors... fearfulness and trembling horror has overwhelmed...I would hasten my escape from the windy storm..'

HE wrote of suicide!

'...For it was not an enemy...but you...my companion...'

How much a closer companion than a husband!

'...has put ....his hand against...has broken...covenant...words of his mouth were smoother than butter But war was in his heart: his words were softer than oil, Yet they were drawn swords...'

He is talking of Joe! God is going to carry me and look at what Joe will get – ooh He is far better equipped than me to give him what he deserves. I've got too many other problems anyway...

Psalm94 –'...unless the LORD had been my help...'

So that is why I am still going!

Then Psalm 139  'Oh LORD You have searched me and known me....'

Oh my! And still Jesus died for **ME!** More talk about wanting to die, so this guy knows this feeling too.

'...For You formed my inward parts...You covered me in my mother's womb...Your eyes saw my substance, being yet unformed and in Your book they are all written; the days fashioned for me when as yet there were none of them....'

I am not a mistake, not a means to an end, something to be used **BUT** thought of, planned then made by GOD!! *I* matter. *I* have a purpose. *I* have a worth....perhaps.

September 30. Neighbour looked after kids while I saw solicitor. My heart is screaming no; my head, yes. God help me, the last few days feel like years.

October 2. The silence hurts more than his anger. If not for the kids I'd curl up and die. Note pushed under door, 'called and collected stuff from shed will need to do a few trips'.

October 6. He rang, 'What are we buying Tyler for his birthday?' He wanted to know when and where the party was to be and me to forward any bills or other stuff to his work. I feel so lonely inside despite my friends. Part of me dreams of him walking in and holding me tight and kissing me senseless BUT the other part knows this won't happen and I grieve. It hurts so much. Yes I packed but he said it was 'fricking over......we are fricking finished for good'.

October 9. He turned up unannounced to see the kids. Tyler was at Joey Scout's as usual so he waited outside till I brought him back. Joe handed over a large wad of money to the kids for them and household expenses. Hardly spoke to me but spoke to the kids outside. They tell me later the date and time that they are going to see Joe's parents.

October 12. Tyler's party. He is eight. I'm so sad for him that I could not keep us together but I'm so proud of him. Joe came during the day with his Mum and took a trailer load of stuff from house. He came in the evening to the party with gifts and a card 'from Dad and Mum'! He did not speak at all to me the whole evening. He did speak to Sonja, a mutual married friend, who he flirted with all during the meal, 'feeding' her and providing drinks and laughing with his arm across the back of her chair. They talked at length outside. She said to me that his comments gave her the impression he had not expected me to involve lawyers. 'If they want a shit fight they've got one' and that he 'was finding the extra travelling inconvenient.' I wonder what he thought would happen! I don't think my spirit is going to survive. I miss the loving Joe so much it hurts. I miss being able to reach out and touch him in bed. I want to curl up and never move or feel or think again. What of Tyler and Alyssa though?

October 13. Solicitor rang. Joe is not going to cooperate with property settlement so will have to go through the courts if I want to ensure I have the house and children in the future. I broke up bad, so back to counsellor. Why do I still love him? Why do I let him constantly hurt me? I have to get the strength to proceed. Has to be settled legally. This eggshell, fearful life, is he going to go or stay, stressing over how I can keep the peace, is no good for kids or me.

So Lisa enters a world she never had expected to in her lifetime. Court, the big city one, men in wigs and a new language to work through without the use of a dictionary! Part of this process was that the court chose a mediator they had to see together. The aim of the court was to try and not be needed. It was a 'have to', a nonnegotiable; however they had a wait till the court appointed a mediator and sent them to their area.

Joe rang Lisa and let her know in very colourful language that he was not impressed.

October 25. I took the kids to the local show. Should have seen their eyes pop when I got down and milked a cow!! They were all smiles and laughter on the merry-go-around, I felt queasy. Note under door, 'called 9am NO one home. You'd better call when I can see my kids'. Rang his mum as I had no contact details for him. Joe was there. He spoke to the kids, then to me to tell me he would be around Monday, at five after work and that he was not happy that no one had been home as 'his weekend, his Saturday to see his kids.'

Because of the way things were between Joe and Lisa, she took notes, wishing she could remember those shorthand classes at school, as fast as she could during phone conversations with Joe, just so she could remember what he told her he was doing and what she was to do and just in case....

November 3. A phone call from Joe – Can you talk?
Yes.
This thing you filed with the tax department

Child Support Agency?

Whatever. Do you know the amount involved, have you discussed it?

No, they work it out from past tax.

Yes, yes, but doing overtime then, about eight thou, a one off. Well they want $730 a month, ridiculous! I won't be able to live!

Well they decide the figure and if you don't agree you can counter file and explain.

Yes, yes got heaps of forms but not necessary, we can decide ourselves. I don't mind paying maintenance but a reasonable amount. You work it out and we'll negotiate. Would have to get two jobs to pay for this amount and live. You're responsible for this property stuff as you threw me out.

No. You said we were finished.

Don't blame me for this mess. We have to consider the kids now. What you've started, going to a lawyer, is going to cost us money, eating into kids assets. There's no need to muck around with them. We can divide up property ourselves. I want my share; have not worked the last 20yrs to get nothing.

Would expect you to.

Will be putting my hand up for what's mine. You should not be spending money that the kids should have on these people. Come up with what you think you are entitled to and we will deal with it directly but we have to settle this maintenance thing first. Let me know by the end of the week what you think is reasonable.

And he hung up.

Lisa rang the Child Support Agency to make sure she had understood them correctly. They informed her that it was compulsory to have a child support assessment because she had put in a request for the Single Parent Pension. She could have a private agreement, though this was not advised, and it would not be allowed to be less than the assessment they made using his last tax return.

Lisa rang Joe back.

He would not believe her that she had no control over what

these people did and, 'yes, he knew it could be settled quickly but in his lawyer's opinion' – Lisa's brain was spinning, his lawyer? She had thought he had said no need for these! – 'it was too early for a settlement. That was why they had not sent any of the necessary information to yours.'

Joe's phone calls continued day or night. His conversation was always the same complaining about Lisa using lawyers, wasting money and maintenance issues. Desperate after a couple of months of these aggressive and threatening foul-mouthed calls, Lisa mentions them to her lawyer.

Joe apparently should not have been doing this and a letter was written. The calls stopped.

She also mentioned how Joe still had free access to the house, yard and shed and it was obvious he was exercising this freedom. She had been informed by legal advice she'd sought earlier from a different source that she was not allowed to change the locks till all the property was in her name. This advice was apparently wrong, so the locks got changed that very day. Sleep came a little easier that night.

November 10. Tyler rings Joe. Yes he will see the kids for tea. It's hard talking or seeing him. He is so cold and distant yet I want to throw myself at him and beg him to love me and for us to try to fix things. But I am beginning to seriously doubt he has any desire for this. It hurts terribly but his actions or lack of, all point to the marriage being over. So I must keep on with the legal side, though my very being is dying.

Lisa wanted to talk and fix things so badly between herself and Joe that she saw their family doctor. He was willing to mediate and see if there as any chance. When she rang Joe to let him know, he just raved on about a multitude of issues and demanding to know how come he was not allowed to talk to her about them. This conversation came with an abundant serving of cussing. I guess she got her answer.

November 13. Trying to study but keep thinking about and missing Joe. Miss the feel of him, the sound of his voice and smile. The bad times are fading; all I can remember is the good. Now there is no future, just loneliness.

# THE MAKING OF A JEWEL

November 15. Court mediator is a female. Joe told her he 'has not loved me for a long time; however he would not leave as loves his kids. I went out and got outside interests and friends, not that I actually neglected them but you know how it goes. I was not home like I should have been.'

Lisa remembers the mediator requesting Joe to step outside for a moment. Lisa had not yet spoken, had not been able to. When Joe had reluctantly, almost angrily left, she, while writing on a slip of paper, spoke to Lisa, 'I want you to get up and walk out. Go to the nearest book shop and buy this book, go home and read it. It will describe your husband and you will begin to understand.'

Lisa felt a bit bewildered, this was not how she thought mediation worked but this lady was not one you would consider questioning. Still, Lisa thought, she could not possibly know what he was like let alone anyone else understand what it was like being with Joe. No one understood. No one that Lisa knew saw him like she did. She was alone and going quietly insane.

The diary entry for this day continues. -- Joe had the children that night. Joe picks the kids up. He is no longer wearing his wedding band. It hurts almost more now than it did living with him. Doubting I did the right thing. I can cope with life but there's no joy, no meaning left for me; only the kids.

November 20. Alyssa is four, out for tea with family, friends and Joe. As we were leaving all I wanted to do was to hold him, he looked so good, and never let him go and have him kiss me and tell me he would never hurt me again and that he loved me and that in time we would work it out together – dream on Lisa! He walked away in silence, never looked back. In fact he never spoke to me all evening, even Sonja and her husband commented on his 'rudeness'. It HURTS. I still love him. I just could not handle the hurting and anger. NOW I can't handle the loneliness and empty future. Please help me God, please.

November 21. Really upset today. Cannot see any future for ME. I want out. Cannot handle the pain and missing Joe. Want him to hold me and make everything right.

December 5. Letter from solicitor, Joe wants the kids

permanently!! Why? He could not be bothered with their day to day care before. He had threatened me with losing everything if I continued to use lawyers to settle legally so I guess he is going to carry it out now.

December 9. To doctor, I'm experiencing 'ventricular ectopics' due to high adrenaline levels because of stress,' scary but harmless apparently. It does not feel harmless! Doctor said that if he 'heard from Joe, though he doubted it, he would tell him to get his head out of the clouds and be sensible. What he is doing is proving what I've been saying about him'. Thanks, I needed to hear that God.

December 10. To solicitor, depending on how difficult Joe is going to be it could all be settled next week, next year or in 3 years' time. Why, when he no longer loves me? Is it to punish me? Fine, but wish he'd leave the kids out of it.

December 14. Marriage is over so why do I still wear a ring? In hope? In memory? For guilt, punishment, reminder of how worthless I'd become? Took it off and put away with engagement ring, my 'star of hope'. His weekend but not heard from him. Had court mediation yesterday. Did not work. To court I go.

Lisa did purchase the book the mediator had told her to, *'Men who Hate Women and the Women who love them'*, by Dr. Susan Forward,[5] but did not get the chance to start to read it till travelling with Dorothy on the train for her first date in court. Pencil in hand she could hardly believe what her eyes were telling her brain. The introduction, a personal account, was describing her, Lisa! And Joe!

It talked of 'walking on eggshells'. Lisa had thought no one could have known this, this was her phrase! It talked of feeling crazy, that there 'were other people out there who understood'. Surely not! Yet – This is too close, I need to but can I read on?

She did – '...whirlwind courtships, romantic blinders,

---

5  The quotes on the following pages 69-73 are from Dr. Susan Forward and Joan Torres' book *Men who hate women and the women who love them. When loving hurts and you don't know why.* Bantam Books 1986

rescuing, rationalising his behaviour, Jekyll and Hydeing, blaming yourself, gaslighting techniques and shifting the blame.' Then this – '...with the misogynist: The longer the partnership continues, the less caring and concern there is about her feelings and the more he's liable to criticise her desirability as a woman.'

'Financial control, Control of contact with your family; good feelings about self are dependent on his moods.... It was incredible how different I felt at work, compared to at home. At work people respected me and I had a feeling of intelligence and competence. The minute I walked in the front door, however, I fell to pieces. I couldn't do anything right...' Oh Yes, yes, I know this!

Under the section, headed 'Stockholm Syndrome', Lisa scribbles – I think I'm a basket case.

'Self-image.....a common denominator among...women... who were with misogynistic partners ...they all carried with them from childhood a profoundly negative views of themselves. It was this damaged self-image more than any other factor that set these women up to accept abusive treatment from their partners'

In the chapter that dealt with 'How are you feeling?' Lisa heavily underlined many statements like – 'no one has the right to judge how we feel or to devalue our feelings...' Really?

'... became confused about what she was supposed to feel... had begun to disconnect from and to doubt her emotions... believed she was supposed to 'tough it out' when she was hurting. Paying attention to her pain meant to her that she was 'wallowing in selfpity' But I've believed this since a kid! A check list. Let's see –

- Do you feel sad much of the time? Yes
- Do you feel afraid of your partner? Yes
- ...hopeless and overwhelmed? Yes
- ...enraged most of the time? No
- ...confused and bewildered about how you are supposed to behave? YES!
- ...overpowered by your partner? Yes
- ...guilty and always in the wrong? YES!
- ...selfhatred? YES!

- ...frustrated? YES!
- ...trapped? Yes

'If you have answered 'yes' to 6 or more of these questions you are clearly in a great deal of emotional pain.' Whoops! Okay, another list, let's see where this one takes me --

'How your partner has been behaving :

- Does he insist on having control over your life, your thoughts and behaviour? Yes
- Is he unrelentingly critical of you and always finding fault? Yes
- Does he intimidate you by yelling or by threatening to withdraw his love or to leave if you don't do as he wishes? Yes
- Does he frighten you into submission by threats of physical violence? Not exactly, but the guns are there.
- Does he switch from charm to anger without warning? Yes
- Does he make derogatory comments about women in general and you in particular? Yes
- Does he withdraw love, money, approval or sex to punish you when you displease him? Yes
- Does he project the blame for all his failures and shortcomings onto you or other people? Yes
- Does he attack your character through insults and name calling? Yes
- Does he devalue your opinions and feelings? Yes
- Does he accuse you of being too sensitive or of overreacting if you get upset when he attacks you? Yes
- Does he confuse you by refusing to confront issues by denial, by changing the subject, by rewriting history or by acting as if nothing has happened right after a bigblow up? Yes
- Is he in competing with your children or other important people in your life for your attention? Yes

- Is he extremely jealous and possessive? Not obviously
- Does he insist that you give up what is valuable and important to you to satisfy him? Yes
- Does he constantly criticise the other important people in your life, such as your family and friends? Yes
- Does he belittle your accomplishments? Yes
- Does he belittle you sexually? Yes
- Does he force you to participate in sexual acts that are unpleasant or painful for you? Yes
- Has he had extramarital affairs? Yes
- Is he inconsiderate of your sexual needs? Yes
- Is he charming in public but apt to launch into a tirade when you are alone together? Yes! Yes! Yes!
- Does he humiliate you in front of others? Yes

If you have answered 'yes' to 10 or more of these questions you are in a misogynistic relationship'. Try 19!!!!

The train had arrived and Lisa, with Dorothy leading had made her way to the courts. Now as the waiting began for her case to be called, Lisa read faster.

She read the section headed 'What makes a good relationship' – '...mutual respect...concern...sensitivity for each other's feelings and needs.' All missing.

'If required to lose our best qualities in order to keep the peace, something is seriously wrong.' OH!

Then under the subheadings – 'Picture your partner behaving at his worst with someone else, Change the way you see your partner', the author suggested to '...picture your partner at his worst, with someone else', and, yes, as she said, Lisa saw his behaviour was not acceptable. Then came the questions –

'Why is it not OK for her to be treated this way but it is OK for you? Aren't you just as important? Don't you have the same rights to good treatment and kindness? ....picture him behaving irrationally and ask yourself would any reasonable person get so upset over such minor incidents?' No.

'Are constant criticism, picking and blame shifting part of a loving relationship?' No.

'Does anyone have the right to treat another human being the way he's treating me?' NO

Then Lisa was called in, it was time, and what timing!

She was not insane, or any of those other things she had thought, had believed for so long....perhaps.... There was now enough doubt and light to strengthen her for what was going to begin and continue...

Looking back, I don't think that besides God's Word, the Bible, has any other book impacted and changed my life as drastically as this book. It opened my eyes, strengthened my resolve, affirmed and made me wonder that just maybe I was not mad; and all just before I had to face him in 'payback' mode in the court room.

December 18. Court. Nightmare. I had told kids we were going to court as dad and I had grownup stuff to sort out and we needed the help of a judge.

Lisa's memories of that day, of what happened in court are only of pain filled blows that did not let up, shock after shock after shock Fear...pain... Dorothy, sat with me on the train, parents relieved as they did not have to do so, as I read and read, who stayed with me except for going into actual court room......of my solicitor's firm cool hand on my arm and his whispered, 'sit still, don't move your face or make a sound, he's not worth it'... Joe's lawyer, saying what Joe had instructed him to, was painting a horrifying, lie filled caricature of me...me... ' I was not quite like a lady of the streets or a druggie but for how I cared about him, his children and the home he had worked so hard to provide, I may as well have been...I thought more about my career than them.' Dorothy's calmness...who took one look at me on exiting that room and saying nothing marched me around the CBD till I could walk no further and it was time to catch the last train home....

December 21. Tyler yelling. Hysterical tonight. This time because I refused to read to him unless he sat still and quiet. He kept on yelling over and over, 'you do as I say....you hear...you listen....fat pig do it now'. Unable to reason with him. He would ask a question. I'd answer and he would ask the same question but louder and this kept on going regardless of me answering or not. Took over two hours for him to calm down. I went into his room after he gave permission and asked if he was upset because of dad and me – 'Daddy loves you Mum. He wants to come home but you won't let him'. I replied that we did not love each other as a married couple should and I felt that the hurt for everyone would be worse if we stayed together.

Lisa's college mates had been a great support in the early months of uncertainty and anxiety.

At one time, when she became too fearful of going home alone because of Joe turning up unannounced and taking stuff, some of her mates decided to follow her home. The look on Joe's face when Glen, a big burly, rugby-type, stomped outside asking, 'Who are you and what the hell are you up to?', was priceless!

Contact with these mates faded over time though, as it has sadly with most people from this period of Lisa's life.

Final exams were held between Lisa's court appearances. To her enormous amazement she passed, and with a High Distinction again! Not bad for a 'fricking, stupid, fat idiot', she thought to herself.

For the first six months after the separation, Lisa made herself unavailable for any nursing shifts. Later she would get evening or night shifts while the children were at Joe's on access. She also assisted in teaching massage techniques to help with the pain during pregnancy and labour at the local hospital's 'huff and puff' classes.

## Chapter 3

Lisa had no rule book for 'how to do life as a single parent'. She was as a tottering baby, falling often and bruising, sometimes bleeding.

She also feared that she was too absorbed a lot of the time in what had to be attended to and her own pain and confusion, especially in the early months, to really understand – if this would have been possible – how perplexing and wounding this time must have been for her children.

She never got to like access, despite it being her only break from the constant demands of parenting and living.

Alyssa started kinder and Lisa did the weekly cleaning there to help reduce the costs. She then moved on to the world of primary schooling, readers, homework and excursions over the following years.

Tyler moved up the grades, being so very excited that he'd 'made it', by completing Grade 6 and beginning his secondary education.

What else? Let's see.....

Holidays with the children to the mountains, snow, beach, as well as some interstate exploring.

Visiting the Circus when it came to town as well as a trip to the Zoo; Judo, basketball, dance classes and swimming for the children; becoming involved with Joeys and Cubs, where Lisa was talked into being trained as a leader. Luckily they just needed a female presence not a female adept at knots!

Tyler became accepted into the Children's Choir.

Guinea pigs, rabbits, dog, cat and fish; garage sales, teaching Sunday school, Lisa that is! Oh and garden and house renovations. Sewing clothes and costumes, even a couple of pintsized bridesmaid dresses for a friend.

Sleepovers and birthday parties; school holiday programs – a must for a working mum!

Head lice for all three and Lisa was roped into being a checker for the School because of her nursing background. Chickenpox scars for the children. Dental visits. Asthma and teaching Ally how to do chest percussion on Tyler. Gastro, flu, fevers, more asthma, bronchitis, sinus and ear infections – actually the children always seemed to be sick and Lisa was not much better, migraines, hay fever, sinus and chest infections being common place. All fairly normal activities for a young family really….

However Tyler and Lisa did the counselling rounds over the following years Tyler through his school as well as privately. Lisa supported by Tyler's counsellors, did all the school run parenting, relationship and conflict type programs that were held. She also attended a Church based grief and loss program, with private followup. It was this last counsellor who encouraged Lisa to write. She filled pages in exercise books or scribbled on whatever bits of paper are handy at the time of of need -- Parenting course brought up some disturbing feelings, opening up a whole lot of stuff, none of it comfortable, in fact very uncomfortable. Fatigued afterwards, and angry at self. Conflict and resolution – well acting as a peace maker just got me turned into a doormat that Joe kicked when wiping his feet was not enough! ….

Apparently it's not what I do but who I am – Okay so what's the answer someone? Who am I? ….

Not possible to increase kids self-esteem or confidence if mine is nonexistent – great my fault again! …..

Parenting after separation course, 5 minus 1(me) of us bitching about ex's, unsettling. I want to be beyond this point. I want to move on and get on with my life…..

I am tired of feeling sorry for myself, of burdening others with my feelings. I am fed up with feeling like a victim. I want to forget it. The only good from fourteen years is Tyler and Ally and sometimes they don't feel so good.

January 8. Sixteen years ago I first went out with Joe. Wish this nightmare was over. Wonder when or why he stopped loving me. I wonder how long it will take for my ring mark to leave my finger. Both kids having wet beds. (This was to continue on and off for a couple of years.)

January 13. Joe showed up unannounced, organising activities for kids on the weekend; icecream and pictures. It's as if the 15th is not happening. I can hear him talking to the kids outside about how 'all mums and dads fight but do not do what I'm doing and that I must ring him if going anywhere as had not known we were going to be away last week.' Well both the solicitors had known!

January 14. Phone call from solicitor, Joe wants court deferred till judge up here in a few weeks' time. No. Why do this when we are due in the city court tomorrow?

January 15. Court. To decide where kids will live till final decision is made in one to one and a half years' time. I don't understand how I can still feel the desire to hold him, to love him, after what he is saying about me, after the pain he is still causing me. Why? After all it was you who stopped loving me. You make it very hard for me to keep saying nice things about you to the kids but I must let them find out for themselves the truth. Interim orders settled, kids with me except for access.

Lisa's memories of the actual court hearing are hazy. She had to travel alone this time. She arrived in the city early. Finding a church that she had to walk past open she sat inside and let the quiet fill her. Of her sadness that she could not rest there on her way home to regain a little of that quiet; trains do not wait.

January 26. This weekend has to happen but it's the first time the kids have been with Joe for so long without me around, totally dependent on him. This is the person who proudly told anyone who'd listen that he 'had no intention of ever cooking; Alyssa would when I got too old to do so' for him. What are they going to eat? He's never even given them medicine. Tyler can do his own puffer but needs reminding, and what of Ally's eardrops or cuddles if hurt or when going to bed? So of course I'm worried. Keep them safe God please. Packed some of their favourite toys and books to keep at Joe's.

So access began every second weekend and alternate Wednesday nights and half of all school holidays and alternating days each year during Christmas and Easter.

More often than not, when the children came back home,

# THE MAKING OF A JEWEL

Tyler would hurt Ally till she cried and yell names at both females. Lisa would more times than she should have, 'lose it' and do her share of yelling and name calling as well as smacking. Not knowing what else to do, when all she had and was being instructed to do by the 'experts' did not help. Mind you, she decided this smacking when too emotional did not help either, but then nothing seemed to.

The children would settle by the beginning of the second week, just in time to flare up as going again.

They would also frantically devour whatever they could find in the cupboard that was sweet as soon as they stepped into the house, though they were meant to have been fed before coming back. If Tyler could not find anything, not even cooking chocolate, he would mix up icing sugar and water and eat that. Lisa gave up and made sure there was always cake or biscuits, preferably of the chocolate sort around.

February 11. Joe comes to Ty's school interview. Ally runs up to him and tried to cuddle his leg. He just kept on walking and talking to Sonja. Ally fell over his feet and rolled on the asphalt. He did not even pause. Ally picked herself up.

February 19. Property settlement may not happen if Joe is still fighting to get kids full time. He has requested I sign papers to sell the family car, as it's in my name.

March 1. I feel as though I'm being punished. I am guilty of marriage breakup, of dividing kids, of causing this pain. I do not feel worthy enough to be forgiven by God or anyone.

March 15. St. David's church. (Around this time Lisa had changed churches). Sermon, 'we are not alone, Jesus is with us till the end.'

Church, even this one she changed to, was not exactly overflowing with women of similar situations.

Most of the ladies wore skirts and pearls; the men, suits and ties. Lisa's age group was not well represented, though there was a small group of children. She actually felt a little sorry for the folk of St. David's. She felt that they were a little lost as to what to do with this woman who wore baggy jeans and jumpers, whose hair was shorter than most young men's, who would not shake hands and had rather unpredictably behaved children. There was a small group of older women, however, who seemed genuinely interested and happy to talk to the children and feed them. And an even smaller group who wanted to encourage and challenge Lisa spiritually and involve her in their activities and lives.

The minister, the Reverend Daniel Hankey paid a visit after a while, to answer a question that had arisen from a sermon in the previous church where Ally had been baptised –'Should a woman, an 'emerging' Christian, stay in a marriage, regardless of her husband's behaviour towards her and their children?'

Daniel's answer, without any hesitation, was a firm 'NO', not what other Minister had been saying. After praying for her and the children aloud, he left. -- The thoughts he put into words for healing and moving on, were a little overwhelming. No one has ever done this for me before. Thank You, God for bringing into my world the things I need, when I need.

March 19. Sonja tells me, Brad her husband has been seeing Joe's car parked in the bush by our home several times, late in the evenings. Maybe I have not been imagining the footsteps around the house at night, is this how the gas hot water service got turned off?

Tyler and Alyssa, with eager faces, help Lisa plan a weekend holiday during March. – It did not go to well. Lousy evening. Tyler hurting Alyssa, she is screaming. Tyler is hitting and pushing me when I scold him, back answering and arguing with everything. Refusing to settle to sleep, it's very late. I was getting angry so went outside. Tyler started screaming hysterically for me, racing around the unit like a mad person. Perhaps Joe is right, perhaps I should just let him have them and never see them again; forget I ever had kids as obviously I am not a suitable parent.

Lisa was to think this often and what she saw and heard only seemed to 'prove' these thoughts. At one stage it got to be so bad, that driving home one night, the oncoming semitruck lights approaching at high speed seemed to beckon, to give an answer. But what of the sleeping children in the back, did she have that right? End her life, yes but theirs??

The steering wheel never got turned. -- Every time I think I am doing something they will enjoy and we will have some fun it ends up a nightmare. I cannot handle this anymore. I don't know what else to do. I feel as though everything is against me; even God, for I was wrong in breaking up my family. They would not behave like this for Joe. If they did he would belt them or order me to. I hate him for what he has done to us and yet I cannot blame him now. Now is my mistake, my fault, like always. I am tired. Tired of trying, fighting, coping with everyone's problems and behaviours. Oh God why do I allow ALL my fears and worries to crowd in till I explode at the children? I blew everything, their inability to sleep, out of proportion, making things worse. My poor kids, what must they think, feel? How much damage do I do? Yet no one seems to have answers about how to treat or discipline them. It's no good talking to Mum or Dad; 'you just have to make him behave and not rev up'. Fine! How?

'We would never have spoken or thought to speak like this to our parents.' Fine! Why not?

How do I get mine that way?

No answers, just more guilt for me, more feelings of inadequacy, bad parenting, my fault, my fault, my fault...NO!

Later this month Sonja thinks Lisa needs a different sort of evening while the children are at Joe's, so she borrows a R+ video and armed with chips, bourbon and coke she arrives at Lisa's – Having very disturbing thoughts after watching, really watching and listening to a part of this video, the part where there was only one male and one female. Most of what they did were 'copies' of what Joe and I did, after several years of marriage, after moving up here, especially after having Tyler. Joe's lovemaking changed overnight to this sort of thing. No cuddles or mouth kissing, but lots of positional changes, dirty words or comments, rough stuff I was not comfortable with at first, but got used to. I acted so well I lost sight of what was real and what was not. I don't think I associate sex with love. Cuddles, yes, but not this; I think I have a big problem here. I wonder what it is like for a 'normal' couple, how/what do they do? Sonja says 'not that!' So maybe my deeply buried feelings of being used, unloved, prostituted, dirty, have some grounds. Yes, during it my 'body' felt good, but my mind hated its response. It was awkward, embarrassing, selfconscious and afterwards cold.

April 1. Court. Joe will not agree to anything. His Barrister (so they had to find me one there who was willing for that day) with long blond hair and a tight pink two-piece very short skirted suit, kept going on about Grandfather's will, how I was to inherit around a million in the future!

Joe seemed to know a lot more about Lisa's future than she did, and her monetary worth. Bill, Lisa's Dad, had to become involved now. He had to supply the documentation, family secrets, to prove this was not true. This did not improve her relationship with him.

April 7. Tyler aggressive, violent, hysterical, 'Dad said you killed Tom' (the family pet) Yelling for Joe, refusing to go to his room. I'm scared he will really hurt Alyssa or me in this unreasonable rage. Yet he does some of his best school work today and apologises tonight. Ally now spitting at me and screaming for Joe if I scold her. Great!

Tom had lived several years longer than his type were meant to. He had though reached the stage where his back legs no longer worked and he had fecal incontinence. Lisa was the one who made the decision it was time to have him put down by the Vet. It was the only time during their marriage that Lisa saw Joe cry.

April 24. Solicitor discussed how court is dragging on. I want it over so going to put in for far less than half to get settled, but want house and car (birthday gift one) if possible. Joe picks kids up almost an hour early. Last time it was dropping them off early! He was very jolly, new shirt, looked great. I felt lonely and sad. Sonja tells me they had met down the street; he 'was very angry as had made me a very generous offer and could not understand why I was doing this and why I would not talk to him and discuss stuff.'

May 10. Joe 'lets' me see the kids on his Sunday as Mother's Day, nice but I'd had a shift at work booked. He brings them back thirty minutes earlier than had said. When I have to return them a couple of hours later Ally gets upset, refusing to let go of me after I finally had prised her out of the car. Then when I got free and in to drive off, she hung on to the front of the car so I could not go. Joe kept washing his car, not even looking up. Tyler eventually stepped in and held her firmly as she continued to scream so I could drive off safely. Why could he not come and hold her hand or cuddle her? Make it hard for me fine but not them.

May 11. Tyler upset, 'Dad says he wants to be reconciled (big word for Ty, a new one and he could say it!) wants us to live together, Dad does not understand why you won't let him Mum'. Joe, leave the kids alone or are you completely mad!

May 12. Solicitor, Joe will not go above $20,000, this is probably not even a quarter let alone a half share. He is also demanding reduced contact time with the kids. 'No Judge can make him be more involved.' Anyway if I could he would only take it out on them. So yes, I'm agreeing to all his demands for my sanity and hopefully the kids', though just for once I wish I could beat him, say 'No' and get what I want. But then I have, I'm free. I don't have to deal with his anger or problems daily.

May 30. Sonja tells me she has seen Joe. He told her he 'supposed I would be getting a divorce at the end of the year, probably got a boyfriend already' Ha! There is no one else and the way I'm screwed up probably never will be. He must think I'm like his mum and will do as she did.

It was during this month that Lisa got involved in catering and collecting food for a local dance as a fund raiser for the Cubs. Esther and Lisa also do the setting up and clearing. As a result they get to stay and dance. Esther rings Lisa asking if she would like an escort for the evening. Lisa's violent 'NO' shocked even her. She almost did not want to go, so upset and unsettled were her feelings. But she did go, and go alone. Esther though gets her husband (these guys are competition dancers!), to get Lisa up for a dance – The first time in thirteen years I've really danced but this the first prolonged contact, arms around me for about a year or longer, the first nonsexual contact or contact that will not end in sex for well over two or more years. It is as if my body and mind do not know there is another sort. I don't understand, cannot name the feelings. I want to run.

The decreases in his access that Joe had demanded begin, yet another change for the children to deal with. It was not easy for any of them.

June 7. I had just started a rather late tea when I heard Tyler yelling and knocking on the door. He and Ally were crying and upset, saying I 'had told Dad in a note we had to come home tonight.' When they had sort of settled, after cuddles and food, I sat down with them and tried to explain the changes Joe had decided on. They were now only going to be sleeping every second weekend and midweek night with me picking them up and taking to school and only for two weeks of all the annual holidays. Confusing enough for me to explain, so not sure they understood. Ally had thought they had to come back after breakfast this morning. Joe had not got out of the car to check if I was home, I had not thought this change started this weekend, so could have been working.

June 14. Sonja was telling me she saw Joe again a couple of days ago. He was agitated and angry. Not happy. Saying he ' may as well buy a new home and give it to her at least she would appreciate it...his family will never forgive me for what I have and am doing....it is not right for a man to come home to a cold house, no one to talk to, no tea, no support, cold bed... had had someone else for a short time...never thought about it now though I had accused him of it....had bought a computer for us....supposed I had someone else already...he'd not be staying in town as not allowed to see his kids except for one or perhaps two weeks over Christmas, that would have to do....' Sonja said he broke out in a sweat, could not stand still, and kept on going on about money; she felt scared and just wanted to get away. Oh boy, if this is what he and his mum have been like with the kids, no wonder they are stressed. And the lies!!

I thought I'd brought our computer. Where's that bank statement? Yep I did! I thought it was he who refused all the time he could have had with the kids. He's not missing me, but what I provided. Sonja had suggested to him to ring or visit me over coffee and talk – she really does not get it. He's the heroin. I'm the addict. If I am to survive and move on, make a life, it has to be over. He had over 18mths of me begging him for us to get help, to

# THE MAKING OF A JEWEL

talk and he would not. It is over. It has to be.

June 25. Joe changing settlement again, he now wants sixty days not thirty, and the remainder of monies in the joint accounts. Accounts?! Bank had told me earlier there was only $110 in the one I knew about, is that worth fighting over?

Lisa struggles with emotions that often swamp her and pull her down. Writing till she cannot write anymore helps sometimes to pull her mind back into focus. The following is an example, originally done sitting at the new computer at night, the children peacefully asleep as Lisa rediscovers typing skills learnt at school.

July 26. I have always said I felt sorrow not anger at what happened between Joe and me, but today I began to feel a burning all-consuming rage. A rage I do not know what to do with. It involves Joe, the kids, me, his parents, especially his mother and You God. Though part of me acknowledges that I did many wrong – no sinful things, from when I knew Joe. Why, I'm not sure, perhaps because I had an overpowering desire to be needed and loved by someone, to belong, to have children by, to share my life on earth with, someone to hold, who would hold me and support me. I still have these feelings and now no one to share them.

FORGIVE me God, for I know You should be and are meant to be all I need. So my sin is all the greater. The guilt all the more. For not only have I failed my husband, my children, my family BUT You!

How dare you Joe, treat me like you did. I never thought about anyone else, desired anyone else (when things were very bad and confusing I did wonder what it might have been like with someone who could argue but still show he cared in other ways than sex but that was all).I always wondered about Carol, things there were not right and you told Sonja that there had been someone. Then when I was pregnant with Tyler? Or when I was trying to keep us together, no matter how you treated me and the kids? Did it give you pleasure to have so eroded ME till I thought I was insane? Did it make you feel like a man? Though I felt used, sex was the way you tied me to you. You marry the person you do this with. It was the way you apologised, the way you forgave me when I had not met your expectations. It was the only way I could get comfort. To make the things I was trying to ignore, that were wrong, to go away. If this was good our marriage was and you would not leave, you still cared if doing this. How sick is this twisted logic? I wonder if I really know what love is like because I am sure we did not experience it together. Lust at the beginning, from then on I'm not sure. Towards the end, well domination and control IS NOT love!

I wonder if I will be lucky enough to experience it my God, for if it even comes close to what You have made me believe it can be, it will be nothing like what I have known. You know I no longer feel anger towards You. To be honest, and that is after all why I am doing this, the peace I am searching for, that I once had is here, sometimes in glimpses yet sometimes overwhelming. But enough to make me fight. At the moment it is a fight to even find me. I pray that the girl called Smiler, who had enough for all those she cared for, whose spirit never really felt tired and weighed down like now, is still there, that I can find her again, for I really liked her. I need to find her strength, her confidence for without it, without You, I feel that neither me, Tyler or Alyssa have much hope. I am so tired. Fighting against the negative stuff that the kids have to deal with, the lies I have no answer for, the stuff I can't fight against as bad as I feel he is, I try very hard not to say so, to speak evil of him if You want, of him to the kids. After the initial demand to have them full time he could not seem to care, unless it's for appearances. He once said he washed his hand of Ty, would never forgive me for giving him a son like that.

I am waffling You are truly helping, for at the moment I cannot remember how this started out. Forgive me, forgive him, his mum and help me to also start to forgive them and myself. Help me to live again, to care for others, to be happy, for my children to be happy and at peace. To not be scared, but to trust. I am beginning to believe that this may be possible because of what You have let me achieve in the last ten months. May it be Your desire and may I continue to find peace in You and my children also.

To be able to return to You my marriage was lost. I pray not my children.

Yet – and I pause here to make sure I am really going to say this – it was worth it, for now I am alive! Thank You God for the ability to write, to get rid of hate and anger. Thank You for waiting for me, for not forgetting me, for being there, for stopping me from committing suicide when things were really bad and the thought beckoned. My belief, rusty as it was letting me make it to another day then another till I found You again. Thank You for carrying me when I could no longer manage, forgive me for taking so long. Thank You for Your Son, for Your strength and Your never ending love and peace. Amen.

June 31. I'm trying to tell Joe as he picks the kids up that both of them have barely begun to recover from a bad bout of gastro. But he's not listening. Talking over me while handing me a note I 'must read and think very carefully about as he's signed over the house today'. He has written that he wants to reduce the maintenance even more, the agency wants it increased. If I was working full time and earning his income I'd tell him where to shove his!

August 3. Kids back. Ally is croupy, vomiting and screaming with ear pain. Tyler says just like at Dad's. To Doctor, he lets me look. Her eardrum is ready to burst.

August 5. When trying to tell Joe about Ally's ear drops, he states ' she never had pain , there was nothing wrong with her all weekend, no problems at all so don't blame me smart arse, don't put it on me you bitch' – in front of the kids, then still in a very angry voice, 'you had no pain Alyssa did you?' Ally gently shook her head and in a quiet dead voice said, 'No Dad'.

August 12. Another note from Joe about decreasing payments, this time with forms completed and highlighted where I had to sign. I rang the agency. If I do not agree with decreasing it I don't have to do anything. I rang Joe and told him I would not agree, 'Do you want a hearing then, court again?' I replied that he could do what he felt he had to but I was not going to agree to less than the agency had settled on. Joe then started raving on in a threatening voice telling me what I had to do, I gently hung up.

Dorothy encourages Lisa to have a party for her birthday, mostly for the children's sakes. Dorothy proceeded to do a lot of the work, getting the children to make decorations and taking them shopping. She did this every year, while they still lived next door to her. She opened up her home as a safe place for Ally and her heart to her three neighbours, taking them under her wing, helping and encouraging Lisa to gain courage and personal strength. She was just there, calm, quiet and strong, an expert at building camp fires and cooking damper on sticks in Lisa's veggie patch.

August 18. Letter from solicitor, Joe is unable to have kids midweek, due to work commitments till further notice, starting tomorrow. I tried to explain this to them. They think I am stopping them from seeing him.

September 4. Tyler is unhappy living with me, 'but Dad does not want me till I'm twenty, then I can live with him.' Ally thinks we 'should just say sorry and would love each other and be together again.' I try to explain that that will not happen, that I do not want to live like that again.

September 13. Kids back early again, glad I was home. I had been discussing with them about getting overnight bags for them so they could take what they wanted to Joe's then bring it back, as I could not afford to supply both homes with clothing, toiletries, toys etc. Ty brought back a sale catalogue for kids clothes from Sports Co, trousers $30, shoes $100, marked and highlighted, 'Dad gave to me for you and you will have to write him a note Mum as Dad will not allow us to bring our clothes home, he has to keep them.' I had spoken to Joe and asked for the kids to bring their clothes home, Ally only had two pairs of overalls that she lived in, and they were now both at Joe's.

September 16. The $20,000 has arrived and the title for house, though expecting it, it hurt. I was lost and unsettled. Get to it Lisa and pay the solicitor's bill now, and it's all over.

September 29. Well it has been a year. Sometimes easier, sometimes harder, sometimes in limbo, numb.

October 8. Tyler upset, wanting to live with Joe, blaming me for stopping him from seeing his Dad. Big tantrum. I'm sorry to say but I lost it and called him a few names back.

October 9. Today at 1400hrs I was served with divorce papers. Joe had signed them on September 30, as soon as the year was up. Will be heard in court, I'm told, in November. If I agree I do not have to do anything. Think the guy was a bit bemused at my uncaring response. If Joe wants to spend the $500 he can, I was never going to bother, no need.

When Lisa attended St. David's, sometimes with eyes barely open as she had just finished a nightshift, she felt as if Daniel was speaking directly to her, about her. She found this a little unnerving, yet comforting. One sermon this month spoke so loudly to her that she summoned the courage to request a written copy so she could think further on what it was saying. What follows are some of the 'loud' bits --

Hebrews 11:23-29. Exodus 14:10-31. Some final verses of Samuel Taylor Coleridge's poem, *The Rime of the Ancient Mariner* were also used. The Rev. contrasted two scenes one of isolation, and one of being surrounded by people within a church.....

'Perhaps in some disappointment or difficulty – you have felt like the Mariner when he says, 'So lonely 'twas that God himself scarce seemed there to be.'

Perhaps that is how you feel even in the circumstances of your life today...Stephen Hawking has concluded, 'we are such insignificant creatures on a minor planet of a very average star in the outer suburbs of one of a hundred thousand million galaxies... that it is hard to believe in a God that would care about us or even notice our existence'...

I'm sure that each one of us here this morning, has been to the Red Sea at some time or other in our lives. We have all faced a situation, a brick wall, a deadend in our experience of life just as the Israelites did when they stood before the Red Sea. And so we despair. We are distressed. We are discouraged. The great medieval figure Dante tells us of a time of grief in his life and he says: 'I sought for consolation and I found faith'... Heb.11:29 'By faith they passed through the Red Sea as by dry land, whereas the Egyptians attempting to do so were drowned.' And this is what we need to learn today as we face the different challenges and the changing circumstances of our lives. We need to know how to go forward 'by faith'. The consolation that God offers you today in your circumstances is faith in Him and in His Son, Jesus Christ...The Israelites were trapped...but by faith they moved forward...trusting in God's faithfulness...they walked... without panic, trusting in the God who cannot lie, they walked through...And if we will believe – if we will walk by faith this morning, then we can rise from our pews and go into this new week in our lives. And we can face that problem or that person or that disappointment – not with panic or despair – but we can walk forward trusting in the God who cannot lie.

Sheldon Vanauken, a friend of C.S. Lewis, lost his wife to cancer when they were both quiet young...in the end he realized that he had to make a choice. He either had to accept Christ – put his confidence in Christ – or reject Him. He saw himself as caught in between – on the shore between the Sea and Pharaoh's army we might say. Vanauken says, 'There was only one thing to do once I had seen the gap behind me, I turned away from it and flung myself over the gap towards Jesus...I wrote to C.S. Lewis: 'I choose to believe in the Father, Son and Holy Ghost – in Christ my Lord and my God. Christianity has the ring, the feel of unique truth.'

Remember how Jesus asked His disciples: 'Do you also want to go away?' At that time when so many were turning away... Peter said: 'Lord, to whom shall we go? For You have the words of eternal life.' Where can we go? Where can we turn? You alone have the words of eternal life. We can't go back. We believe – we are sure – that You are the Christ, the Son of the Living God.

And this is what we must now believe as we stand on the shore of the Red Sea, this morning. We must believe that Jesus is the Christ, the Son of the living God – that in Him all God's promises are 'yes and amen'. The meaning of the word 'exodus' is literally 'a way through', and this is the Christian message –that in Christ God has provided us with a way through. Even for the greatest dead end of all – death itself...In Jn.8:51 He says 'Most assuredly, I say to you, if anyone keeps My word he shall never see death'. Jesus says that...you don't even see it. We can walk down to that sea. We can step into those waters and we shall find that we are already on the dry land of Heaven's shore and we never even got our feet wet. In Jesus we find a way through.

And this is true for all our experiences. God does not promise us exemption from all trials and difficulties of life, but what He does promise us is that in Christ there is a way through. In Cor.10:13, Paul says, ' No temptation has overtaken you except such as is common to man; but God is faithful, who will not allow you to be tempted beyond what you are able but with the temptation will also make the way of escape, that you may be able to bear it.' He will make a way through.

Christians suffer bereavement. Christians suffer depression (Really??) Christians have disappointments. God does not promise us exemption from the ordinary pressures and difficulties of life. Paul says these things are common to all men. We'll often find ourselves as Christians at the Red Sea. God does not promise us exemption from these things. But what He does promise us is an exodus – a way through. With every trial God provides us with a way through. When everything is driving us to despair – to distraction – God will provide a way through. That is the difference between the believer and the unbeliever. Christians go through, Egyptians go under...

It is interesting to see in Ch.13 of Exodus that it was God who actually brought them to the Red Sea...it was God who had brought them into this impossible situation...He didn't take them the easiest way. And God doesn't do that for us. He doesn't take us the shortest way or the easiest way. But we can be sure if we are following Him that it is His way. It is the path He has prepared for us. What did the patriarch Job say? 'He knows the way I take and when I am tried and purified I shall come forth as gold.'...

God is an Ancient Mariner; He knows the end from the beginning. He knows us. He knows the way that we take. He will guide us to His chosen destination... 'I commit my life to Him that made me...to Him I resign myself'. If we all – like Lord Nelson – could make this our prayer, what storms, what battles, what disappointments we could face – if we knew and believed that in Jesus there is a way through....'

November 6. My third or fourth counselling session, I 'lifted the lid' and I'm still here. In a way it was a relief to have someone listen who did not know Joe, who did not judge, who I could not hurt by speaking my feelings.

During this month Lisa has a health scare -- Unpacking groceries, blinding right occipital pain. Severe tingling across face and down left arm. Fingers not working that well. Esther got me to the Doctor after organising kids to be looked after. He said 'was severe muscular spasm and inflammation. Xray had showed marked degenerative arthritis in the cervical region. No more nursing, could end up in wheelchair by 40'! God I can't, what of the kids?

December 6. Feeling lonely tonight, deep inside. Sometimes I can ignore this and other times I cannot. Feeling down and self-pitying, want someone to hold me. I had loved Joe. I had wanted to grow old with him. Now I am alone. Why did he have to treat me like he did? Why did he begin to hate me?

Lisa and Joe's first Christmas with access arrangements was fast approaching. It had always been difficult juggling between the families and now emotions on each 'side' were heightened, so it was probably understandable this was not going to be at all easy.

December 18. Joe's picking the kids up and questioning me, What's the go for Christmas?

You have the children from 5pm. on the 24th till 2pm. on the 25th.

Yes, yes but at your Mum's or here?

I tell him to bring them back here.

Can't do, later say some time around tea time I can do.

I made the mistake of reminding him that the agreement he had made was for 2pm.

You fricking bitch. Mum won't have lunch ready till 1, you stupid bitch! I'm not going to rush all the way back here and have an accident, and kill the kids. It will be all your fault, fricking get out!

I was doing up Ally's seat belt, she had not been able to.

Do what you bloody want but they will not be coming

back.

Tyler had his hands over his ears, cowering in the front; Alyssa was trying to hold the sobs in. I can't fight back and make it worse, so I just said 'Okay', not knowing if he was going to return them at all now for Christmas.

Lisa remembers the amount of alcohol that Joe always consumed over Christmas lunch and during the afternoon watching television. Still having no contact number for Joe, Lisa waits till she thinks he'd be at his mum's and rings, 'Not here' was his Dad's reply and he hung up. About ten minutes later Joe rings, before Lisa can say anything, he curtly says, 'I'll bring them back but you'll just have to hope no accidents; Deb (the sister-in-law) is putting lunch on and as you know she is always late.'

No Joe, I am ringing to tell you I will come down and pick the children up. Right, Deb's at 2. And down went the phone. Amazing how first it was Mum doing lunch and not dishing up till after one, then it is Deb! Wish I had not got so upset with his hate filled, aggressive tone and stopped thinking and instead suggested I'd pick the kids up despite order being for him to return them. The kids would not have had to sit through that exchange. Why does he have to name call? He is still controlling me, making things suit, be convenient for him. When or will it ever stop?

During these last few months Lisa had been getting irregular phone calls late into the evenings where no one spoke, they just hanged up after she spoke. She was beginning to feel a bit unnerved.

December 23. Joe's lawyer managed to get the divorce papers sent just in time for Christmas. Not sure if I'm as upset as he would have hoped, in fact it's a relief! I showed them to the kids and started to explain what this meant. Tyler spoke up, 'yea yea Mum. Dad's already told us you did it because you want to get married.' It did not seem to matter that there was no one around who I'd be doing this with, Dad had said, so that was that.

December 25. I had worked last night. Went to church then slept. Driving the hour something trip I got stressed about what 'ifs' and how to knock, knowing they'd all be rather 'merry'. As

I was a bit early I parked in the bush and waited, listening to the Christian radio, praying and praying. The kids were waiting on the porch, so much for my fears of entering the lion's den, the front door was shut and all the curtains closed. Tyler was angry and aggressive, unable to sit still; Alyssa quiet and 'invisible'.

Lisa's counsellor had been encouraging Lisa to do something nice, special for just herself, and sometimes she had bought a bunch of bright yellow flowers, but for the New Year Lisa purchased a gift slightly more costly for herself, one that would last many years and be used often enough to wear out and need replacing. She bought herself a Bible. On filling out the flyleaf she presented it to herself on the occasion of her 'Salvation', dated January the 2nd. And wrote a quote from Selwyn Hughes: 'You don't know what you are until you know whose you are.'

During February Lisa writes –

Dear LORD,

It is as though You got everything prepared then You waited. While waiting You added finishing touches and waited and waited...then caught me as I fell and held me safe till I could stand supported and You will support me through to eternity unless I throw You off, then You may wait for me again, such is Your love and grace for a sinner. What did I do? All I did was call Your name in anguish and despair and in calling reacknowledged Jesus' birth, death and resurrection for me and my sins. Amazing Grace. My life is changed. I pray forever. That I will never know that blackness again and yet that I will remember and so be grateful for NOW.

February 24. Tyler again aggressive and hysterical, refusing to do his homework but when I just let it go with an 'Ok', he starts screaming that I won't help him. He was complaining of a sore back. A first – he threatened me with the big kitchen knife. According to the counsellor who I spoke with later, it was only because I did not give him enough attention when he told me about his back – my fault.

Hugh, the school counsellor, is going to see Tyler fortnightly to try and increase his selfesteem and ability to recognise his feelings and trust them.

During this period Joe seems to have been telling the children that Lisa is going to be selling their home and that he would miss it as he still loved it. He also seems to have told them that the car she is driving is his and that he can take it back anytime he wants to. The children who are telling her these things are concerned about how they will be able to get to school if Joe does this.

April 11. Problems with my parents taking over and organising, making plans for me that involve their friends when I have made no concrete decisions regarding an interstate study weekend. My chest pain is back, not really surprised. Sensing a lot of similarities between Dad and Joe. Distressing. I need to make a decision, mine. I talk it over with Dorothy and decide. Pain goes. Dad's not happy with my decision though, so I have to do all the explaining and unorganising with his friends. And apparently if the kids don't do as they are asked by their grandparents I will not allow Bill and Irene to look after them again. More lies!

A bit later on one night while her children were sleeping Lisa found herself writing what flowed from her heart as she struggled to work out what was swirling around in her head – I don't know how to accept or to handle help, understanding, and sympathy any more than comfort or hugs. Not sure this counselling, talking is so great. Have so many things to do. None of Tyler's camp stuff is ready; ironing (yuck); housework, garden, baking, preserving, organise holiday program, study – all I want to do is crawl into a hole and sleep. I cannot dwell on how good this would feel. I may never come out! Every time I lift the lid, this fatigue, futility starts to take over covers up everything else I am feeling I don't like this. Each time the conscious effort to pick myself up and get going is harder, more of a struggle and slower to take effect. The more lid lifting I allow the harder it becomes. Part of me says, 'stop being a melodramatic bitch, get going, stop complaining, look at how lucky you are, look at how much you have achieved'. In my head I do know how far I have come ON THE OUTSIDE, but the ME deep inside has only gone a little way, enough to leave Joe and survive court, the lies, but then all my strength was gone and I went no further, had no fight left.

'Oh stop wallowing in selfpity, you are luckier than most,

your kids too. Stop looking for problems where there are none', a voice in my head says.

Shut up, I'm tired.

I do not have to explain why groceries cost so much, why I used the phone, that I can turn the heater on for the whole day if I and the kids are cold, that the kids and I do need new underwear, clothes, shoes, that I can go out and spend more than ten dollars on a meal (though perhaps I should not) and not worry about my behaviour or conversation or dress, or what will be said later about my companions. If I am so intelligent how did I let myself get in and stay in a situation so destructive? I know what advice I would have given to a friend or client in such a situation years ago so why not me?

Sympathy? NO. I don't want this – it won't help.

Understanding, empathy, yes and help. Perhaps this is why I have never really told all my feelings of fears, besides sounding completely loony...comfort, hugs, too scared of breaking....I hide when in pain, when confused, others cannot help so why show them, besides I'm too scared to face it myself! For some reason the thought of showing my pain, of letting go, especially to my parents or someone who loves me, means letting them down. I feel if they could see the mess inside, the real me, the madness, the craziness, the fear, I'd be locked away. There is more peace, the most since I was free to watch sunsets and roll in the grass as a kid but the madness is there too, lurking, waiting.

I'm searching for an identity, for ME. Everyone who knew Mum at my age mistakes me for her, calling me by her name. Dad even gets confused, one evening going to the car pinching my bum thinking I was Mum. I am ME. A small part – a part that has grown smaller yet fights harder – will not accept that this is how my life is to be. I don't have to be an empty, mechanical shell reflecting what is expected. I have a right to be loved not needed. A right to be held for no other reason than that is what I feel like.

This tongue tied unable to speak selfconscious embarrassed person is not me. I am the free running child galloping on her horse climbing rocks watching sunsets able to be still without

# THE MAKING OF A JEWEL

fear able to feel like I did when Tom kissed me and to know that it is good and all right to feel this way and yet not having to depend on this to live to be happy free and still. To feel safe to express feelings and not be criticized for doing so.

But I've forgotten how to find ME. There are a lot of doors each one bigger and heavier than the last. Is it all right to ask for help to open them? Is it right to use your help, as a counsellor and not struggle alone going nowhere, even though I have God? Seems to be a constant pattern of who I love always letting me down – not counting my feelings as worth anything. I seem to accept bad behaviour towards me more easily, seeing nice as suspicious... Is this because of all those years of 'stinking thinking'? I need to lose completely this fear I have of what would happen if I expressed my feelings or needs.

What do I fear would happen if I was truthful and expressed these honestly? – ignored, devalued, ridiculed, put off till a more convenient time, stop whining, grizzling, complaining, don't you know how lucky you are, how dare you want or need more, laughed at, made fun of, used against me later, made to look a fool, embarrassed, treated as an idiot, don't know what you're talking about, invisible, work is more important, things have to be done first then if there is time, don't be so stupid! Of course I/we do (love you meant but not said) –

Where did this come from? I feel more but no words. Do I need to look at it more like anatomy and physics, to step outside and look in – so I don't truly feel, just see the possible causes, problems then set about solution finding in a clinical almost detached way as though it's not ME but someone else who I'm fixing? I cannot blame my parents or Joe for I let them do this to me. I gave them permission over and over and yet I cannot blame myself for I knew no other way at that time. I did not know that I could let alone how to stop it. Now I do. So let's not look at blame but solutions and preventions. In time I hope to be ready and able to step in and be ME and feel ME.

*Ah, Smiler*
*You hid my spirit*

*Hid it deep enough not to be destroyed*
  *Ah, Smiler*
  *But now it's time*
  *Time to be ME*
  *For me*
*Goodbye old Friend*
    *Goodbye*
        *For now.*
            *L.*

April 26. Tyler crying, not wanting to go to school, it's the day after access. Complaining of 'headache, dizziness, sore back, stomach, feeling sick,' he went from car to school gate crying 'as missing me.' What am I to do? Things were easier when first separated.

April 28. Brought up my concerns about Tyler's stress and aggression and Alyssa's binge eating and other behaviours before access with Joe, at the school's positive parenting program – it was suggested I contact Child Protection as soon as I could. I spoke to the principal, she will meet with Hugh. Tyler's teacher tells me that he 'is very stressed and worried and confused with what Joe is saying about me.' I wonder what he's saying now?

May 2. Mum rang, wanting to talk to the kids. She hung up after a tearful 'keep in contact anytime you need anything or want us, I love you.' I believe you do Mum as best as you can but I have to start standing on my own. I cannot run to you all the time.

This last episode with her parents seems to open up a whole lot of stuff for Lisa, from childhood all the way through to now. Again she writes and writes, working through all her thoughts and emotions as they appear, ending in making some very assertive conclusions that she struggles to live by, for now anyway. -- I am nearly forty years old. Why cannot I make a decision about my life and have acceptance, if not support and understanding? Why do I have to do what I think others want me to or else? The else being some sort of punishment. Reading *'Women Who Love*

*Too Much'* by Robin Norwood.[6] Bill and Joe. I did everything I could to avoid criticism, anger, to make him happy or get approval – though sometimes I did deliberately try to blow everything up – but I never really succeeded. Hooked into game playing. 'Rescuer, Persecutor, Victim.' This sounds very familiar when described for both the child and adult me. 'To play any of these positions, whether in conversation or in life, keeps the focus off yourself and holds you in your childhood pattern of fear, rage and helplessness....less of the 'If it weren't for......' and more of the 'Right now I am choosing to ....' YES Oh, YES! The fear I have of what would happen if I alienated my parents more – how would I cope with noone to help with the kids is equivalent what I had with Joe. SCARY. Of course I would cope – find another way around the problem! I am mature enough to be responsible for myself, my feelings and actions and my ability to learn to express them. I have seen and felt things my parents have no hope of understanding. I have the right to be seen by them as an adult, an equal, they do not have the right to treat me as though my feelings do not matter, as though I am a child. They should be mature enough to be responsible for their feelings, this is not my responsibility.

Several days later Joe phones Lisa and converses in a lovely friendly voice. -- What's going on? This is the old Joe that I loved. He had decided that Lisa could have the children overnight till nine in the morning for Mother's Day, 'unless she had other plans of course.' Joe also informs her that he had moved temporally and giving her time to find a pen informs her of the address and contact phone number. -- I got the feeling he wanted to keep talking; I was not comfortable with this. His voice remained friendly, interested. I felt confused, off balance, scared.

May 8. Mother's Day, I lay in bed listening to my two giggle and whisper – loudly – in the kitchen. A tray appears with flowers and food: Tyler made coffee, Alyssa toast.

Later that day, after the children had returned from access Tyler hands Lisa a note saying, 'its bad stuff about me, mum.'

---

6  Robin Norwood Women who love too much. When you keep wishing and hoping he'll change. Pocket Books 1985.

Lisa keeps the note folded and asks Tyler what happened. They had slept the weekend at Joe's Mum's, Tyler on the lounge sofa and Alyssa in a bed in the spare room. Tyler had soiled himself while asleep.

Dad hit me and said I was dd...ddus....

Disgusting?

Yea Mum. And Ma yelled.

Lisa asked him how he had felt -- Bad.

Alyssa pipes up -- Yes Mum, Ty was very naughty.

No, he was not naughty, bad, disgusting or anything else horrible. He does not do that deliberately. It was an accident, Lisa responds firmly. Cuddling Ty Lisa now looks at the note. Joe is informing her 'that if she did not have the time he would find time and do something about this problem' Ha! Will he now go to counselling to stop screwing his son's mind! But there was more. Joe's temporary accommodation was not suitable for children and as a result he wanted access deferred promising he 'will make it up over time, commitments allowing of course.' Of course!! Lisa was to inform him of what she thought. Tyler was devastated when I told them. He is convinced it is because of him. Oh yes I'd like to let Joe know my thoughts but would he like to hear them? – I don't think so! What about my commitments? – Fully booked at the Spa that weekend to massage. I cannot 'dump' kids on someone else so I can work, do my thing; they already feel abandoned by Joe. In a sad, dead voice Tyler asks, 'Why is this happening to me Mum?'

A few evenings later while cuddling and reading stories on the couch before bed with both children, Alyssa blurts out 'You know Mum, Ma said she would wipe Ty's nose in it like a dog if he poohed again and she meant it Mum.'

Lisa said the first thing that came to mind – Do you think that was a very nice grownup thing to say?

No.

Hmm. What if I said something as silly? I could say, I'd go down there and wipe her nose in it if she did that to our Ty.

Tyler gives a little grin at this.

How would your child feel if you were the grownup?

They both answered together -- wouldn't say it.

Lisa had learnt that Tyler may exaggerate or not be truthful about things that happened on access. But if Alyssa said similar in private or backed him up at the time Tyler was telling the story it was usually right, it happened.

Ally's nightmares and screaming out during the night were worsening. She tossed and turned so much she often flung herself out of bed. She was also becoming clingier, more reluctant to go to Joe's. Lisa speaks at length to Hugh and is advised to contact the Child Protection Unit.

I spoke to Mrs. S. of Child Protection and Adolescent unit. She tells me I 'am describing a child or children who has or is being sexually assaulted'.....Oh God where has all the air gone???

Is this why Ally has suddenly started wearing underwear to bed?

She instructs me to get a referral to a Paediatrician but to talk to him first before he sees the children and describe their behaviour to him as I have just done to her.

I feel as though I've entered – no, been hurtled into a nightmare/confusion of despair. Knowing that even if I scream at the top of my lungs noone will listen. It is as though it is all inside my head and only I can see/feel it, so how can it be real? How can I make anyone feel, understand and believe my fear?

Sexual abuse – NO. I can't believe that even if I want to believe the worst of Joe's family – and yet as a nurse I know that is what everyone in that situation says.

How could I let that happen?

And how can I prove that anything is being done to them?

I know how Joe always comes out looking good and I am just crazy, imaging things, making trouble. He is too strong, too good, I cannot go against him and win and yet God if he or someone there is really emotionally or otherwise abusing Tyler and Alyssa I have to, don't I?

I feel as though I've been thrown to the bottom and he is pushing, pushing me down and down. If I don't fight I will die. Yet I have no strength left, great rocking sobs rip out of me and yet there is no clean air. Get me out. Hold me up. Let me find a grip, not for me but for them. I should never have married him or 'made' him have kids. I deserve it but they don't. I am so tired, so very tired.

Lisa's doctor writes out the referral to the paediatrician but tells her that Mrs.S. had given her the worst case scenario as ongoing severe stress can also cause these issues.

Tyler is terrified, he believes he will have to have 'needles' like Dad and Ma say they 'used in the olden days.'

May 14. Palpations. Legs will hardly hold me up. My hands are shaking like an old lady's. Chest pain, stomach pain, and it has been over an hour since I read his letter. Some anger but mostly fear and panic. He is going to have the kids this weekend after saying he was not. Thought they would have space, I'd have space to work out what to do after having the kids talk the other day and having to speak to Child Protection. Rang solicitor, Joe has court order for this weekend. If I refuse to send the kids I'll be in trouble legally. I tell him what Tyler told me, but he 'feels this is not the problem but Joe having them – upsetting my plans is the real problem.'

I don't know anymore.

Is it my concern for the kids? Is it because of Joe ruling my life still, controlling it?

The kids want to see their Dad. How much damage will I do if I cause a stink? If I don't cause a stink how much more can they take and still turn out okay? How much longer can I wait? I was relieved he was not having them after what Alyssa said on top of what Tyler had said. Am I concerned as I have to have control or am I concerned for their sakes? Who is going to be caring for them this weekend?

I want to run and run but when I stop it will still be there. I am feeling just as helpless to help them as I was me. Dear God, show me what I must do, show me the way I have to go.

Tyler had been unable to sleep. He came out for a cuddle. Lisa asked him why he was having difficulty --

Worried about Dad.

Oh, what's worrying you?

Going there, having him yell at me, calling me names and

hitting me.
 Oh, but Tyler that only happened last visit, you told me.
 No Mum.
 What do you mean, No?
 It's all the time.
 Why?
 Cos I have the skids. (Faecal incontinence)
 What about when you are at Ma's?
 She calls me a f...f...you know Mum.
 What do you think you could do?
 Nothing.
 Silence. Lisa was trying to think, to say the right things, not the wrong, whatever that would be!
 What would you do if you were me Tyler and it was happening to Alyssa?
 I'd hit him.
 Oh. Would that change things?
 N..o.. but it'd stop him Mum. Tyler was crying now, cuddling, and burying his head into Lisa's side. I like playing with my cousins Mum. I'd not see them if not with Dad.
 Hmm. I've said I'd take you and your sister. I thought it would be better without me around for you with Dad. I have hit you too Tyler.
 Yea Mum but that was cos of him. It's got worse since Christmas, since you had that fight with Dad.
 Oh.
 And then I had an accident and Ma was going to...you know..
 What's Alyssa doing when all this is happening?
 Standing by Dad, laughing.
 Oh. Do you think she may be scared that Dad may hit her if she does not?
 Well he's never. She still rubs his back and picks his pimples all the time.
 Why don't you?
 I'm a boy and I chew my nails.
 After a long silence they just talked of nice memories. After

about an hour Tyler went back to bed and to sleep.

May 19. Tyler's teachers and aide talk to me. They are really concerned about his deterioration; he is not coping at all, bursting into tears and sobs over the smallest thing. Last term they would have stood up for him over complaints of hurting etc. but not now. His behaviour in the playground is really a problem as is the constant lying; they are also concerned about the smell. I decide to stop the aperients the doctor ordered a few months back and wait till we see the Paediatrician.....

I am really scared, afraid, so full of guilt, so tired, tired of everything, so scared that soon there will be nothing left to give – then what will happen to Ty and Ally? I wish Ty could be 'normal' – it is such a struggle all the time to just get ordinary things done EVERY DAY: wash face, clean teeth, get dressed, have your puffer, go to the toilet. If I fail him what then?

And I am.

I had him. I put him in this situation and I cannot help him.

I cannot cope with the responsibility and guilt, with the futility and frustration. At this moment I don't want to exist for ME, yet I have to for them.... The overwhelming anger, resentment, frustration, selfpity, and responsibility he – Joe – can go off and do whatever he desires, no hassles, no commitments, and no responsibility – I can't even work regularly – but then it's always felt like this. And when I let him know I have a life instead of rolling over and playing dead, I fear the kids are going to suffer. I should have just said 'Yes Joe, no problems Joe, whatever you want Joe', instead of saying 'Yes, but....' What payback are Ty and Ally going to suffer this weekend?

It is as if someone knows when I feel I'm beginning to get my life on track, as though I am beginning to feel I have some control, say over my life, some hope for the future for the three of us and they decide to smash it all up and cause havoc so I have to start all over again – just to remind me I have no say, no control, no hope....I know I have to be consistent, reliable, calm etc. for Tyler but HOW, when I'm being yelled at, abused, threatened by a child?

Using Xrays Tyler is diagnosed as having severe constipation and he is prescribed a long regime of treatment, tablets and disposable enemas; the mum has to be the nurse, not a pleasant job for either Tyler or Lisa. The Paediatrician does not consider there is an abuse issue or that Ally needs to be seen.

Joe is not that happy. Tyler becomes scared to go to school in case 'Dad comes and gets me and takes me away to a new Doctor who will use a big needle like he and Ma said would have to happen to fix me.' Lisa wonders where she would stand legally if this was to happen.

Her friends across the road have moved to another suburb and now Sonja and her family are moving over eight hours away. She wonders why she is always losing supportive friends and whether the effort of making friends is even worth it. Lisa is still struggling with the weekends she goes to bed not being able to kiss her children goodnight.

June 15. So full of many mixed negative feelings and so tired. Up, down, up, down and just when I start to get the hang of things and see a little hope the rules are changed again. I am fed up with him controlling me. I truly wish I did not have to depend on his money. I hate what he is doing to me, yet there is nothing I can do. And yet perhaps it is me – noone else seems to see him as 'bad'. Why can't I get on with my life and stuff him? Life for me would be easier if I had not continued it – perhaps I should have walked away – the kids want him –scream about how much they miss him, that's it all my fault they can't see him. Tyler wants him back in this house. Why do I keep struggling? I could not survive without them yet it would be easier just to give in and say it's my entire fault, I'm a bad parent, a worse wife and walk – hand them over to the better parent: let him have the minute by minute responsibilities that apparently I take too much on board and stress about. I love them so much and yet I am such a failure. Now I have to manage on $300 less/month. He has enough to buy one or two motels depending on who is talking, but not enough to give me to help care for his/our kids and he still demands that I buy new boots, more clothes etc. for his house.

Should I just dump the kids and go back to work despite the welfare agency saying 'NO', as care for the children costs them more? No, everything in me is against this: but perhaps he's right, perhaps it is because I'm too lazy. I don't think I'm strong enough to survive another 10-15 years like these last two, yet what choice have I got? I can't even fight back.

Tyler has just come in and asked if he can watch Better Homes and Gardens with me, wanted a cuddle too. Perhaps it is worth all my personal pain just for brief moments like these.

In other diary entries over the following months and years Lisa notes some of the comments over money that her children or Joe have made or written -- Dad is unable to have a proper house because you take all his money...Dad was unable to buy us a McDonald icecream as he had to buy chocolates for your birthday (The kids enjoyed the chocolates.).....Dad can't sponsor us as pays you all his money.....'Lisa, with the clothes would you please try not to send over clothes from the OP' (Opportunity Shop is like a cheap second hand shop) shop. Given the level of support something a little better to keep here would be appreciated...'...
..'Please note I have had to buy PJ's for the kids. Given the child support I pay I think it's unfair. I think you need to help out here and provide me with some good clothes etc. If not I will be making my position clear to the child support people.' (If I was earning his $30-40000 income I'd tell him where to go with his money and threats and he'd lose the joy of control.).....Joe cannot come to Tyler's first Choir concert in the city, cannot afford to unless I pay for his ticket as well as mine and Ally's...

July 13. Great day. Tyler did all his jobs and more, no reminders. Both kids helped make sausage rolls, no fighting. Ty washed dishes and helped me with Ally's reader then we played UNO together.

Brief moments, but oh so very brief.

Hugh wants Tyler in his grief counselling program and tells Lisa she 'must show her emotions to the children.' The teachers want her to work with them, so Tyler is 'receiving discipline at home as well as at school to not let him get away with hurting people.' – Ha! What do they think I am trying to do! Both Lisa and Alyssa are sporting bruises. Some of Lisa's entries of Tyler's behaviour this month tell a little of what it was like -- Throwing punches at my head and chest for several minutes while Alyssa cowers and I deflect. This has to stop......I refused to do up his buttons this morning so he threw forks, book and pillow then kicked and punched out at me. Then cried most of the way to school as 'wanted time at home with me as misses me too much' – talk about confusing.....I would not allow Tyler to play with my headphones and tape player I used for choir because of how he asked and I had stopped him from visiting a friend the other day because of pinching and kicking me, now he was again because I refused to do up his buttons which he can now do himself. Refusing to go outside and cool off. Ally scared and crying. Ty refusing to go to his room, so I get hold of his ear – woops! Explosive rage, throwing everything, breaking glass, incredible strength and hate on display, screaming over and over 'Ya don't listen, ya don't care, I'm asking ya something.' When I asked what he just kept screaming these statements. I don't know to do. Ally is terrified. I don't know how to stop it. Someone please understand how bad it is and help us. First time I've never been able to kiss him goodnight. I just could not bring myself to go into his room and have him start up again

Lisa again discusses these events with Hugh, the school councillor. He wants to meet with Joe and Lisa together – I get all shaky and teary just considering this but will if there is any chance it will help Tyler. Joe though refuses to meet Hugh if Lisa is present as 'she has not had a friendly dispossession towards him since the separation.' Joe also tells Hugh that he 'is happy with the way Lisa is bringing up his children but because he is very busy with studying and the business he is not able to help.'

Over these and future years Tyler keeps trying to have more time with Joe. Hugh tried to set up several meetings with Joe to discuss what Tyler was hoping could happen. But Joe would find excuses work or study, refuse or even not show up despite having agreed to do so. Somehow Tyler always saw it as Lisa's fault that he was not allowed to be with his father.

Hugh began to voice a suspicion that 'perhaps some of Tyler's undesirable behaviours were connected to his not so good a relationship with Joe as well as what occurred during access.'

Tyler's teachers had a different opinion, telling Lisa that they 'felt his behaviour was due to frustration at not getting his own way.' Lisa comments – I hope so. If it is not related to Joe I can work through it. If it is I cannot. I can't make Joe do anything. I'm tired of having my energy wasted on 'fixing' problems created by Joe. Would sooner focus on here and move forwards.

July 23. Last night in bed after reading my Bible and while praying I felt this incredible warm calm cloak like Grandmother's eiderdown made from real down, fall and wrap itself around me, embracing, safe. I had not wanted to move in case it went, not even to open my eyes. I stayed still and went to sleep in its cocoon. Tonight it is back.

It is not only Tyler who is giving Lisa heartache. Alyssa is beginning to say things that trouble Lisa greatly.

July 27. Concerned. Ally came into the bathroom, she usually knocks but did not this time and saw me in the shower. Asked why I had 'fluff like a boy there', pointing to my pubic area. I asked her how she knew that boys did, instead of answering her question. 'Oh I just do. You don't have a penis jumping around.'

Lisa again asked Alyssa how she knew. Her reply was, 'because I do.'

Lisa's stress levels reached a new high, if this was possible. She recalled Joe prancing around their bedroom, naked, very erect, making it 'jump' and being very smug. It was not a pleasant memory. A couple of days later she writes – Unable to sleep. Flash-backs,, smells, sounds, the works, of our sexual relationship, most of it very unpleasant. If this is how it is with 'normal' couples I don't ever want to again.

Tyler develops a big pus filled pimple on his forehead. Alyssa announces, 'Dad has lots on his back and I have to push the yellow and red stuff out.' Lisa is not pleased to hear that this is still occurring and it's not just the concern that Ally may catch something. Joe used to get Lisa to do this on the couch after the children had gone to sleep, and she remembers what he would want after --

Alyssa is a little girl not a replacement for me, for what I had to do. He should get another grownup, not his daughter!

Things for Alyssa during access did not seem to be improving. Her nightmares and screaming during the night worsened. She would sob, begging Lisa not to make her go to Joe's saying he had told her that 'it was up to your Mum not me if you come or not.' Even Tyler was showing concern about his sister, firstly that he was worried about her not being allowed to see the cousins if not with Joe. But as Ally gets worse and the sobs more obvious he begins to insist that Lisa speaks to 'Dad and tell him she does not want to go mum.' Lisa replies saying that she 'already had and he knew that Ally was not wanting to go but still insisted that she did.' Great - Lisa thinks to herself - let's do everything Joe wants regardless of what you want.

During these months Lisa is being nagged by Irene on several occasions, 'It's not good for you to not be going out. You should be out and about, considering having someone.' Shows how little Mum knows, or understands despite my efforts to explain. I'm just not heard. How could I risk it again? How could I put the kids through it again? That part of me is dead. Joe thought so! It will remain so. Life is kids and work.

Lisa is acting as a locum for a well respected masseur while he is overseas for around six weeks. While she loves the work, sometimes putting in twelve hour days, she is torn. Friends, neighbours, afterschool care, holiday programs and her parents help with the care of her children. She comments – Tired, sore but fulfilled. I not the mum, not the ex but I was actually worth something.....School holidays, I'm still working. I'm missing the kids; their laughter, talking, yes even the fighting not to mention the cuddles. Work is not worth missing out on this – but can I have it both ways? I want to cuddle and kiss them so badly and listen to their chatter, while watching the expressions flitter across their faces. I rang them. Ally gossips away over every little detail: Ty just tells the bare bones but it is good to hear their voices.

Yet regardless of all that is happening around this time Lisa is still struggling with feelings for Joe. Late in September she writes -- How screwed is my mind? Enough that this morning I sobbed in the shower because all I wanted last night when Joe picked the kids up was for him to get out of the car and cuddle me and never let me go. He looked so good, yet so untouchable now. He has been the only source of emotional comfort in my adult life and now there is nothing. Good Christian that I am! God should be enough and yet I cried because I wanted to be held, comforted, understood, supported and loved. A tiny voice says, 'well you had it and threw it all away because it was not 'right', you wanted more, perhaps something is better that nothing?' NO! NO! NO!

I am alone, terribly alone but I am alive! I have a life, the days are good. God give me the strength to live, live this lonely life now. I love my kids more than life but they are not a soulmate.

November 18. I still have no contact number for Joe, so rang his mum to inform them that Alyssa has the chickenpox and is very miserable. Four hours later Joe rings, he spoke to Ally then to me. He spoke in a calm, pleasant manner as though to an employee with only half a brain, wanting to know if it was still okay to take the kids out. I said yes, but best not to mix with other kids.

He is still having them for weekend access, does not understand Alyssa's problem -- perhaps someone has been saying things?

I suggested that perhaps they were not happy having to stay in bed till after 10am and then watch TV for the day.

What crap (tone now harsh, angry and impatient). You can't believe a 6yr and a 10yr old, you should know that by now, we do things with two active children, you have to, we do lots together, noticed Alyssa has had problems the last 4-5 visits, don't know why.

I suggested that watching a movie about spiders may have.
Rubbish!
Well even the teachers have noticed her checking the walls
He did not argue the point as no longer just my view.

Had to go to work for a few minutes and got caught up, kids disappeared and put TV on for a few seconds before I realised, you know how it is, you can't watch them all the time, what do you want me to do, you have them for 10-14 days, I only get them for 2, of course she does not like leaving you. Don't you want me to see them? I want Alyssa, I want to work through this problem.

I replied I would not be putting her in the car like before again. Joe did not say it but his whole tone of conversation was that I was causing the problem between him and his daughter and that I cannot believe **anything** the kids tell me. I don't believe they could tell such constant untruths.

When I told Ally that Dad wanted to have her as he wanted to see her she started crying and begging me not to make her. What do I do? She ended up promising me to get into the car if I walked out with her. I had not been doing this the last few times as just too hard with his unpredictable anger.

Again Lisa speaks to Hugh at school. He feels that Tyler 'does not cope with any change or threat of change well as he associates it with bad things.' Joe had again changed the weekend access dates. Tyler had worked out this change meant that they did not get to see Joe for several weeks, till Christmas. Again he believes it is Lisa's decision, not Joe's.

Tyler is now pulling his hair out, creating bald patches. Hugh is 'really concerned about Alyssa and her feelings about access.'

So how did this year end for Lisa?

December 15. Thoughts after watching *Mathew*, a video of the Gospel Mathew at the manse. Uncomfortable that because of my sin Jesus had to suffer like that. I wish He did not. Who am I that a stranger should go through hell for me, instead of me? I did not ask for this – for someone to suffer like that. But who am I to refuse a gift from God?

But with every day decisions, problems, how do you know what God wants you to do? How do I tell the difference between GOD's desire and mine? Like with questions about nursing, access, massage and even smaller stuff?

Got a lot of stuff, voices in my head and some are not good confuse, cloud issues, causing problems I don't need.

Prayer – my way or Barb's? Are both right? Or is she right and mine are not giving enough honour, reverence? Do I have to quote scripture? Do I have to be 'nice'? David in the psalms he penned was not always. If God knows what I am thinking and feeling before I work out how to phrase them verbally and say them 'rightly' why can't I just be honest and spit it all out? God what is what You want of me? Give me...can You give me understanding, words, actions etc. because I don't know how to. Perhaps I do treat Him too much like a friend, not enough fear, but...

Bill and Irene agree to come to church when their grandchildren, Tyler and Alyssa are involved in the Christmas Pageant. The negative comments and feelings that swamped Lisa following this service gave her much to ponder.

December 19. I am writing again, I have no one to talk to, to share with. I found myself in church today, unwilling to share or be with my parents. But I did the right thing and I could feel myself taking on my Father's ideas. I could feel the fight in me to stop them. Instead of the warm comfort I usually feel in church, even when challenged and reawoken to my sinful state I felt the heavy oppression of negativity. So instead of introducing, conversing I hid in the kitchen or over attended to the kids.

When home – we left early before I could share in the cleaning up that I enjoy and the conversations I hear during this time because Dad was very restless and edgy – the subtle complaints and niggles started. 'This woman introduced herself, the one you said worked on radio and wanted to know if we were new to the church, if listened to the radio. Your father replied 'NO' and soon put a stop to that sort of conversation' 'Biblebasher' was the unspoken words. I explained Barb's unique and envied gift of going up to people, especially in trains and starting up such conversations – 'yes well some people are just pushy'.

Dad had fallen asleep, so resting on Sundays came up and how ridiculous this notion was for all sorts of people from farmers to garden lovers. I said that people in church have differing ideas on what to do on this day. Lynette loves working with God's flowers yet Daniel does not see this as a Sunday activity. 'Yes, well', Mum said, 'things do get taken much too seriously.' Unspoken comment 'don't you get so carried away!' When I said the answers are found in the Bible she said, 'Oh well I don't understand that. I used to go all the time before you came.' So not only am I the cause of Mum not going to church I now feel like a naughty, disobedient child to be seen and not heard. I cannot witness to my own parents, I feel shut out. They have all the answers. Theirs is the only right opinion – unspoken or spoken. All this is okay if helping me cope short term, a 'crutch' while I'm broken, as long as I don't get 'brain washed' or 'sucked in', too seriously involved. I don't belong.

They are so wrong, but I can't tell them that. I can't hurt them but I can't be silent. I won't bury myself again, deny HIM again. I need to find a family, a surrogate 'Mum and Dad' that I can talk, share, open up to and grow with. How do I do this? I can't even talk to Daniel, he is a 'he', the past gets in the way, and I get tongue tied, awkward. And it did not help when Kay in a stagewhisper as leaving church and about to shake his hand said, 'perhaps he's the one!' I can barely look at him so fearful that he may be thinking I am 'the one'. I don't know how to behave with other men either for the same reason and I find myself saying, acting in old ways that I know are wrong ....

Lisa now got distracted by another thought and writes –

Consider the angels. The Baby, born knowing He had to die. As a mortal. As an unholy, sinful person. We – NO – I am Judas. I kissed Jesus. For the world, money, sin. I killed Him. I betrayed Him......

Bill had been scathing in his attitude when realised Lisa was putting money into the plate but relieved that she 'showed some sense' and only put in $5; 'only lining the minister's pockets and he doesn't look as though he's going without.' Daniel was a little on the portly side. Bill's comments and tone troubled Lisa, she had been studying Malachi, a minor prophet of the Old Testament and tonight she was reading Chapter 3. She read it several times – Is God challenging me to 'Try Him and see?' Why not?! Tenpercent, a tithe, of the monies I receive as well as earn and before anything else gets taken out, is quite a lot, around $40-50 a week. The kids needed new shoes, clothes and school books soon, not to mention the bills.....NO. Let's see if this 'promise' works, is real. If it does not and the kids start to go without, I can always go back to putting $5 in the plate that is only the price of a pair of work stockings, which I needed!

You, my dear Reader will have to keep on turning the pages if you are curious to see if God proved Himself trustworthy in this for Lisa. But before then, would you like to know if Lisa found her 'spiritual' Mum and Dad?

Well it was more of a case that Charles and Lynette, around the same ages of her physical parents, saw her need and stepped in and just became. They began by mentoring Lisa and taking her through the required studies before she made her Profession of Faith in the New Year. Charles took to minding the children so that Lisa could attend prayer meetings or the Ladies Group meetings. He also attended as a 'grandparent' for school activities of Ty's. They opened up their home and hearts to this lost family. They were played with, fed and cuddled; physically, spiritually and emotionally warmed. Lynette gave the biggest, bestest hugs, warm, enveloping and soft and she cried and prayed with and for Lisa and her children, as did Charles.

## Chapter 4

The New Year began on a difficult note. Tyler was to have stayed at Bill and Irene's with their other grandson for a few days. Murray however did not want him there as he felt Tyler was a bad influence on his son and so Lisa had to bring Ty home.

Irene has several times told Lisa that Tyler is cut from the same cloth as Joe and 'a leopard never changes its spots as the Bible says'.

Lisa does some searching for herself, refusing to believe there is no hope for her son.

Jeremiah 13:23, 'Can the Ethiopian change his skin or the leopard its spots? Then may you also do good who are accustomed to do evil.'

*Mathew Henry's Commentary* says of this: 'It is morally impossible to reform and reclaim these people.....But there is an almighty grace that is able to change the Ethiopian's skin, and that grace shall not be wanting to those who in sense of their need of it seek it earnestly', and so Lisa hopes and continues to pray against her parents reality as well as the reality she sees, for her God to show His power to reverse the impossible. I still am.

A little while later, following an access visit, Tyler announces 'Dad has a girlfriend and she is going to be my stepmum.' Alyssa was also excited about this wedding as she she was going to have a part in it. While driving home from Irene's with the children, Lisa sees the lovers.

Joe could not have planned it better if he had tried. They were just about to step over the kerb to cross the road at the 'Stop' sign where Lisa had to, well stop – Saw Joe with girlfriend, arms around waists walking, waiting to cross. She is beautiful, young, flowing, glossy hair, trim, shapely, figure hugging jeans matching Joe's, carefree happy lovers. Joe is Mr. Cool, tanned, suave, tight jeans, white tee and sunnies, strutting, big grin when realized it was us, me. They look good together; suit each other, the 'beautiful people'. Amazing how much can be absorbed by your mind in seconds! Going around this town like we used to. Is he parked in the same spot? Going to the same pub? Why did he stop loving me? Why did he start to hate me so much? I feel like when Murray punched me in the stomach hard enough to drop me, I feel just as Joe described me so many times: 'a fat, ugly, stupid bitch' old, frumpy, haggard, useless, discarded, hated, unwanted, unloved, despised, ALONE. Why can't I get on with my life? Why do I feel as though I am marking time, just surviving, going nowhere, meaningless, worthless – But how can this be? God is with me, holding me up. He has given me life so I am NONE of these things. I should not feel as I do!

February 1. Tyler exploded this morning, physically violent to me. I had told him off for hitting and punching Ally who was now under the table, and to go to his room. It was really bad till I said, 'okay I've got my hands behind my back (I'd stopped defending myself) punch and kick me as much as you want.' He stopped immediately, actually surprising me. Hugh rang later – I had spoken to the school staff when I'd dropped kids off – he 'feels it is a response to his fears and worries over the girlfriend and will talk to Ty.'

February 3. Have mixed and confused feelings with kids going to Joe's this weekend. I hope they like her and yet I'm scared they will like her more than me: the perfect family unit... and me. Yet Joe is not all powerful. He does not destroy, GOD does. So he cannot destroy me as much as he may desire to.

February 4. Kids eager to go, full of questions – 'What do we call her? Mum? No that's you, so what?' I reply 'whatever you and they are happy with.' I go to Lyn and Charles's place for tea with Daniel. Study and discussion, very interesting, actually one of the best nights I can remember. I just need the courage to get my feet up front and stay there while everyone prays for me after I've made my Profession of Faith.

Joe having a girlfriend brought numerous changes to the access routine. Things would come up where he could not have the children. Saturday nights for example, but wanted them for the rest of his weekend. Lisa found herself having to refuse or cancel hospital shifts that would have given her a couple of hundred dollars extra income to 'babysit' free of charge but with bonus stresses. As her availability to work became unreliable Lisa was called into work less and less.

February 17. My Profession of Faith. The warmth most of the church especially the ladies gave me surpassed that which I have ever experienced from family. They wanted nothing of me, they took no credit, and they felt joy, emotion for me. They were not demanding anything for themselves from me, they were not needy, they were pleased for me and what I was experiencing, the hugs, and the emotion I felt from them to me was incredible. Gives a different insight into 'who are my mother, brothers, sisters....these are...'spoken by Jesus (Math.12:47-50). I love my parents but have never experienced peace in their presence or support without strings. Thank You God for Your grace, for the life, family and friends You are leading me to. Grant me wisdom not to throw it away as I did in the past.

March 7. Barb comes to tea, giving the kids a copy of the Bible she had as a child. She was very encouraging to Ty, spent lots of time talking to him about the Bible and how to pray. He sat and listened, seemingly taking it all in. Tyler amazes me sometimes with his responses and behaviour.

Barb has encouraged Lisa to attend BSF (a ladies only Bible Study Fellowship) and to join her and some of the older ladies in a BYO lunch and talk afterwards. Lisa loved the singing. She had been involved with a choir for a while, singing at weddings and public functions but these were songs of freedom, peace, her God and her spirit soared on eagles' wings. Lisa writes – My life is now so different, so fulfilling, and full of learning new things nearly every day.

Bill, her father, is not impressed with her new understandings. Lisa is eager, maybe too eager to share and Bill challenges her to 'prove there is a God, as no one can!' Well how can you respond to a challenge worded like that? Lisa decides no pearls before.... well let's say she just decided to remain silent.

LISA DENNY

# *A Meditation on Psalm 121*

*I lift up mine eyes to the hills –*
*From whence comes my help?*
*Not from the world*
*With all its fleshy lures*
*Not from the people*
*Who cannot understand.*
*Not from me*
*With all the tumult within.*
*My help comes from the LORD*
*Who made the heavens and earth*
*The caressing wind*
*As it goes where it will*
*The rhythmic ocean*
*As it goes out and comes in*
*The starry heavens*
*As in awe I gaze up.*
*And my soul is still.*
*L.*

March 17. Joe arrives to collect the kids. I erred in saying he should have let Hugh know he could not attend the meeting they had set up. He became very angry, swearing aggressively. I turned away but he started to get out of the car, so being scared about what could happen when he got out I turned back to face him. The kids were watching, bugeyed. I'm sick of my life, of still reacting to him, still dependant. He only wants Ally for Friday nights now as she is constantly upset every access. He has said nothing about this since last October. The girlfriend's gone. Ty is demanding that I take him to visit her.

Lisa finds herself unable to sleep, so pen in hand she sits up in her bed and starts writing at four o'clock one morning during this month of her God's love for her and therefore her worth – To experience love from my parents I had to 'earn' it. Earn their respect, earn their willingness to listen, earn their willingness to help. I had to make them proud of me. I had to aim for their shifting expectations, their ideals, and goals. I did not matter.

There were no open arms to hold me, to make me safe and give comfort. I never succeeded. To experience love from my (ex) husband I had to have sex. Sex was my comfort, my security, my only way of feeling that he saw me, listened, understood, cared, that I mattered. I hated myself. I sold ME and got nothing.

To experience love from God, I do nothing. Just accept His view of me as a sinner and take what He offers. Is this where the fear comes in? He knows me as the world sees me – unlovable yet He sees more, worse, all my sin, everything, thoughts and all. So much more than anyone else, me included, yet there is no rejection, no 'strings', only His love, His wisdom, His understanding, His security, His comfort, His peace, His safety – how could I not love Him! HE has given me HIS all, including the death of His Son. I have given Him nothing, only pain and disappointment. And yet He loves me. ME. He will never reject me. His Son will fight for me. And should I become lost and confused yet again He will search tirelessly for me and rejoice greatly when I am found. It is scary – but a good scary – what He is doing for me in this life, as I know it. He is in control. I can let go and soar free without the fear of falling, failing, being alone. Who can understand such love? Not my parents, not my (ex) husband, not even me, fully, except that I am no longer running away from these arms but fighting to crash straight into them with all of me forever.

April 1. Who am I? Have I been so busy being who my parents wanted, who my teacher wanted, who I thought I needed to be to be suitable wife material, who Joe wanted and his family me to be and who all contacts expected me to be that I no longer know? Yes, I like my cat and dog, even with the extra hassles. Yes, I like classical, rock, gospel and hymns. Yes, I like soppy romance films: no violence, bloodletting or sex. Yes, I like singing and I can hold a tune. Yes, I like nature. Yes, I like kids and oldies. Yes, I like helping people without expecting or wanting anything in return. Yes, I believe in God. Yes, I believe a man should cry, should be able to touch, cuddle and passionately kiss a woman without having to go further. Yes, I like the person emerging: fat and all!

*Who can know and love me?*
*Surely the mother who bore?*
*With her power to reject fearful*
*Her inability to see*
*Her conditional love*
*Bruising.*
    *Who can know and love me?*
    *Surely the husband?*
    *With soul exposed*
    *Stripped bare*
    *His knowing a weapon*
             *Battering.*
*There is no one*
*Who knowing me can cradle with love.*
    *Yet One did.*
*Knowing seeing loved*
*giving His very blood Cleansing freeing clothing*
*Covering me with Love eternal.*
    *L.*

May 4. I met with Ty's counsellor at CAMHS (Child and Adolescent Mental Health Services). She feels 'that any counselling involving me telling my story, which is a pretty bad (Really?) one of aggressive emotional abuse, would amount to re-traumatizing self, so not on'. Whew! No counselling until I'm ready to talk, sounds good to me! To become more assertive and increase selfesteem 'Yes you are a beautiful woman, with lots to offer'. Ha! 'See what I mean!'

June 6. Reading a book on biblical parenting.[7] It's a dream. Can this really work in real life? Only catch is this house has no 'father head to teach, discipline and lead' – just me. Can I be used as Your instrument to bring my kids to salvation? Book suggests 'a sharp smack but not given in anger for fighting, hurting, back

---

7    Standing on the Promises. A handbook of Biblical child rearing. Douglas Wilson. Canon Press 1997. Note: as with all other references Lisa does not necessarily agree with all that she reads in a book and so does not expect her dear Reader to either.

answering, disobedience and disrespect.' My hand let alone their bottoms could not handle this, I'd be smacking before I got out of bed and after I went to sleep!

Lisa gets talked into going out one evening while the children are on access by her group of non-church friends. They take her to a local pub, and unbeknown to her a blind date has been organised, a bloke they think is suitable for some 'light fun' – I froze as always. He did not fit into my 'safe box'. Fear, panic. Feelings that were impossible to fight though I managed not to run. Are these emotions protecting or hindering me?

The Reverend Daniel Hankey had been loaning Lisa a range of books and she had also been raiding Barb's and others' libraries. She was devouring Christian literature, factual Biblical based theology doctrinal, all the 'big' stuff but no fictional, romances or the like, as she had once devoured Mills and Boon.

Through these books and the sermons she was hearing on Christian radio as well as Daniel's preaching and studies, Lisa was beginning to develop an understanding of what a truly Christian friendship with a man leading to courtship and marriage should look like, along with a lot else, and it was not, did not belong in a pub atmosphere!

Daniel preached a sermon on 1Corthians 14:33b-40 and Lisa writes – If I knew a godly man I hope I would have no trouble being submissive. The Biblical idea of this actually seems pleasant.

Feeling that God may have been softening her up to make her consider the possibility of marriage again one day Lisa decided to 'agree' but on her terms. If her old nursing friend, Lil had thought it was all right to make a list, Lisa could!

Firstly, he had to appear in her church. She was not going looking in pubs, cafes or anywhere else, as she was not looking!

Secondly, he had to be tall, blue eyed, older – that meant probably been married, probably had children, so these had to be older, okay with her appearance in their dad's life and not needy.

Thirdly, he had to be really strongly grounded and mature in his faith and knowledge of God, a regular church goer, well liked by others, not into the social scene.

Fourthly, he had to be okay with her kids – well more than

okay.

Fifthly, he had to belong in her 'safe box'.....

Get the picture?

Lisa was determined to make it impossible for God to find the 'right' man. She should have known better by now!

Hugh is running a program over several weeks in June, *Raising Boys,* specifically for single mums. To break the ice those present share photos of their sons and a brief personal history and then break for coffee, nibbles and more of a chat. Lisa writes – While I was on my knees searching thru my bag, one of the women introduced herself, 'Hi. I'm Joe's ex.' The 'gorgeous one' I'd seen. I just sat there and sobbed. Probably scared the daylights out of her, I was scaring myself! I could not stop shaking. I wanted to be sick. She wanted to talk, 'could bitch for hours....'

It felt as though I was being ripped open and apart. Is there no where I can go and be me without his shadow following?

She felt that Joe was a 'hard, cold man, especially towards his children. I could trust her and talk freely as she would not repeat anything.' Buddies? Bitching buddies?

Oh no, I don't think so! The desire to be sick was so strong I had to go outside into the winter's night and freeze, make myself numb. It's not her fault or her problem.

Lisa writes the next day – I've had to deal with the children's reactions and stresses as a result of her relationship with Joe, with their 'noises' at night causing questions I did not need and escalating Tyler's violence yet again. Alyssa's belief that their break up was 'all her fault' was making her clinginess and tears worse. And how can I 'now feel free to discuss everything as she's not seeing Joe now. You can trust me.'

Trust? Trust another human, Ha!

She said I'd 'be able to see the funny side tomorrow', well I can but it does not cause me to laugh, it causes another pain my body has to deal with that he has caused, even if indirectly.

Hugh wants me to talk to her. Oh God how can I? I don't want to know, like her, I don't want to deal with his exwomen. I don't want to, cannot deal with the pain and confusion and hurt, it is like having to face everything from the start again and I don't want to.

Perhaps it is not wise to keep everything buried, but the numbness is better than the pain.

All right Lord, You threw this one at me, or allowed it. You have promised that all things will be for my good (good = whatever makes me more Christ like) let it be so, just please help me to cope with this agonising pain. Should it hurt this much if I no longer love him? I wish I could remove him from me, then this would not hurt, then I could get on with life, with being me.

Lisa's level of distress did not allow for a good sleep and she is awake before sunrise the next morning, wondering if she needs to go back to counselling – Perhaps I should contact Daniel and see if he knows of a Christian counsellor. Right! If it is meant to be he will answer the phone, it's midmorning now. There was no answer. I fought to trust. Trust and obey for there is no other way....

By the time Lisa arrived at the BSF meeting that morning she was distressed and teary. She sat in a back pew and thought – Okay, I know this is not the right way but I'm going to just open my Bible – speak Lord!

Psalm 121 'leapt', verses 3, 7 and 8 'screamed' at me --

'...he will not allow your foot to be moved; He who keeps you will not slumber...The LORD shall preserve you from all evil; He shall preserve your soul. The LORD shall preserve your going out and your coming in from this time forth, and even forevermore.'

Lisa glanced at the rest of that page in her Bible and the end of Psalm 119 caught her eye so she started from the beginning.

Verse 24 – 'Your testimonies also are my delight and my counsellors.' How much plainer could I want?

Then verse 28 –'My soul melts from heaviness; strengthen me according to Your word...; v.50 -- This is my comfort in my affliction. For Your word has given me life...; verses 65-68 – You have dealt well with Your servant, O LORD, according to Your word. Teach me good judgement and knowledge, for I believe Your commandments. Before I was afflicted I went astray, but now I keep Your word You are good, and do good; teach me Your statutes...; v. 73 – Your hands have made me and fashioned me; give me understanding, that I may learn Your commandments...; v. 75-76 -- I know, O LORD, that Your judgements are right, and that in faithfulness You have afflicted me. Let, I pray Your merciful kindness be for my comfort, according to Your word to Your servant....; v. 92-95 – Unless Your law had been my delight, I would then have perished in my affliction. I will never forget Your precepts, for by them You have given me life. I am Yours, save me; for I have sought Your precepts. The wicked wait for me to destroy me, but I will consider Your testimonies....; v. 114 – You are my hiding place and my shield; I hope in Your word..; v.116-117 – Uphold me according to Your word, that I may live; and do not let me be ashamed of my hope. Hold me up, and I shall be safe....; v. 132-133 – Look upon me and be merciful to me, as Your custom is toward those who love Your name. Direct my steps by Your word, and let no iniquity have dominion over me....; v.143-144 -- Trouble and anguish have overtaken me, yet Your commandments are my delights. The righteousness of Your testimonies is everlasting; give me understanding, and I shall live...; v.146-147 – I cry out to You; save me, and I will keep Your testimonies. I rise before the dawning of the morning, and cry for help; I hope in Your word...; v.169-176 – Let my cry come before You, O LORD; give me understanding according to Your word. Let my supplication come before You; deliver me according to Your word. My lips shall utter praise, for You teach me Your statutes. My tongue shall speak of Your word, for all Your commandments are righteousness. Let Your hand become my help, for I have chosen Your precepts. I long for Your salvation, O LORD, and Your law is my delight. Let my soul live, and it shall praise You; and let Your judgements help me. I have gone astray like a lost sheep; seek Your servant, for I do not forget Your commandments.' And the peace became louder again.

Lisa had begun to realise if she was not looking squarely at God, if she was looking elsewhere, if something was taking her focus away, the peace she felt deep inside became quieter, harder to 'feel'.

The class then started with the hymn, *Amazing Grace*, Lisa's song, followed by another favourite from her childhood, *How Great Thou Art.* YES!

The speaker then retold a tale that had been given to a congregation by an elderly man – 'A father took his son and the boy's friend fishing. There was a big storm. Even though father and son were experienced fishermen they were unable to keep in the boat. Father had one life rope and two boys. And only seconds. He knew his son was a Christian. The friend was not and had shown no desire to be so. So calling out to his son, telling him he loved him dearly, the father threw the line to the friend. The son's body was never found. The father knew his son would have eternal life in heaven. He could not face the thought of causing the friend to have an eternity in hell. Afterwards two teenagers politely spoke to the old man, telling him it was a nice story but a bit unrealistic that it was done in the hope of the friend converting. 'Yes,' the elderly man agreed, 'except I'm that friend', as he held on to a worn Bible, the Bible that had been his friends!' The size of my pain withered. I still have lots of questions and fears but I'm glad Daniel did not answer the phone this morning. One lesson from this – increase my trust, increase my faith, increase my amazement and awe at how He works, increase my willingness and trust to depend on Him. I am still not short of money despite tithing and God is decreasing the pain and confusion without stirring up victim, selfpitying feelings.

Note tonight's reading was Psalm 71:18. 'In You, O LORD, I put my trust; let me never be put to shame; deliver me in Your righteousness, and cause me to escape; incline Your ear to me, and save me. Be my strong refuge, to which I may resort continually; You have given the commandment to save me, for You are my rock and my fortress. Deliver me, O my God, out of the hand of the wicked, out of the hand of the unrighteous and cruel man. For You are my hope, O lord GOD; You are my trust from my youth, by You I have been upheld from birth; You are He who took me out of my mother's womb. My praise shall be continually of You. I have become as a wonder to many, but You are my strong refuge. Let my mouth be filled with Your praise and with Your glory all the day.' Keep in mind there are no such things as coincidences or luck for a Christian – me anyway!

Lisa went to the next session of *Raising Boys*. The 'gorgeous one' was there also and despite there being plenty of empty seats she sat next to Lisa, who fought a losing struggle against thoughts of her being with Joe. So she did the only thing she could, she prayed. The 'gorgeous one's' phone rang. She left and did not return that night or for the rest of the sessions.

June 30. I hate smacking. Tyler just hits and hurts his sister more. What am I to do Lord? Show me. I feel as though I'm failing in all areas.

July 2. Both kids now asking to come home from access Saturday nights, so can come to church with me; I say 'Allright by me but will have to check with Dad.' Oh God let me cope. Hardly any break. Let my Father in heaven arms enfold and hold me as my father or husband never did. Let me rest in the knowledge that He loves me just as I am and forever.

Sunday's sermon struck a chord with Lisa's position at this time and also challenged her. What follows are the sections she underlined after asking Daniel for a printed copy. --

Ecclesiastes 9:1-12. Believe it. You have a choice of whether you want to be glad or not, whether you want to be joyful or not. You have a choice on how you look to others. Sure there will be times when things are bad but how you react to those circumstances is still in your hand...

Knowing there is a purpose to these trials and tribulations helps us to act differently, in fact it helps us to rejoice and to be glad. 1Peter1:6. The way we react is up to us. It will depend on our attitude and how we look at what is happening to us...

Worry selfdoubt, fear and anxiety – these are the culprits that bow the head and break the spirit... 'for it is now that God favours what you do'. How many of us recognise this fact? God favours us now. Not tomorrow, not after we die as Christians but now, this instant...

How can this be true? I'm really suffering and there is no way that I'm in God's favour because of all the things that are happening to me at the moment.

When we find ourselves thinking such things there is one

antidote... ' Count your blessings, name them one by one'... 'go eat' God supplies your food...All that we need...also drink, clothes...everything needed to live...even a marriage partner.... an ability to love, to be glad, to be filled with joy and the ability to enjoy yourself...but these we take for granted...see them as 'normal' parts of life , as something we do for ourselves...

Many couples are in love but are not companions, enjoying life together...others have wrong ideas about relationship...a husband who lords and treats his wife as a slave...making it not possible to enjoy life or be companions...

Do we thank God for His blessings...Now if God's favour is on us why do we worry?...Why do we let worries stop us from enjoying life?...Mathew6:31-34...get priorities right. Put God first. Can start to do this by remembering and counting the favours He has given already... 'this is your lot in life'. God first. Partner second, then the rest....

Next we should do everything to the best of our abilities... So how should we live life...with all our might...giving it our best shot...What is stopping you from achieving things? Too scared to make a mistake? Too frightened that you won't be able to cope? What is stopping you from doing everything with all your might? Nothing should be because you are in God's hands, God's favour is on you now and God will provide everything you need...

Life does not have to be meaningless but if you ignore God or reject His way to live your life it will be meaningless when the time comes to face God...

July 24. Alyssa is having nightmares about 'a bad man not letting her or Tyler get to me'. Tyler rings Joe as 'wanting to spend every weekend with him and just every second Sunday with me so can go to church.' Ty says Joe 'can't at moment as has to go to hospital.' Tyler is scared 'Dad will die and he does not believe in God', so he prayed for him tonight. In the morning Ty was glad Jesus had not come.

But within less than a fortnight Tyler had changed his mind again about wanting to be with his father. He is also calling Lisa a liar again, this time because he says that he 'had never wanted to be involved in the choir, was just pushed into it', and he 'hates' her – I am so tired of this nastiness. Not a day goes past that Ally is not in tears because of him...feel overwhelmed and under pressure then when he acts up I cannot control the situation and I revert to the way I was brought up. Not what I want to do!

      FEAR DOES NOT EQUAL RESPECT!

Hugh advises, no tells Lisa, 'to tell her children next Friday, just before Joe arrives that they will be staying with him for the whole weekend. She needs a break as she is not an endless supply of energy. She is not to tell Joe till he is picking the children up. And she is not to feel guilty, as there is no reason to, and she is not to get into his mind games but to go out and do something for herself'. Hugh challenges her by saying he 'expects feedback and is quiet excited for her' – I wish I could be. Fear of payback, kick back already.

There was none of this, it was Father's Day and the children were 'pleased to finally be allowed to stay the whole weekend' with Joe. As to the 'doing something for herself', well Lisa spent the whole weekend in bed with the flu. Not what she thinks Hugh had in mind but still a luxury for her.

Tax time comes around. Lisa carts all the required bits of paper into the accountant: he is 'amazed that anyone can live on so little'. Lisa knows how. Her Father has opened the 'windows of Heaven and poured out blessings' just as He promised in Malachi 3:10, remember my dear Reader?

The need to write often over these months and the coming ones continues. In her writing Lisa is talking to her Father, trying to work things out. She sits in her bed at night, the house quiet and still. Tyler is asleep, not jumping around throwing himself on the floor screaming that she is pushing him.

But Alyssa is having trouble sleeping. She is become nasty and angry, shoving and hitting Lisa, almost like Tyler, shouting that she 'can do as she wants as she is the boss' not Lisa. What follows are a sample of these longer writings, of what Jane would much later refer to as 'Lisa's buzz buzzing in a bottle till she becomes exhausted, till falling to the bottom and is ready and able to hear God.' And my dear Reader, please remember these are more feeling based than doctrinally correct statements about our

LORD God. I have chosen to leave the errors of Lisa's thinking in for our sanctification takes a life time on Earth!

August 8. So much confusion. So much internal and external war. No wonder the coward's way out, throwing everything, in holds some appeal – at least for the short term. I'm tired. I'm torn. I can't. I don't want the burden, responsibility every day, every minute of my life or the kids.

I'm resentful. Why me? Why should I? Why can't I dump them on him and go and do my thing and just see them one night out of fourteen but only if it suits me as he does?

Because it's not in me! It's against everything that is me – worse luck a voice says – it's not fair.

I'm back to the same old same, I want someone to hold me, to share a game of chess with, to dance – just to be, to have fun I've forgotten how to do that with an adult who cares. I don't think I could one on one now, I don't think I ever have. I am no fun. I am angry, resentful, envious, frustrated, confused, using Christ's name as a swear word – I'm no good under pressure, show true colours and they are evil. Depressed, a failure. I know how I should be and yet daily I know, I am shown what I am, and it's not nice. How can I be a Christian? Who am I to show others how to live – I can't even get it right for me without mentioning kids or others? Who am I to think I have something to offer, show, teach other people's kids?

Leave me alone. Let me be. Let me hide.

I hate myself. A stranger looks back at me from the mirror. How can God love me? I am a fake, a fraud, a hypocrite. I don't want to go back to BSF, to mix with others. I don't belong, I don't belong anywhere. For a while I did, as a student nurse but it was gone before I knew. I don't belong. I feel uncomfortable with others. I think He is getting great delight at showing me how far I am from Him. How I don't belong. Tempting me with the thought that this struggle is in vain.....

I am butting in here my dear Reader with a question for you to consider. Keeping in mind that sanctification, that is the process of becoming more like Jesus in character is a lifelong process Is it God who tempts or something, someone else? Maybe you could check out James 1:12-17 before you answer.

Now back to what Lisa is writing – Why not just give in and just be? I have never personally achieved recognition for anything in this life, never been anything but a failure: in this I want to succeed, I want to be Yours. As unworthy as I am, I don't want to let go and give in but it is so hard and I feel so alone. It is so hard to believe that I am Yours. Yet I have to, for if I don't then how can I believe that You will not let me go no matter what: and if I can't believe this then there is no point to life, to being, no reason, nothing.

I am a failure because I am still trying to do it by my power. I don't know how to let You do it —make me good on a daily basis. I just know I cannot do it. I have tried but my mind is cunningly evil and always fails me on a depressingly, frequent daily, hourly rate.

There has been nothing in my life to show me to trust in others despite my true self: do good, be rewarded, do bad, forget it. How can I understand, trust Your love? There is nothing in this life to compare it with. I even fail as a parent as I cannot love my children as You love. You daily show me Your goodness and love towards me. Why, when I more frequently show my hate, sin to You? Why me? There are others more worthy, more deserving, more able to love, obey and serve You. I will never please You. I cannot. I am too lazy, tired, pathetic, greedy as I want LIFE. I want Your peace how dare I when I can give nothing in return.

Don't forsake me. I'm not strong enough. I feel guilty for being thankful that You forsook Your own Son so that I would not have to experience that. Don't let me go – keep Your promise – even if I do let go in my weakness. Hold me tight. Fight for me as I cannot. Thank You God for friends, even though not Christian -- who am I to judge -- that support and care that make the darkness of aloneness not so thick.

I fear hell – yet that is where I belong. I want to walk with You, yet I do not trust that my faith, such as it is, is capable of saving me from hell. But yet, is it my faith? Is it not Your saving grace? Your promise, that in this I can trust because it is so impossible to understand, comprehend and yet so simple. You spoke and it was so. So the 'trick' is not to trust me, not to believe in my faith but You. Though I don't trust me for have I not seen how fickle this is? – I don't seem to be able to let go of me and truly turn fully to You. There is too much of me in the world and not enough in You and no time. I'm scared for self and kids: hear me my LORD. Save us, I pray. Not necessarily from this world for it is short, time moves faster as you get older, but from eternity in it, in hell, eternity without You.

    August 23. I belong. I am not alone. My LORD and Christ died for ME.

Leave feelings behind. Just know this.

If this was not so, how come I have got this far? By my ability? I think not!

Remember the pit? The death wishes? You hit rock bottom. You could not help yourself; neither could anyone else! Most were not even aware of your pain.

Remember the numbness, the ability to shut down so you could do what had to be done; remember when you became aware that this was not some ability but your LORD shielding you, taking your pain on Himself?

Remember all the answered prayers; there are no coincidences. Know the peace now as compared to before.

My LORD died for ME, because I was, am, will be unworthy, because He loved ME. Because He chose to love me, despite myself and what I am, do or feel. And He will NEVER stop loving me. He will never leave me. He will only do what is best for me. His love knows no end, has no boundaries, and has no restrictions, buts, conditions, payoffs. It is given freely, endlessly. All I have to do is grab on and hold tight. He will never reject or despise me.

It is enough. Know that it is this simple. The simplicity is what is hard, especially in this world. It is enough. All else will follow.

God forgive me. Thank You is not sufficient – but thank You for Your love; I accept it. I accept the death of Your Son as payment for all my sinful deeds, thoughts, past, present and future. Teach me wisdom. Teach me forgiveness. Teach me so I may become as He, so I may be worthy.

August 24. Render = give in return, give back, pay as due. Psalm 116:12-14. 'What shall I render to the LORD for all His benefits toward me? I will take up the cup of salvation, and call upon the name of the LORD. I will pay my vows to the LORD now in the presence of all His people.'

Is that all? In some ways it seems too little compared to what He has done for me. So simple. Why do we make it seem so hard and complex?

September 7. My thoughts on Death and Dying. What is it that causes the fear? From twenty years of nursing, listening, observing and personal thoughts, surprisingly even for an unbeliever it is not usually the being dead, it is the dying.

Unbelievers either think they go to the great fishing experience or heaven; there is little fear of a hell, or they truly believe that there is nothing after, nothing. To be honest I think a lot of Christians, me included fear the dying. Dying grace is not given till we need it to begin with. Apart from this, why, what is it about dying? We were not meant to originally, so in a way it is unnatural. What else?

1. Pain.
2. Loss of control over bodily functions, being dependent upon others, pity, embarrassment, shame.
3. Disfigurement.
4. Aloneness.
5. Concern over those you are leaving behind.

On the surface, especially with some terminal illnesses sayings can appear trite, meaningless platitudes. E.g. God only lets us experience what we can handle...Christ suffered as us, He knows and understands. But wait, let's consider this: that Christ suffered these things – remember though God, He was crucified as a Man. He felt pain for example as you or I would.

1. Pain. Physical or emotional.

Luke 22:44. Mathew 26:67, 27:29-30. Mark 8:31, 9:31, 10:33-34. As with a terminal illness He knew what was before

Him and yet like us perhaps He did not really know because He had never experienced sin.

Mathew 16:21, 17:22-23, 20:18-19. Mark 14:65, 15:15, 17, 19. Imagine the pain of having nails hammered through your wrists and ankles. Then the weight of your body pulling on them as you hung in space. This would be enough to make most people incontinent. Imagine the pain and fear as breathing becomes difficult due to the constriction of the diaphragm. The struggle to push up to breath the fight to breathe, the fight to live: these guys died very quickly when their legs were broken because they could no longer do this action.

2. Loss of control.

You have no say, others making decisions. Pain does cause incontinence, hallucinations, ramblings of mind and speech. This 'king' was treated as a low class criminal. He could not even carry His own cross. He may have also been completely naked, hanging there for all to see; as the Romans deliberately did this to increase the shame and so the torture, especially of the Jews.

3. Disfigurement.

The beatings and scourings made Jesus 'marred more than any man' (Isaiah 52:14) almost unrecognisable as a man. The pain during crucifixion could also twist and contort features.

4. Aloneness.

Rejected by all His disciples, they could not even keep Him company that last night, during the night watch. He was rejected and mocked by His own people. Even His God left Him. We may feel alone dying but if a Christ-follower, we will not experience God leaving us. Christ travelled a pathway no believer ever will have to. He was alone; we will be surrounded by our Father's presence.

5. Concern for others.

Mary His mother was not only needing physical help but spiritual. This is perhaps why it was John instead of the next eldest son, who at this stage was not a believer. John 19:25-27.

His concern for the disciples, us and the world, John 17:6-20.

So I believe Jesus the Man experienced the process of dying as we do -- though He chose to do so voluntarily -- the same fears, emotions and abstract feelings. But because God hid from Him, His dying was so much worse, so much more than we will ever face. Have courage, know that God will be there for you, that it will be okay: for it is, unless you are alive when Christ returns the only way into Heaven, only way Home.

October 26. Yesterday Tyler was yelling angrily, physically aggressive, gesturing and eventually grabbing a bag containing a cauliflower off the bench, swinging and throwing it to hit me in the face. Today not a cauliflower but a glass bottle, just because I scolded him for hurting his sister. I rang Joe, asking him to have just Tyler this weekend. No, but he will talk to him, had not been aware he was hurting us. What's the use of Hugh's communication book idea if Joe's not reading it!

October 31. Spoke to Hugh. Advised to speak to Joe in Tyler's hearing and get him to have Ty as often as able. Here we go again. 'No, not possible. No free days or nights, including weekends as studying and exams. Have had no holidays in last three years. And none in near future. He sees them for the required amount of time I can't and should expect nothing more.'

Daniel visits as a result of my phone call to him and strongly tells Tyler that his anger is not to result in hurting me or his sister, that no man does that but a coward.

Mum rings and I share a little of what's been happening, including Daniel's visit. 'Your father could say the same thing to him but we are worried about Joe hearing and causing trouble, not allowing us to see the kids' What a terrible thing to be afraid of!

November 8. Tyler's teacher tells me to 'get counselling for myself as it is my attitude to Tyler that is not helpful. Yes he may be treating me similar to Joe but I am reacting to that past stuff rather than to Tyler and his behaviour.' – Oh really!

Lisa is no longer able to walk the children out to Joe's car.

He has been getting too angry and aggressive in stance as well as verbally. She is scared and does not want the children to hear or see this behaviour.

They have Boxing Day lunch at Bill and Irene's. Lisa is asked by her mother to say grace; she uses the one her Grandfather said at every meal, one they all would have known – 'For what we are about to receive, may we truly be thankful. Amen.'

Murray is scathing, telling his sister she 'needs to get a life'. Lisa replies that she has one now because of Christ, because of Christmas and Easter. In an I-know-all, you-know-nothing voice that stops any further conversation by Lisa, Murray states that the 'only people without a real life are Christians.'

The year ends with Tyler being hysterical. Yelling for new socks among other things and bashing his bedside light against the side of his bed till it broke.

Happy New Year!

Lisa's reading was Romans 15:13. 'Now may the God of hope fill you with all joy and peace in believing, that you may abound in hope by the power of the Holy Spirit.' Pen in hand she wrote her thoughts – Hope belongs to fairy tales, not me. Hope, hope for a 'normal' life, someone to love me in this world for me. Someone to hold me and rock me when things get tough and not to criticise, finger point, blame but someone I can feel safe to argue with – this hope is a dream!

The hope that Christ will return seems easier – He has promised it and since history is not over it has not been disproven. But my history has disproven such a hope for me, over and over and over again. I want someone to hold and comfort me so much and yet I cannot take kindness in thought, action or prayer easily as it weakens me – this I don't understand! It seems to let the pain become stronger – the pain of aloneness. Just the ability to hold a conversation and to keep company with a man like 'normal' women do, without being uncomfortable and selfconscious and worrying about what he is thinking or how he is interpreting me would be an enormous step for me.

The Reverend Hankey is diagnosed with a life threatening illness just as he is preparing to marry Ruth. And Joe has glandular fever, so will be unable to see the children until further notice. As Lisa continues to bow her head ever so slightly and silently to say grace at her parent's table or wherever she is, her brother's aggressive and loud use of God's and Jesus Christ's names as swear words continues to escalate.

Tyler and Alyssa are understandably concerned about their Dad, they write letters and try to ring him but without any answering responses from him. Ally cries till she makes herself sick. Towards the end of February they finally get to speak to Joe on the phone and are told that he will take them to his mum's for Friday night then back to Lisa's Saturday.

February 6. Tyler angry, yelling and crying because I won't dress him for school. Tonight it was like he snapped, no warning, no reason. Yelling, demanding me to help him remove a harmless mole off his back then and there. I am unable to reason with him. So he throws a kitchen chair repeatedly on the floor, then charges into his room and begins to jump up and down on his bed, screaming, and then rushing out to start bashing the laundry door open and shut till it is almost off its hinges. God what am I to do? How can I help him? Is this because Joe's unwell?

February 7. Yesterday never happened. No trouble at all. A different child.

Another weekend beach holiday is planned and organised. Lisa though, becomes concerned about money. There is less in the account than she thought. Kay visits because she is suffering from a migraine; she pays $50 for the initial treatment as well as for two more in advance. Lisa goes for treatment herself as her back and chest are troubling her again. She is asked to do a swap as the practitioner she goes to, also needs treatment. No money changes hands as a result.

The holiday gets off to a great start; the children are helpful and well organised, even doing all their homework. Lisa still worried about finances and is feeling like a miser as she refuses to buy the children icecream. But walking the beach the following morning there in the seaweed was a five dollar note. Her God was watching, was understanding, was capable of providing. That note was placed in the offering bowl and Lisa bought the children icecream the next day.

Then Tyler, against Lisa's wishes, tries to move his bed to make it. It breaks. Lisa is upset and lets him know she is not happy and wished he would listen when she says 'No' – He got hold of a very heavy based lamp and went to hit me over my head. I ducked instinctively. I saw his eyes and I knew that he knew he had won, I had lost and for good. I was terrified. Part of me wondered if I'd be writing this if he'd had a knife or a gun instead of a lamp. Later, when at the beach playing I looked up and he was sitting on Ally's head. She was under the water. I had to shove him off her as he did not respond to my yelling 'get off!' at him as I ran towards them.

Next day they drove back home. Tyler as usual slept most of the way. Lisa made lunch for the children when they got home, then commenced to unload the car – Tyler began to demand I stop and teach him how to make custard as he was still hungry. I refused to do so till I had finished unpacking. He started to toss stuff out of the pantry cupboard, yelling. I asked him to go outside and cool off. My voice was getting softer, deliberately but his louder. He picked up a chair and came at me screaming, 'I'm gonna to kill you.' Ally ran to get Dorothy from next door. I rang Joe and told him to get here and take Tyler as I did not want him in the house. I told Joe what he was doing. Joe refused. I then rang Hugh. I could only make these calls as Dorothy by now had somehow got Ty into a corner and sitting on the chair. Hugh told me 'to ring Joe again and tell him he had said that Joe was to take Tyler for two weeks starting now.'

Joe marched into the house, no knocking, as if he still owned it and sat himself at the kitchen table which was in the lounge as I had started painting the kitchen before we'd gone away. Tyler was one end of the table and Joe the other. No contact, not even by eye between them. Joe proceeded to tell him how 'ashamed and disgusted' he was with his behaviour, 'bad boys like you get locked up; put away.' I stayed up the other end of the house with Ally most of the time, only hearing snatches of the conversation, the one way conversation. 'If he heard that Tyler was behaving like this again he would take him to the police station, no TV there mate'.

When I asked Joe to take Ty as he rose to leave he said that he 'could not as had a full time job so I could have maintenance, unable even to take for the night as had to get straight back to work' checking his watch yet again.

He asked if Ally was okay, but did not want her for the weekend access coming up till she spoke up saying she wanted to go. 'Would mean a bit of a shuffle', he said, 'she'd have to sleep in his bed, and he'd have the couch, as did not think it was right for them to share a room'. And he was gone. Under thirty minutes. 'Done the best I could with what I have', though he did manage to give approval of my painting and the changes I'd made of his home.

Hugh visited a little later, 'disappointed with Joe's lack of responsibility.' He talked about other options, 'perhaps foster care, as Tyler would have to be removed next time he threatened me'– not 'if' but 'when' Hugh kept saying! He also spoke about psych and academic assessments through CAMHS as Tyler has been under their care for a while now.

I function but I'm numb. Where is my bubbly, loving little boy in red gumboots gone? Worse, where is he headed?

Dorothy commented later she 'had been scared, shaking by the time she got home.' She also noted that Ally did not stop eating the whole time.

I can't hear You LORD – don't let me do more harm to the kids. Let me make the right decisions for them. I am so alone.

Lisa leaves Tyler alone; he remains quiet, looking through childhood photos over the next few days. On returning from the weekend with Joe he is weepy and upset, as he does 'not see enough of Dad, as he can't because of something to do with child support. What's that Mum?' Tyler also tells her that, 'he does not want Lisa spending money on more swimming lessons for them as it should be spent on clothes for Dad's house, as Dad said.'

April 21. Tyler 'busting', barging into the toilet while Ally was in there, squeezing his very erect penis, it's dark purple, to 'stop wee', then running in yelling at me in the bathroom, before charging outside still exposed and holding himself screaming 'as if let go see, see'. Do other eleven year olds behave like this?

April 26. I lost it with Tyler tonight. I'm so frustrated! I've had enough of his constant yelling, abusive putdowns and blaming me for his father not having him Wednesday nights and two weeks holiday each year. When he refused to go to his room after hurting Ally yet again I hit him across his face, only bit I could reach. I hate myself much more than he will ever hate me and a little voice says yet again that perhaps Joe is right and I am not a suitable parent for them or anyone.

Because Lisa sits in the back pew at Church she notices new folk who come and not return, or keep coming to 'her' church.

She had noticed a tall, straight man, who always seemed to sit in the same seat, come and go on and off over the last few months, but had not really paid much attention. However one Sunday there was a bit of a commotion when another couple had to almost carry him out, one either side with their supporting shoulders under his armpits.

Lisa thought he must have been in quite a bit of pain but she was more concerned at that time about how to get Tyler's name on the manse lawn mowing roster, Daniel is unable due to the treatment he's receiving. Lisa has been told that she needs an adult male to supervise her son doing this chore. The tall man's name was Luke and Lisa's first entry in her diary about him follows --

March 18. Luke's back is better. He sat next to me. I tensed ready to fight against my usual tenseness and fear but oddly this did not happen. I felt no desire to run. He will ring if wants Tyler's help with the manse lawns.

Luke did get Tyler to help with the lawns and take the rubbish out to the tip before Lisa and the children went interstate for the school holidays. Charles and Lynette had helped her organise and plan this adventure, as well as encouraging her that she was capable of achieving this dream. It was a good experience, a lot of fun and memories with only the everyday normal manageable sort of hassles and problems with the children.

She had invited Luke to stay and have lunch with them after he and Ty had returned from the tip all dusty and thirsty, after all it was only the polite thing to do. But Lisa kept the front door open, a detail that did not go unnoticed by Luke, however at this time he just remained silent, observant.

April 24. In general conversation I ask Robert, a church leader, how hard is it to get married in our church. I was thinking of my friend Kay, an unbeliever who had been a couple of times, and wanted a church wedding. Robert asked if I was considering marriage, I laughingly replied, 'do you see anyone around?' He and his wife, Gina, Lynette, Barb and Charles all grinning and in one voice said, 'Yes!' 'Who?' I returned. Again as one came the reply, 'Luke!' I got all flustered. Speaking to Robert, I said that 'if it had taken me nearly two years before I could shake hands and reply to Daniel's questions without panicking, it would take me another thirty before anything else.'

I thought it was just my imagination, my fantasy, my need to have someone, not real, not concrete, so why do all these people think this? I speak to Luke, he is easy to talk to, nonthreatening, have told no one except Lynette about him coming to lunch and giving Tyler his son's old billycart...but there's been nothing slightly 'romantic', so why? Does this mean everyone is watching me and 'matchmaking'?

Lisa was to learn much later that the older ladies of the church, some knowing Luke from other Christian circles, had taken one look at his arrival at St. David's and started praying for him and her. Luke stood no chance!

Poor Luke. If he has no such interest it could be difficult. Do I say anything to him about this? Do I stop talking to him at church? Just as well he did not sit next to me today like I'd hoped. Come to think of it I've had several people tell me or discuss within my hearing what a 'good, caring, gentle Christian man' Luke is. Oh dear! Do they see something I do not? Or are their imaginations as bad as mine? I asked Lynette on the way home if that is really what people are thinking; she said 'not to worry but to pray about it, asking God for a good Christian man.' Yes. If I leave it to God it will be right, for me, kids and whoever and God will see a way to remove my fears/garbage.

April 30. Thinking again about the other night's comments and how closely others seem to watch me at church. How should

I now act with Luke? Troubled, these thoughts intrude on and off through the day. I don't want to be a cause of discomfort or embarrassment.

Several days later Lisa writes – Actually it's a bit of an ego boost to my selfesteem. These people all must think I am a woman who could be loved and wanted by a man! Maybe I should listen to their voices instead of Joe's.

Maybe indeed, what do you, my dear Reader think?

## Chapter 5

May 9. I stopped fourteen years of abuse by removing myself from my husband. How can I remove myself from Tyler? It's like living the nightmare all over again. I can't do this again. Walking on eggshells, waiting to see what he will do. I'm standing at the entrance looking down a dark tunnel. How can I stop entering it? He is my son! And Ally, she feels sick most of the time, worried about him hurting me; not wanting to stay, not wanting to leave and go to Dorothy's. The pain is too much and it has not even started.

And you thought this chapter was going to be about Luke! Well it is but Lisa still had everything else to cope with as well, including her children having to cope with yet another girlfriend. But she had no idea how prophetic the last statement in the above entry was to become.

The 'experts' had organised Carers Support to visit Lisa in her home. This sounded great, respite, oh how lovely, space to breath. But when confronted with the reality of a stranger, male or female, staying overnight or just during the day, with her in the home, Lisa just could not do it. The thought just caused panic.

May 30. Restless. Conflicting emotions about my personal feelings and relationships with others. Me, as a woman, not a mum, an ex, a nurse, but just me. I wonder what the point is for much of what I'm feeling, doing.

May 31. Very low, lonely and confused. I've had nightmares the last couple of nights. I am going to be alone for the rest of my life. I ended up in the shower (as it muffles sound) sobbing. Wishing I could touch, feel, hear God/Jesus as He is the only One who will never leave, hurt, or destroy me. The only One who wants me. But then one day I will be able to, I'll be with Him. Gave it all to Him. His choice. His will. My gain. My peace.

Two days later, yes two days, at church Luke asked Lisa

if Tyler could help again with the manse lawns in a couple of weeks' time and could he take them all to the children's favourite takeaway for lunch. Before Lisa could reply her little shadow, Ally piped up, 'Hungry Jacks?' So of course Lisa said 'Yes'!

I leave it to God, the confusion and worry about me and men and look what happens: I have a 'date'! Well sort of. Who says miracles don't happen! Lord if nothing comes of this lunch at the moment I feel anyway that it will be okay, because the main joy is because You heard my loneliness, my feelings of undesirability and of never being wanted and gave me this hope and for now that is enough. What am I that You should so beautifully answer my despair? You are my LORD, my ROCK, my ALL in ALL. I am not 'a fat, ugly bitch that no one would want let alone look at'. I do not have to be 'grateful' to Joe for being the only one who could want me.

June 4. The joy in God this morning was almost painfully touchable, so acute was it at what He has done. In a way one of the most painful remarks of Joe's was that 'no one else would ever look at you' has been wiped away by Luke asking to take us out. Romantic? No. No hint of anything else but because it is not my doing but God's it is enough, a final seal if you like, of me being worthy for just being me.

The 'date' was well nice, comfortable, safe, no fear.

Tyler was going to be assessed by a Professor, to see if he was within the Autism Spectrum. Lisa wonders if a label will help. She tries to speak to Joe about this development but he makes no comment, just went on about how she will 'have to buy PJ's for kids to keep at his place' and if she doesn't help out he 'will be reporting me to the authorities'. Lisa contacted the 'authorities' and was told she 'had no legal responsibility to provide any stuff to keep at Joe's house. Both parents have a moral responsibility to insure their children are clothed and have a home like environment.'

Lisa wonders if she can excuse Tyler's latest outburst on his stress over this upcoming test. He became loud and smart mouthed, 'Why don't you lose more weight, you're taking up too much space. Ha! Ha! Ha! I expect my jeans to be washed by tomorrow morning.'

Deuteronomy 29:29. 'The secret things belong to the LORD our God, but those things which are revealed belong to us and to our children forever, that we may do all the words of this law.' – was tonight's reading. I don't know my future but God does. It is enough for Romans 8:28 – 'And we know that all things work together for good to those who love God.' It will be only to my good.

The end result of this assessment was that Tyler was suicidally depressed and placed on medication  Where have I been!

Tyler's been 'boxed' and started treatment. Things should improve. WRONG! The medication lifted his mood but in doing so the 'brakes' were taken off and his behaviour got increasingly worse, not better.

June 17. Tyler covering Ally's head with the beanbag and jumping on her. She is afraid, so am I. Great! I'm glad God loves me. How could anyone else?

August 5. Luke apologised for not asking till now, but has wondered about Tyler's test results. He appeared interested, concerned and caring. Lord he is so easy, comfortable to be around it scares and attracts.

August 8. Bad morning. Ally sobbing as Ty screaming over and over 'Up yours Mum', I felt numb for rest of the day. Troubled by flashbacks of Joe saying similar stuff. I don't want to go back into the house after being out seeing clients. Not wanting to cope with Ty alone tonight, but no options. I don't know him. I can't help him. LORD I'm terrified for him and Ally. Wish for once Joe would put kids' needs before his own. He tells Ty's teachers he wants to be more involved and spend more time with them but I don't see it. I can't raise Ty by myself. Lord help me to find someone who can help Tyler please. I have chest pains. I have a very long, hot shower and good sob.

Later in the month during a meeting with Hugh and the CAMHS councillor Joe is praising Lisa up as 'a good mum and of course he is willing to support her with the children.' Lisa never knows these words as actions however.

August 12. It is not my job, responsibility to ensure others happiness, pleasure etc. to my cost. I am not God. When we know God stands with us it does not matter who stands against us.

Lisa's birthday is coming up. Her children with Dorothy in charge are planning a party, inviting Luke and Madge. She is one of the older ladies within the church who has befriended them and calls Lisa 'my sweet girl'. Charles and Lynette are away. Lisa begins to become apprehensive – How to act, what will they think etc. BUT then I stopped. I do not need to do this. I worried most of my married life what to do, say, think so I'd not upset Joe, so he would love me, if this is God's will it will happen regardless of what I do or don't do. Luke is a grown man, he can say 'no'. I can be free to be me, the me God wants. As a result I can live life like never before; I can have truly abundant life and not be afraid. How could I not love You, my Shepherd, my King, my Companion. You know my tendency to jump in and do things though. You don't need my help to make things happen. I pray that I will not give You a helping hand to move things along but that I trust You to give freely all good things when it is the right time. Love and companionship and sharing of Your Word will occur with who You choose!

The Reverend Hankey has been watching more closely than Lisa had realised and deciding that she needs to know that Luke is a 'good' man tells her how he came to be single. Luke chose to put God first and to be obedient to Him in all of his life. Lisa wanted to hear what Luke had to say, so asked him -- He had walked deliberately away from God as a teenager, causing much grief for his parents. Married and had two children. Life was wanting and he knew what was missing. He also had a fair idea what would happen and so delayed as long as he could but living without God was not for him. Having her husband love God more than her, alcohol or cigarettes was not for her, she left taking the children who were little more than babies. 'Choosing God,' Luke said, 'will always cause life changes.'

The current CAMHS councillor, Helen is a Christian. She speaks to Lisa about respect and what this means. 'God made us all, therefore all humanity deserves respect.'

October 12. Kids upset. This girlfriend has gone. Ally is

crying during the night again. Tyler just lost it, trying to jump out of the car as I was driving to school, demanding I 'give him a new family by the time school is over today or else.' Helen tells me 'not to lose self-confidence so easily, not to debate with Tyler, not to get sucked back into love/hate relationship with Joe.'

Despite asking her father and Joe to teach her how to change tap washers, Lisa has never been shown and now she has leaking taps and Bill is away. Luke to the rescue! But not till he had ridden Ally's pink bike, despite having the legs of a man who was over six feet tall! Ally, not yet five, and so much shorter, was riding her Mum's bike, leading Luke along their obstacle course through the bush. Laughter.. Tap washers done. Luke is very easy company, natural, despite being slightly sore! I don't deserve life so good, so abundant, but thank You.

Lisa is again losing her voice due to another severe throat infection. Lynette's daughter is concerned how she can cope without a husband to help – Did I ever really have one to do that? God please don't let me become dependent on a man for happiness, security and be let down, hurt again. Let me enjoy what I have, whatever that is, with Luke but look to You to meet my needs. Ha! Seeing I've stayed home hoping he'll ask me out. Be careful Lisa. Thank You LORD for teaching, showing me how to accept and be greedy for the blood of your Son and the life He offers. Thank You for keeping me alive, for Tyler and Alyssa, for bring me to here.

November. What is there really between Luke and me other than 8 meals in 9 months? Lots of laughter and fun to begin with!

December 1. I rang Mum, her conversation and tone upset me. She was asking me 'what is a Christian?' yet saying I had no right to say that someone may not be. 'Suppose you think your old mother is not'. I had told her there is no life without Jesus.

Later this month Lisa is at her parents' home for tea, it was not a comfortable evening  In an almost proud tone – perhaps it was defensive – as coming to the table Mum stated, 'In this house we don't say grace, just thank you.' Oh, Mum I thought, who to, and what else is grace but thanks. She went on to say that 'her parents did so just to get the kids in order.' 'Yes,' I replied, 'there are some side benefits, look to God and He provides everything.' Mum then went on to say her grandma had a saying, 'The Lord helps those who help themselves.' 'But,' I said, 'none of us can really help ourselves.' I had heard this saying a lot as a child, funnily I had forgotten it. The unspoken meaning being that God's only interested in selfsufficient people, the ones who cope in their own strength with the life He's given them, who are not needy. Boy am I glad this is a lie!

I felt as though I was being tested, my beliefs questioned and then casting them away as she was right and I wrong. I did not continue this conversation. Help me, my LORD to deal with her halftruths in a way that will glorify You and keep my faith intact. Open her eyes and heart fully.

A conversation during morning tea at church one Sunday between an older couple and Lisa sent her into a bit of a spin. She had looked up to Ray and Vera, and they had been encouragingly supportive and helpful. But today Ray was telling Lisa that, 'if Joe became a Christian it would not matter who she was married to she would have to divorce him and remarry Joe'.

Daniel was not impressed when he heard. He reassured Lisa that this was unbiblical and gave her a book to keep called *Second Chance*[8] by Ray Sutton.

It was revolutionary to Lisa's thinking, liberating in fact. Remember she actually had no real 'evidence' yet that Joe had been committing adultery while they had been legally married.

What follows are extracts from this book --

'...marriage is a convent of companionship; ...covenantal death in marriage definitely encompasses physical death. But, it also means that if the spouse breaks the moral terms of the covenant, he will die to the relationship, and the marriage would be dissolved; ....covenantal death is an ethical or moral separation of some sort....death to a person's relationship with his spouse kills the marriage bond. Covenantal death releases the innocent party

---

8     Ray R. Sutton Dr. Gary North, General Editor. Second Chance. Biblical Principles of Divorce and Remarriage. Biblical Blueprint Series. Dominion Press 1988

from the jurisdiction of the guilty party, making the innocent party free to divorce and remarry without being classified by the Bible as an adulterer; the capital offences of the Bible are divorceable offences. If they kill the person's relationship to God they kill the marriage covenant....sexual sins...murder general classification includes...physical abuse, desertion (physical and sexual); ...the 'one flesh' phrase also indicates a condition of death...it pictures a human body being torn in half should the covenant bond be broken; ...remember, apart from repentance, there is no forgiveness, meaning no true restoration; Jesus literally overcame the dead (Old Testament) covenant through His own death and Resurrection...event that makes a New Covenant possible. It offers a second chance to man, but is also the theological basis for the concept of *remarriage,*'

So Joe had 'died' as far as their relationship had been concerned and shown this in his actions and attitude towards her! Lisa's feelings and her response were validated by God's Word. Wow!

Ray had challenged Lisa earlier about having a 'catholic cross' in a very prominent position in her home. Lisa did not know what a 'catholic cross' was and Ray was happy to explain. Apparently 'they' have a crucified Christ but 'we' are meant to have a risen Christ therefore an empty cross. A friend, Rainie, from Lisa's nursing days had passed it on to her at the request of her dying mum as a 'thankyou' for helping care for her.

Each morning when Lisa got up after her time in her Bible and praying, and came down the passageway to start the daily routine of getting the children up and feed, she saw her Christ crucified so she could have life. If He could go through that for her, she thought, surely with His strength she could get through whatever would happen that day.

However Lisa could see Ray's point. She did worship the risen Christ, the One who had torn the veil and given her direct access to her Father's knee. After some days of consideration and still with a slight reluctance Lisa took the figure of Christ off the cross and rehanged the cross (well re-Blu-Tacked it actually!) empty but still there, first in her vision each morning. At this period in her life, a much needed 'in-her-face' reminder.

December 8. I'm feeling. I'm scared, overcome with emotions that Luke and ghosts are stirring up. Lynette reminds me not to worry as all is in God's hands. Psalm 56:11 'In God I have put my trust; I will not be afraid. What can man do to me?'

What is real, what is fantasy Lord?

December 20. Ally asked Luke to have tea with us. Laughter and more laughter. It's like an empty space here now he has gone home. I'm scared LORD; I'm liking his presence a lot.

December 25. Realized during last night that despite seeing and hearing my kids not at their best Luke still asked about a day out together next week. Church friends and family for lunch, I could talk freely of You – all this as well as life GOD?! – Thank You.

December 27. Dorothy asked me when I'd 'last gone out for a day and had to do nothing but go, no food preparation or kids'. I can't remember! God it is hard to believe that tomorrow will happen. I'm excited but also scared. No kids to hide behind and a sister, an important sister, to meet. Let me be me, no games, let it be okay for Luke and Jean.

December 28. Luke takes me and Jean to Tree Tops Christian Convention. I have around fourteen hours with Luke. Tyler went to Mum's and Ally to Lynette's. Luke bought me a Max Lucado book. 'If I did not accept it I'd have to walk home' he said! He came in for a cuppa when he did bring me home, asking if he was to shut the door or leave it open – he'd noticed! I had been wondering each morning when I woke what You will bring into my life for that day. I asked Luke if this is right or should I be wondering how I can serve and glorify You instead. He replied 'that this wondering is glorifying You.'

I remember my initial surprise, shock when I walked into the convention's auditorium that day. It was big and it was full to overflowing. There were more people my age and younger and a lot did not 'look' Aussie. My God was *big* and very much alive and active! And the messages! How could Luke and Jean not want to hear what was to come the next day? Oh, Luke bought the recordings of the messages! He lent me the ones from this convention and *all* the others from many previous conventions. What a feast! I also discovered how good it felt to have Luke's arms tightly around me as well as praying and singing together The New Year had not even started LORD and You did it! You have topped it all in less than 3min. by leading Luke to hold me. Cuddle me! Our first cuddle. What is going to happen next LORD? I can only lean on You and wait in wide eyed wonderment like a child. Thank You for loving me and bringing me to You. Whatever happens LORD keep my by Your side please. Luke said that if you pick up one grain of sand every 100 years, off every beach in the world, when you have finished and there was no more sand, Eternity would hardly have begun. This heaven is where I ache to be but I thank You for the joy here in this moment also.

January 1. I'm curious LORD; each year gets better and better. What or how can You do better this year when You excelled over abundantly last year and I feel as though I have done nothing. How could I possibly feel more joy in living, be more eager to live, yet be almost content to die? The peace, joy and hope You have put in my life this past year is overwhelming, so much so that sometimes I have been put to my knees sobbing. I have never known the strength of these 'good' feelings; I don't quite know what to do with them. Glad I can talk with You. I pray that You will continue to make me walk Your path. If it is like this here, how much more will heaven be?

Looking back I can only recall one time that I was 'put' to my knees, by my bedside and sobbed. The children were not around, perhaps at school or access, may be I'd just made the bed, I don't remember now. But I do remember suddenly 'seeing' what I'd done to Jesus, who I was beginning to know and love. I had put Him on that Cross. I had caused His Father not to be able to look on Him. Yet look at all He had done for and was doing each day for me now! My sorrow, guilt and thankfulness all tumbled around in the tears that flowed. I have not to my memory felt such a strong compulsion to kneel again.

January 3. God would You whisper a hint of how good it could be only to take it all away? Let him hold me forever, let him love me. **NO** I don't **need** him I **need** You but...Oh shit

## THE MAKING OF A JEWEL

I don't want this I don't want to be hurt again...I feel this way after one brief cuddle! How could I feel after more? How would I feel if he kissed me? LORD if nothing is to come of this STOP IT NOW please before the hurt, before the hunger becomes too great, before he holds me again and NEVER let me feel his kiss if it is to end. Yet I thank You for bringing him into my life, that I'm not dead inside, that I can be looked at by a man however briefly as well as the faint hope that the future here is not meant to be alone, that I can have a friend. Luke has brought fun and laughter as well as a sharing of You into my life.

January 4. First time we went out without the kids, he kissed me. I can see questions and problems but LORD I'm beginning to believe that anything is truly possible when it's okay with You.

Tyler and Alyssa seemed to be a bit confused, they appear to believe that cuddling means 'you're going to do the s...e...x... thing' and that 'kissing was sex.' This, despite Lisa giving Tyler anyway a full on sex talk; not exactly what she thought a mum should be doing but there was no one else. So she gives them both a 'heavy' talk this time.

January 5. I'd been reading, *And the Angels were Silent*[9] by Max Lucado – '...betrayal...where there is opportunity for love, there is opportunity for hurt...the best way to keep your balance is to keep your focus on another horizon' – the Kingdom of another World.

January 10. Shopping for a dress for Kay's wedding at a secondhand shop, but got three others as well. So much for never letting a man influence me again! Where did the desire for pretty dresses come from? The need to hide is diminishing. Amazing the change, the increase in selfconfidence and esteem and feeling good about self and looks that occur when you know (because he tells you) a man finds you attractive especially when he has seen you red faced, sweaty and dirty, dressed and working like a bloke! Why do I believe in Christ? He has given me a life, saved me and I see Him in it every day.

---

9    Max Lucado. And the Angels were Silent. The Final Week of Jesus. Multnomah Press 1992 Quote from chapter 22, When your world turns against you.

January 13. Now what? Fair enough he could not come tonight but unable to come any night?! Ally's not the only one confused. So, is the door shut? All the old voices at not being good enough scream at me. But would Luke be the type to say one thing and do another just because Joe did? Would God open the door wider than I could ever believe possible only to slam it shut and cut me in two? Perhaps, if it was for my 'good'. I had not realized how much I'd hoped for or cared. He may have only held me 3 times and kissed me 2 but he has already taken part of me and I hurt. Why did I see him as a future husband? I have no idea. Help me to abide by Your will.

January 14. A verse from a hymn yesterday at church keeps running through my head – 'My help in ages past, my hope in years to come' – somehow this and Lynette's wisdom brings comfort from You my LORD and I can thank You for the pain. I would never have thought I would be able or capable to let anyone in, to care enough to be hurt. This shows me yet again how far You have brought me – so I thank You. No matter what I will not be bitter. I will not build walls. I will not regret. You are in control, there is a reason and it is for the good of all.

January 18. I ring Luke; this is not me, me would have gone into hiding. Polite small talk till I felt he was going to finish off then I asked him what he had 'to be sure about' and how was he going to do this when not seeing us – 'my swearing and social drinking of alcohol.' This is what stands in the way of us being close, which is what he wants! 'That's all!' I thought. Then I heard the swear words in my head. Oh LORD help me to remove them from my mouth and head for if I hurt Luke I am hurting You also. In God's eyes I am a sinner of equal standing with Luke, no worse no better. God has forgiven me, will Luke? God will help me, will Luke? He sounded pleased when I said that the last week, not seeing him had not been pleasant.

But I was not about to change myself just because Luke said, just to please another man! Not again! So out came the books to study and prayer sent for clear answers --

Gal.5:19-24 'Now the work of the flesh are evident, which are: adultery, fornication, uncleanness, lewdness, idolatry,

## THE MAKING OF A JEWEL

sorcery, hatred, contentions, jealousies, outbursts of wrath, selfish ambitions, dissensions, heresies, envy, murders, drunkenness, revelries, and the like; of which I tell you in time past, that those who practice such things will not inherit the kingdom of God. But the fruit of the Spirit is love, joy, peace, longsuffering, kindness, goodness, faithfulness, gentleness, selfcontrol. Against such there is no law. And those who are Christ's have crucified the flesh with its passions and desires.'

Eph.4: 17-23. '...that you should no longer walk as the rest of the Gentiles walk....if indeed you have heard Him and have been taught by Him...put off, concerning your former conduct...'

Matt.12:36-37. 'But I say to you that for every idle word men may speak, they will give account of it in the day of judgement. For by your words you will be justified, and by your words you will be condemned.'

Col.3:8. 'But now you yourselves are to put off all these: anger, wrath, malice, blasphemy, filthy language out of your mouth.'

James 3:10-11. 'Out of the same mouth proceed blessing and cursing. My brethren, these things ought not be so. Does a spring send forth fresh water and bitter from the same opening?' No decision really, as my choice is to have Luke in my life and him to be happy there.

Lisa looked at what she had written. There was no thought of God's hurt or what He desired despite having read these verses of scripture. So back to study and prayer – Luke 4:8 '...get behind me Satan! For it is written, 'You shall worship the LORD your God, and Him only you shall serve.' Am I giving a loved one first place instead of You? LORD, help me so this does not occur with Luke. I want and need You as No. 1 but can Luke be a very close No.2?

January 19. Had a very strong urge to see Luke and apologise. Right LORD if I'm meant to, let him be home, if not send him out. He was home and did not seem to be that surprised, asking me in. I stepped in and asked him to bend down; I said 'sorry' as I kissed him. Asking for his Bible I showed him Col.3:8, I had started shaking by now, he sat me on his knee and we talked, including about how short I was compared to him and we laughed.

January 22. Tyler! I got really frustrated. Angrier with myself as while muttering to myself, I started silently swearing great! All I could think was, 'Oh Luke this is not going to work – no one in their right mind would want to be involved with me, us. Only goes to show that if a deeper relationship does occur, it has to be Your work God. All seems so remote, so unreal now like another life – can it join with this one? I don't know but when I'm with him especially without the kids I seem to forget I'm a mum with at least one child with challenging behaviours that no one can seem to handle yet I have to – and just be. Just be to laugh, feel free, feel special...feel loved? Dangerous. Can I really do all things through Christ, despite my sinful actions towards Tyler and my swearing? Can Luke love me enough? – Joe could not. He is worried about my drinking and swearing, I'm worried about how he would handle it if he ever saw Tyler go right off.

Lisa and the children go for another brief holiday before school begins. Tyler spends the night crashing around the cabin yelling and swearing. Lisa puts Ally in the main bedroom as it had a door, and sits on the sofa for the night. In the morning, which did not come quick enough, the manager of the park speaks to Lisa about the many complaints he has had from other campers about the noise and if it continues he will have to ask them to leave, even if it is during the night.

She is so ashamed, embarrassed and fearful of what could happen this next night, despite being sleep deprived, the decision to go that day is easily made. While on the public phone cancelling arrangements she had made for that day, Tyler started to attack her, fists flailing and screaming. While Lisa is trying to prevent Ally from protectively stepping in front of her the manager comes out, sees what is happening and he steps inbetween mother and son. They are told to leave immediately.

There had been a simmering conflict within St. David's over the positions or power that women should have within the church for a while, but now it is escalating and Lisa is finding herself drawn into it and given a 'side'. Her desire to 'fence-sit' means 'enemies' in both camps, but as she considers all those involved as friends to emulate and respect she is feeling torn. Who was 'right'? What was the 'wrong' one's relationship with God like, were they still 'right' with Him? To Lisa it felt too much like game playing, something she promised herself she would never do or be involved in again. This conflict lasted a few years, causing much pain and confusion for Lisa and others, and ended with several people, including the Rev. Hankey and his wife Ruth leaving. Her church was to be vacant, have no regular minister for some time but this is not really Lisa's story to tell, so you my dear Reader will only get a few of her entries and only about her feelings on this matter.

February 4. Luke. Christian = no lies = trust what says, does, feels. 'Ugly fat stupid ***** that no man would look at let alone want' – WRONG Joe! I can't see in me what Luke does but I don't have to do I? I have to reassess a belief I've had for over 12 yrs. If a kiss can do that I'm definitely not frigid as Joe claimed! Am I?.....

February 5. Why God? For I know I have done nothing good that You would reward me – I was brought up on conditional love but You do not operate this way do You?

February 12. My parents and Joe would withdraw their love, affection, presence if I was not good or stuff did not meet with their approval. So I bent over backwards to please. Never worked, never enough, especially with Joe. I could not 'control' the kids. I always got blamed and wore it – suffered for their behaviour. I know it is wrong to put Luke in the same 'box' – it just seems to happen. Because the kids are not perfect, I expect him to withdraw. Funnily enough though I don't seem to expect put downs or verbal attacks from him. These fears, feelings are mine. I need to handle them LORD, I just don't know how. Trust – yes but that is hard, having to fight against past lessons that taught that you cannot as you will always be let down and hurt. The kids are here. They have to be part of what is happening between us. They are not to blame for my feelings, even though it would be easy to do so – not have to look at self. Trust – *TRUST GOD.* He binds and heals the broken hearted, not a God of confusion, a God of love, peace, joy, everlasting, unchanging =

dependable NO MATTER WHAT. Help me, forgive me. Love me, want me.....

'Of course! Didn't My Son die for you? Oh you of little faith' sounds inside my head.

Forgive me my LORD. Forgive me.

February 26. Out of the boat and walk on water like Peter. Reading *If you want to walk on water, you've got to get out of the Boat.*[10] Okay perhaps I'm out of the boat, risking myself in a relationship and yes there is a storm. The storm of brewing problems that flashes across one's mind. The storm of 'what if nothing comes of it?' The storm rumbling in the heart of one's unfulfilled dreams and the fearful feelings of ultimate rejection. I was never going to get involved, never feel again. I got out because I believed You called me. That You put Luke in my life. But with the intensity of my feelings, his attraction and yet saying he has no intention of ever getting 'hitched' again ...... never get 'hitched', none of what I want can occur outside of marriage. No matter what or how strongly I feel for you I owe GOD my life and I WILL NOT repeat past sins, mistakes, despite the intensity of feelings being so much more......Don't let me sink LORD. Don't let me lose sight of You, even when I'm unsure of what You intend, when I am doubting if I ever did know or rightly understand.

March 5. Tyler is saying he 'has to take over as I'm not doing my job properly.'

March 9. Luke takes us all to the beach. He flipped me over in the water just like he did Ally! Well there's a first time for everything! We laughed till it hurt. This feeling of belonging, sharing, laughing is really scary. It's harder to deal with than the attraction. Asked Luke once if there was more to this relationship than sexual attraction, we were sitting on the sofa talking while my kids were getting ready for bed. He sat bolt upright frowning with concentration, 'Yes, if that was all I would not have kept coming around.' Oh good.......

Lisa's grandmother, who is in her nineties, rings Lisa to inform

---

10    John Ortberg. If you want to walk on water you've got to get out of the Boat. Zondervan 2001

her she has been diagnosed with Acute Myeloid Leukaemia.

When the hospital rings in a few weeks' time to let Lisa know of her passing, she and the children go with Lynette's supportive presence to say 'goodbye'. Lynette is astounded at Murray's coldness towards his sister when they meet in the waiting room; he and his wife were on their way out. Lisa writes over this period of time – Luke is like a rock, a hiding place, a place of comfort and security, where it is okay to be me. It is as if he is my earthly refuge in this crazy world, my anchor, where I belong, is this all right LORD?

May 6. Joe never played with us like this nor did he ever plan holidays like this for us, for the kids and me to enjoy and experience and be cared for. Jean is coming as our chaperone, kid helper and part time cook. I have too much LORD and You keep giving me more – why? Help me to handle the happiness. I feel guilty. Help me to glorify You in all decisions, actions and words for without You I would have ceased to exist.

Five minutes later I was reading my edition of *Daily Bread* –'Ps.35:27 'Let them shout for joy and be glad, who favour my righteous cause; and let them say continually, 'Let the LORD be magnified, who has pleasure in the prosperity of His servant.' Comment – Jesus longs to be good to us, to satisfy our deepest longings with His love. We are His heart's delight. He delights in bringing good to you and in seeing you enjoy His blessings.'

God takes delight in us – me? How can I help but delight in Him! Thanks for answering yet another query.

May 11. Tyler came back from access wearing the teeshirt I had bought Joe for his last birthday while we were together. My response frightened me. I wanted to rip it off him and throw it out of the house. The thought of Joe still playing games is frightening.

June 1. Luke discusses us sitting together in church. 'What would others think, what about Daniel?'

Lynette had said 'if this happened it would be equivalent to getting engaged'– I did not tell Luke this!

'What if we stopped being friends after the holiday? Could we just put some distance between us along the same pew,' he wondered.

We discussed how we had both been praying for God to stop this relationship if it was not going to go anywhere and all of us get hurt but this has not happened.

Luke feels that 'we agree on most things so should be able to disagree and still be friends, work through problems, be safe to voice opinions as long as not attacking each other to hurt.'

Really, can this be real LORD? I silently wonder.

'Besides,' Luke went on to say, he'd 'be looking to, God anyway to see if we were meant to stop being friends.' He then wondered which would be better, since I am distracted from the sermon by looking at his head several pews in front of me; 'to sit together or for him to lie along the front pew so I could not see his head.' I was not sure how the Reverend Daniel would handle this!

Wow, Luke is still concerned about my feelings, me not liking sitting down the front.

Luke asks several questions about how things would be if not friends --

Could we still hug if not friends? No.

Could I still come to your place for meals? No.

Would you still come to my place for meals? No.

Well I'd just have to come around and drag you over then......
So again there has been no 'stopping'. Should I begin to trust Lord that it is going to last, that this is truly what You want for all of us?

So we sat together in church.

I think the Reverend had a smile that morning.

June 30. Sermon on euthanasia; choose life not death. He could have been talking about suicide. Me. A lot of feelings, memories rushed back of that certain stretch of road. The truck's headlights in the darkness, unable to decide if to take the kids with me or not, did I have the right to do that? What would Joe do to them if I was gone? Then later, on that same stretch of road, sunshine, music and the song, Power of Your Love. And I am wondering since when was the sky so, so very blue and laughing. Laughing out loud startling myself, when did I last do that? An

# THE MAKING OF A JEWEL

awesome thankfulness that God did not allow it filled me.

Did I choose life, did I choose Jesus? When?

I don't know. At that moment when I shut the door? When I just did not want to go on as I had been, regardless of the cost, what I was already paying was already too high. Nothing to lose, as did not expect to survive.

To have life was incredible. To have so much, even now amazes me.

Christ loved me, not only enough to die for me, but enough to overwhelm me with the beauty and fullness. Overflowing fullness and richness of life – and this before You brought Luke into our lives. I never knew being this side of the fence was so incredible. I wish I could help others see and know this.

I pray that Tyler with all his blackness could experience this joy, wholeness, and that Alyssa will also. Thank You Lord for the grace that has taught me how to enjoy this life and be hungry for more, in fact greedy, that I can feel my life is a prize.

Jer.39:18. 'For I will surely deliver you, and you shall not fall by the sword; but your life shall be as a prize to you, because you have put your trust in Me.' Says the LORD.'

The July issue of the *Challenge* paper had an article by Rob Furlong on *Building better marriages*. Part of this article included the following (highlighting by me) –

'...sex also promotes mutual love between a couple. Moses described the marriage bond as a 'one flesh' relationship i.e. he intended to convey that intimacy in marriage was more than just a physical thing. To be 'one flesh' and 'naked' before another person means to be completely stripped bare psychologically, mentally and spiritually as well. There are no secrets and you are open and honest before each other. This is the foundation for sexual intercourse in marriage. Without such a foundation both parties are cheating each other of all the beauty that sex offers. This is why casual sex, adultery, sex outside of marriage, etc. is so damaging to people...certainly does not promote mutual love. I like the way Focus on the Family describe it: 'every time **you sleep with a different person, you give another piece of yourself away.**'....Tender, loving affection, when present in marriage, will always contribute to a healthy sex life. Affection is not just expressed through sex...'

July 8. To Luke's for tea, I cooked, Tyler played with Lego and Luke coloured in with Alyssa, yet helped Ty when he asked and commented on his efforts positively. Lots of interacting, showing interest, involved with both kids. I sat in his chair with a cuppa and watched hungrily. Watched a 'family' evening I had never seen or experienced. I almost needed Tyler to misbehave – reality – as too much like a dream, a fantasy of wishes for 'normality'. It hurts to watch and want LORD, it hurts to feel and wish. But I'd rather hurt and experience than not hurt and not experience.

LORD how come he always says and does the right things? How come he can ease the pain? How come he can make me feel beautiful, wanted as though I matter?

People tell me 'it's about time – it's my time. I'm owed this good happy life I'm having.' This I am ashamed to confess I sometimes agree with, though I KNOW it's not true. If I'm owed anything by GOD it would be that He left me where I found Him – in my own personal hell of my own making. He most definitely did not owe it to me to give this amount or any amount of happiness, peace, contentment and most definitely not love. I know He could take it all away as rapidly as He gave, I know how close I was to the edge, to being nothing, never expecting to have everything let alone in abundance. Forgive that I do not show enough reverence towards You – but then could I ever? I probably consider You too much as a Friend – a true One who will love and discipline, forgive and teach, but don't let me become too assuming of Your mercy for I deserve none, yet want all. Thank You LORD that in Your mercy You sought me and saved me and gave me life – abundant with hope, peace and love and all good things. Thank You.

Lisa and the children go on the holiday that Luke had planned taking Jean as chaperone. The three of them get to fly for the first time. -- I'm worried. Tyler is speaking to Luke as if he is an idiot. Ally is sulking as Luke is not buying stuff for her. Lord I'm afraid of and for Tyler, for Luke and me. I don't know how to handle this. What to say, how to act, how to discipline Tyler and not make it worse, of Luke withdrawing and thinking badly of us. What of Jean? Not that he has yet, but I'm afraid. I like him and his family too much, it will hurt too much. I want too much....

Luke has had about all he can take today with the way Ty speaks to me, as if I'm dirt. Jean can't believe I can't hear how he is speaking to me. I said I had not realized. I don't hear because I am used to it. Luke did not like the idea that Joe had spoken to me the same way....

Luke still loves me despite Tyler's behaviour, he said so!....

Ally is upset. 'Does not want Luke to kiss me, does not want him as a stepdad. I'm leaving Dad out and he's nicer and better than Luke. Why did Luke have to come into our lives? Why can't I love Dad, he has noone, I have Tyler and her, so I don't need Luke.' Oh LORD I cannot lie but to tell her my truth, I can't do that either....

There is no fear, this is amazing, not what counsellors told me that I'd need lots of support before could have a relationship even start, only a worry that what I feel may not be appropriate out of wedlock.....

Unpacking from this holiday, Tyler got hold of the shovel Luke had bought to dig holes in the sand for him and commenced to bash it on the floor over and over, yelling. Lisa asked him not to use the sharp end then ignored him which caused him to eventually go outside; Luke not being able to believe what had just happened was worried what Tyler may do to Lisa. It was the first time he had really seen what Tyler could be like, 'That boy needs help; perhaps Dorothy's idea about an injection to calm him down is not so silly.' Lisa shrugged and told Luke she had warned him that he should not get involved with her and continued to unpack, convinced their relationship would now be over, her mind racing, crying –

God is this goodbye?

Next day they were meant to clean the church buildings together, but when Wendy rang and offered to help her, Lisa accepted, unsure that Luke would now want to. Later when Luke rings her to see what time they were going to do the cleaning she tells him of the new arrangement and why, hearing Luke clear his throat before speaking she braces herself for what she is expecting 'I feel no different about you.'

Oh! I hear him but believing is hard. I found it amazing that his main concern was for me. The main problem was he did not like hearing, seeing ME being treated, spoken to 'like a dog'. It's not about him but ME! I had never considered this. He had thought I did not want to see him; he was preparing himself, wondering where to sit in church!

August 20. Am I sinning by the feelings and wishes that Luke's kisses arouse in me? Do I speak to him or keep silent and try to rein in my wayward emotions and imagination?

August 23. Sin. Do not commit adultery – not even in thought. NO sex outside marriage. We are not married. As soon as Luke started to kiss me tonight my mind 'knew' how he'd make love – not sex – to me, just like this kiss, taking me to a place where there's only feeling and of an intensity I've never experienced.

August 24. Mum gives me a talking to along the lines of I should get over myself and just live with Luke. I said that because of Luke's and my beliefs anything sexual was out of the question unless we got married. This reply only caused an angry retort and put more distance between us.

Later that night in the quite of darkness I sat in my bed writing, some of what was written follows – We are not married. I cannot ignore my thoughts, my sin. I talk to Luke and tell him of the two conclusions I had reached last night, we both agreed that not seeing each other was out, so avoiding kissing is in. He asked me if I felt better for talking, 'No, I want you to kiss me silly, but....' 'Yea, feel the same,' and he leaves.

Jumble of thoughts...too hard, probably right thing to do, confused, can feel voices 'Play the game right girl, show him what it's like, back away, reel him in'. GET OUT! I do not play games anymore! God get this voice out of my head. I'm tired, confused, cannot fight back.......

A sadness is settling over me that has not been there before. I can see no escape from this unless Luke changes his mind about marriage and yet should he, why would he? To never be able to experience his kisses? Oh LORD! Yet perhaps I never should have. So my misery is a result of my sin......

September 3. I'm still learning that I don't have to do anything to cause a problem – so very different from Joe!! 'If we go to the beach I'll have to dress like those Muslim women we once saw rolling on the water's edge, in full garb.' 'Yep, and I'll still have to wear thick glasses. The problem is not that I'm uneasy with what's between us but how God feels about it'. Yes. But how to go back to being just friends LORD?

September 7. Writing in the quiet of night ...irony hit me while cuddling Luke just before he left tonight. I was married to a man I ended up pretending desire for who I'd never experienced any great depth of sexual feeling for and who I could never with even my best efforts cause him any such feeling that I knew of let alone by being just 'me' and yet here is such a man, one I can respect and desire despite not wanting to and yet unable to marry....no future. Oh Lord forgive me for wanting. Not kissing is not helping, I cannot stop remembering! Lord I'm scared this attraction could destroy me if I cannot get myself under control. In some ways I wish had never discovered how good his kisses could be. But how to go back to being just friends Lord?

Be still. Trust..... Know that **I** know what is best, trust ME, not your feelings. Have **I** not shown you that you can? One day at a time. The future you know not, but **I** do. Wait.

'In You I have put my trust, I will not be afraid.' (My paraphrase of Psalm 56:11)

September 11. I am ill with the flu and bronchitis. Neighbours and friends are taking the kids to school and bringing home. Luke is cooking tea, bringing it over, entertaining kids and cleaning up; I can relax and be ill – another first.

September 16. Tonight we were talking about death and dying. Luke supposed I might miss him.

Yes, remember my dream where you were dying and I would not let you till you had kissed me?

No problem there.

Oh, yes there is, I mean one of those kisses we cannot do!

Oh, not a peck?

No.

Oh, well only half an hour to live, not a problem.

You want to sin just before you die?

Oh.

Yes, see now why I started swearing in the dream and then I realized I'd doubly sinned!

Hmmm, well you can go and get Daniel and we'll get married then we can kiss. Well that would solve the sin problem.

I laughed, Luke asked why.

You'll have to tell Arty when at death's door Stage Three of his 'Three Stages of a Relationship' will have been reached and I will be really angry if you died after that!

Oh.

Luke said that he 'has everything to live for and everything to die for.' I could not have said it better myself, LORD.

October 8. Luke said my lips tasted 'like a flower garden', we had been watching *Songs of Praise* on the ABC with English garden scenery. What a beautiful thing to say but I had to ask if he'd tasted any gardens lately – he nearly choked!

October 24. I had a horrific nightmare last night. Ty and Ally were controlling my life; I woke after crying out to God for help to escape from this emotional prison. I talked to Luke later, he listened. 'They are not going to make me go anywhere.' He is aware Tyler wants to be boss. Lord what do I expect from Luke in regards to the kids if we married? How do I want him to be? And can I let him do it?

A month or so later I write – Do I see Luke as he is or as I want him to be? Joe blamed Tyler for our problems. Luke has stated that Tyler and he would not be able to live in the same house, he is no longer the responsive, and eager-to-be-around-Luke boy he was earlier on. Don't let me blame anyone Lord. You are in control. You are leading, for whatever reason to whatever end. Help me to wait, not to blame, be bitter, frustrated, to do Your will.

What is Your will LORD? Oh God I don't know, I don't know. Is what I feel for Luke real and lasting, enduring or just a fantasy, useless under pressure – Tyler's?

Never leave me, hold me tight, love me Lord and stay despite Tyler, despite me I am not strong enough to endure the stress of Luke and Tyler in combat. I am not confident enough in what Luke feels for me. I still expect him to find fault, find us too difficult and not worth it and walk.

Lisa by now cannot get Tyler to have a proper wash, she's lucky if just getting slightly wet happens and then only once a week. His arms are filthy and his finger nails. His feet are disgusting to look at without considering how badly they smell. And his body odour defies description! So again Lisa finds herself struggling against being swamped by feelings of being useless as a person and as a parent as well as stressing over what others must think of her. Her pride is taking a big hit. Tyler is also refusing to go to church with her and Alyssa or to Luke's home, preferring to stay at home alone, in fact demanding to, but I have let Tyler stay home alone, but now the school is telling me he has been ringing female students and threatening to rape them if they do not befriend him! I ring Joe but he was not interested, so the school notified him, yet he says nothing to me verbally or in the communication book when he picks the kids up for access.

December 17. Tyler home, aggressive, domineering, hitting me so I could 'hear what I say Mum'. I hit back, not a good move. Luke arrived five minutes later. Ty acted as if nothing had happened yet somehow Luke knows this is not so. Luke says that 'telling Ty to leave home if he does not stop treating me like he does, if we were married, would not be an option' – for me it would be! What sort of parent am I?!!

December 25. Tyler says Joe said that 'Luke and I slept together last night and that he has known Luke for years and that he says the 'F' word all the time when I'm not around and that he is just using me and I should turf him.'

December 30. Oswald Chambers (Daily Bread reading) writing on the sadness of what might have been said – 'Never be afraid when God brings back the past. Let memory have its way. It is a minister of God with its rebuke and chastisement and sorrow. God will turn the 'might have been' into a wonderful culture (source of nourishment and growth) for the future.'

January 14. I thought it was God's will to be with Luke but it seems as though God has not told Luke.

January 15. Chuck Swindoll on the radio preaching on John Ch.9 – 'we all have disabilities, some more obvious than others, disabilities can destroy or display God depending on what you do with them. We are the face, showing the characteristics of God to others. Are you a victim or one created in God's image?'
Lord I don't realize just what You have and are doing for and with me. It was not me who decided to no longer be a victim – how could I after being one for so long that I no longer knew I could – it was You. And it was You who sustained me and enabled me to keep fighting not to be, refusing to be what was expected. Life is so full of deep joy, memories touch, disturb then are gone, they are but shadows, events that happened to someone I barely recognise: A relationship so rich, so beyond my imagination and a peace that words are inadequate to describe. I will never understand why me. Oh that You would help others like me. Can I? How? Do You want me to?

January 25. Tyler hitting me in chest, very painful. I ring Joe – 'cannot have on weekend or any other time, unable to help', and he hung up. What do I do Lord? I don't want Tyler here when he's threatening me and Ally. I don't want to be afraid of my own son. I don't want to have to listen to his threats of physical harm whenever I don't do as he says. I don't want to listen to his putdowns, abusive speech to me about me, Luke or You. But I can't make him do anything. I have to leave my home and leave him here lord of all, to break stuff that costs to repair – the phone and now the oven. Joe won't put himself out to help, 'Tyler's your son' he reminds me. How much before Ally suffers if not already, what about Luke and I – is Tyler going to dictate this too? My 'thorn' to keep me humble – perhaps, but do I just sit and take it and offer the other cheek, let him get away with hitting, lying? I feel so powerless and useless.

*Be content in all things*
  *Not anxious or fearful*
  *Not disputing or complaining –*
    *The LORD has allowed it for my good*
    *Therefore I can be.*
  *He is my strength, my refuge*
  *He will give me the words and attitude that*
  *Will glorify him.*
              *L.*

March 30. My thoughts after reading Romans 12:9 'Let love be without hypocrisy. Abhor what is evil. Cling to what is good.' And the comment– 'Live your love, act as you speak. No double standards, this is how a husband and wife should be.' This I know nothing of. Joe's actions did not reflect his words, or words his actions. How can you 'make love' to someone who you believe to be 'stupid, fat and a *****, a brainless idiot, a woman who is not feminine', to someone you can't bear to touch in public or spontaneously hug. God is unchanging, therefore His love is. Ours is not, our moods, emotions are affected by stress, good days, bad days, people hurt, irritate, frustrate yet this is a command. So surely God would enable us to do so? Cling to what is good. Is clinging passive? God is good; He has a sure grip on us that will not slip. Hold on to Him. Trust Him to ensure you do not fall, even when your grip loosens. Love is not passive; it is work, hard work. It is a verb, a 'doing'.

April 12. It is always there but some days it's just more intense. I had to 'run' out and hang up the washing. After asking if it was okay, Luke stripped to his singlet (no, only the top-of-body articles of clothing came off!) to get a haircut, I could not look. If I had, I doubt I would have remained standing. My knees shook. How can he affect me so LORD? There is no logic. How many bodies have I seen and touched in both of my jobs? Never has one body affected me so for such a length of time; no not even Joe's. And Luke, well my legs cause him all sorts of problems apparently; they or anything else never affected Joe that I knew of. So what now LORD? I wait, I learn patience. I learn to live with feelings, desires, needs that cannot be met. I learn control and restraint and denial and not to hurt Luke.....

April 21. Luke takes me to Tree Tops Convention again. I not only believe but I KNOW Jesus lives, for there is no other explanation for my changed glorious life.

May 8. Tyler and Ally do not want a stepdad as 'mean and horrible', but 'stepmums are cool' and they 'want one of these.' They see nothing unfair in this. I feel flat. In **reality** I can see no future change in my relationship with Luke. Then Joe steps in controlling, demanding, he 'cannot afford to travel each fortnight to get the kids' so I have to drop them off once each month, but he keeps changing which day and if it's a drop off or pick up. It's a 15-20min trip – but he speaks and I have to jump. Luke says 'let it go, does not matter.' I sort of see his point but I do not have to do this, he is not restrained financially, why do I have to fit my life around his whims still? I don't want to play games again. I'm tired Lord – hide me in Your wings.

I can't think straight, still too much clouding, too many feelings – bad ones. Struggling against his control, dragging me down into the past. Let me break free and soar in Your clean fresh air.

Tried to pray. Nothing. Then I start writing – everything in me is saying fight against Joe's will, his demands and you Luke as you are saying to go along with him. I am being told to step back into the game – Joe demands, I bow and scrape and jump to his every whim. I can't do this again. I feel as though there is more to this – it's about evil and attacking at all I've achieved through God's grace, pulling me towards the nightmare.

And yet Luke says to go along with it and I've made a promise to myself that I would respect his wishes in matters, to follow his input, advice, believing it honours him and You. Big ask. So stay true to this, to You or fight, run? Being ripped apart. Can I trust God in this – that if I start playing Joe's games I will be safe, I will be okay. I'm ashamed to be unsure. How big is my God? How big is Joe? No contest is there!

Hold me LORD while I wobble, keep my foot sure and safe. I can't play and be safe – but You can and win. So here goes, I choose Luke – his advice, his 'headship', as I believe You LORD desire this. Let me not be ashamed or mocked for this. It's raining, just started. Washing, washing the filth away. I choose You LORD.

Bible reading tonight – Lk.9:23-26 – 'Then he said to them all, 'If anyone desires to come after Me, let him deny himself, and take up his cross daily and follow Me. For whoever desires to save his life will lose it, but whoever loses his life for My sake will save it. For what profit is it to a man if he gains the whole world, and is himself destroyed or lost? For whoever is ashamed of Me and My words, of him the Son of Man will be ashamed when He comes in His own glory, and in His Father's, and of the holy angels.'

Take up cross...lose life...save it...deny myself. My fear. Take up the cross of Joe, Tyler past stuff. Fighting, running will save my life but I will lose it.

Author's comment that followed reading – 'Putting to death our desires and submitting to God's...denying need for more compliant children, more accommodating partners...Accepting our unchangeable circumstances...In acceptance lieth peace. God promises through our dying He will make us more alive than ever before.'

As I had felt like fighting the confusion increased and the 'noise' started. After I had finished the previous page of writing I could settle and pray as the 'noise' cease.

June 1. I asked Luke why he was smiling – 'happy beautiful woman' – I make him happy!!!

Lisa suspects that Tyler is taking money from her handbag. Her personal drawers in her bedroom and her clothes in her wardrobe are also being disturbed regularly. Tyler is still refusing to wash and is often refusing to eat, noticeably losing weight. Lisa finds tins of paint, sealer and petrol buried in the veggie patch, soot covered and almost empty.

She asks Tyler to explain. He refuses saying, 'I can do as I want. My body. You can't stop me.'

June 12. Tyler's quiet. He defrosted the freezer and cleaned up all by himself.

June 13. Sin. Do not commit adultery – not even in thought. NO sex outside marriage. Reading *Fidelity*.[11] Fornication = 'sexual activity in the absence of a marriage covenant....any behaviour involving two people – a man and a woman not married to one another and behaviour which would usually result in an organism for the man. In any such situation, the man is fornicating whether or not he has intercourse with the woman....1Cor.6:9-10... Fornicators do not go to heaven. They do not inherit the kingdom of God. They would be well advised to quit it.'

What has my relationship done to Luke? He has said just sitting in opposite corners of a big room and looking across at me could make him want me too much. It seems this is wrong. Luke for his own reasons is unable to marry me. I want to be with him Lord You know how much but I can't do this to him. I don't want to be a cause of him sinning against You. What to do Lord, what to do? It seems You have shown me everything good only for me to have to lose it as then You have shown it is sinning against You – or causing someone –Luke to sin against You which is worse. Do I have to stop this relationship Lord? How can I? Other than You it is the best part of my life. What of the kids? Oh Lord help me please, show me what You want of me. How do I pull back? How do I not let his very presence affect me? Why these feelings Lord when they serve no purpose but to tear apart, to make weary with constant war with desire/need and You; to hurt confuse and despair? Lord enable me to maintain a friendship with Luke, please grant me that. I wanted so much to lean into his embrace tonight to soak in his warmth, to feel – but what right do I have Lord?

June 15. Tyler is saying how Joe's father is 'giving him a gun and is teaching him how to use it'. His tone and stance are threatening. I'm 'on the third strike and out'.

June 16. Tyler's polite and helpful today, not sullen. Doing jobs to help but $50 is missing from my purse again. I only keep a few coins in it from now.

---

11    Douglas Wilson. Fidelity. What it means to be a Onewoman Man. Canon Press 1999. Quote taken from chapter 3, Fornication, pgs. 3940.

July 14. Tyler and I go to CAMHS. I'm asked if I 'want Tyler to leave my home.'

No, but he does not seem happy with me.

If he would be happy by leaving would you let him?

Yes, if that's best for him.

Tyler and the counsellor go walking. I cry.

July 20. Ally is concerned, scared, not wanting me to say anything but asking me 'did your Dad ever undo his belt and pull his pants down in front of you, Mum? My Dad has so he could check his knee'. I asked her how she felt – 'very uncomfortable.'

August 27. Another request from Joe's solicitor for me to accept a maintenance payout of $30000 to cover the next ten years. This is a yearly total of less than what he is currently paying. What to do Lord? I will seek advice but You allow what is right to happen.

September 3. My spiritual Mum, Lynette, has acute leukaemia. Why? Again? Lord?

September 24. So back to the beginning yet again. I am Eve's daughter. I want it my way. I know best. Rubbish! God does and always has and will only ever do what is best. If I believe that Luke is who God wants me to be with then regardless of how I feel or despite what I want now I must wait on God and therefore Luke's timing as he is or will be my head – 'putting to death heart's desires and quietly (woops!) submitting to God's will, an accepting of our unchangeable circumstances'. I cannot change Tyler. I cannot change, advance Luke's and mine relationship. So – shut up and put up and be glad and rejoice. End of the matter. There is a good and perfect reason for this time and it will be for my and everyone else's benefit perfectly.

### *SO LET ME LIVE AS I BELIEVE.*

September 28. Luke told Ally today that I'd 'never be his servant.' They were talking about who would pick up clothes etc. 'That I'am and always will be his best friend besides You'.

October 3. Kids and I have been on a holiday for a week. I had to go as struggling with my relationship with Luke, hurting and sad. It may be easier for him this no touching, no hand holding, no kissing, but it's only getting harder and more painful for me. Holiday was not pleasant. Tyler spent most of it describing in vivid detail how he is going to kill Luke and I in a multitude of ways. Luke to tea tonight, kids enjoyed his company – they had asked him to come. I did not. I wish I could be as at peace that this is Your will as Luke is. It feels like a slow painful death to me. Tonight was awful. This distance is easier to handle when I cannot see him. LORD if it is Your will to finish this relationship hurry up and do so. No more losing it bit by bit, no slow death. How can he do it Lord? How can he be at peace and so sure? I could see the pain in his eyes when I suggested perhaps not seeing so much of each other because of how I hurt not being able to hold hands even, but how can I hurt him LORD?

October 15. Reading tonight is 1Sam.24:1-15. Where David had the opportunity to kill Saul, God's anointed King who was hunting him, yet chose not to avenge himself, leaving this to God. Comment was – 'There are times when it's best to wait for God to act instead of trying to make things happen ourselves. Is there an obstacle between you and something that you want? You believe it's God's will but the method of obtaining it and the timing don't seem right? Think long and pray hard before taking a bad path toward a good goal. Waiting for God to act is the best opportunity for the right things to happen His way.' D. McCostland.

Okay, okay God I hear You.

October 17. Sermon from the Moody Church on the radio. '1Cor.6:16. Or do you not know that he who is joined to a harlot is one body with her? For 'the two,' He says, 'shall become one flesh.' Sex creates a soul union. 'An alien union is created with adultery, fornication, anything outside of a 1 male and 1 female marriage covenant. You become tied to this person. You are pulled apart when separated; losing bits of self every time you get restuck to another.'

Interesting. Is this why I felt I could not say 'No' to Joe's proposal, how I felt I had to marry him? Dangerous, destructible behaviour.

October 19. A handshake to part! I'm expected to be able to handle this! When I said I may not be able to see him as often or not at all, for a while he had thought I was giving him the 'flick' but this distance hurts too much LORD and I can't trust myself. Confused and hurting. I suspect my every motive. Am I trying to make him marry me now by telling him how this is affecting me? AS well as sharing with him all the 'messages' I've heard and read? I pray not. Don't think I can be just friends, not now. Oh God stop this, I'm hurting myself, Luke and You.

What follows are bits of what was written during this night – I find myself increasingly unable to trust myself not to touch Luke. Find myself doing so without realizing. How can I live LORD if I because of my selfish, selfcentred, sinful need to touch him cause him feelings, longings that are sinful, that could send him to hell? If looking at me and being with me causing problems. Oh LORD can You really be asking me to make decision not to continue in this relationship, do I have to make such a decision? Why? Oh LORD I can't, please don't ask this of me; and yet if it is right, that these feelings are so sinful then what choice do I have – for his sake? Oh, LORD help me – why can't we just marry? Show me before it is too late what You want me to do.

October 20. Not even a handshake. Ally noticed and commented. I think You are turning up the heat, Luke does not.

October 28. Luke is trying to work out how he could protect me from Tyler's abuse if we were to marry.

October 30. Thought came to me as getting into bed tonight – in a 100 years' time none of this will matter. None. It won't matter if we ever marry or not. Daniel spoke to Luke today, Luke did not go into detail, but found it stressful. He listened but did not agree. He will only do as God says and when He says. There is also pressure from others that we should marry despite Tyler. Am I wanting him so much that I am trusting You wrongly – trusting we will be together because I want? But then in 100 years only my walk with You will matter.

October 31. Kay tells me I should just have sex. But I don't want just sex. I've had that before LORD. I want all You promise and I want to do it Your way or there is no point to this relationship at all.

November 2. Pain. Hurt. Being pulled apart and scattered. I could not tell Joe of my hurt with our loss of closeness and other stuff as I learned it would make no difference. Cannot tell Luke. What good would it do LORD? He asks what he can do and I reply 'nothing', marriage is not an option now. Now, when my being is being destroyed, by not being able to touch, be held, to play, to have to be careful, on guard, worried and yet desperate to be held and to hold. I have no choice; help me to go on as though okay. I cannot hurt him or the kids. Seems again I have to deny me, to make it right for others. I had so much more with Luke than ever had with Joe. Having sex would be nothing in comparison. Now it's gone. Right this moment LORD if I did not have to consider anyone else's feelings I would quit. No end in sight. Why is it necessary for me to hurt so much? How much longer before something gives, before this nowhere limbo existence ends?

November 6. Luke rings; he is taking me out for tea Saturday night. I chickened out. Did not tell him I'm seeing Daniel tomorrow. LORD what do I need to ask Daniel to know I am going to do the right thing?

Yes my dear Reader Lisa was going to speak to the Reverend Hankey to see what she should do, if pulling away from Luke would be right for all, if God perhaps wanted this.

November 7. Listened to Daniel. He'd been wanting to talk for about a year now as aware that Tyler was a problem but had waited till sure -- praying and studying – that there was a Biblical basis for not allowing Ty to rule. Tyler does have to accept authority and not rebel so there are no grounds for my concern of being selfish. He knew we were no longer holding hands; Luke had told him and said it 'was because we liked each other too much.' I know Tyler should not be ruling. I have known this before Luke was around, but I can't seem to be able to change this, my efforts have been unsuccessful. So where does that leave me, what do I decide now?

November 8. Tea out. I was not eager to go. Luke probably thought it would lift my mood as at other times. I could not be bothered dressing up, I actually dressed down reflecting my mood. Ordered food, I was looking forward to dessert.

## "Will you marry me?"

I laughed, 'Yea, right you're joking!' Poor man he had to ask me three times, the last time begging me not to expect him to get down on his knees as the restaurant was rather crowded. Oh Boy! Oh my, he was serious!!!

We never stayed for dessert. I could not even remember what it was I had ordered!

Now my dear Reader you have to understand the depth of this statement, I *love* dessert. I mean I **_really_** love dessert! I ate all my mains regardless of what they were as a child just so I could have dessert. But right now dessert was the furthest it has ever been from my thoughts for my entire life!

Luke had decided over a week ago, 'Could not put up with this, not touching, anymore when all he wants to do is sleep with me!'

I had NO idea. I had thought this way of relating was going to last at least one if not more years, till Tyler left home, if ever. Luke said 'a six month engagement was too long, could we organise everything in less than three?'!! Oh my, oh LORD, thank You. Oh, to be able to touch that beloved face, to kiss those lips, to feel those arms tight around me; yep three months was plenty of time!

Lynette asked if I was joking, when I rang her, then she cried. Daniel said the angels were singing. We told the children when they returned from access that Sunday night. Tyler seemed okay. Ally cried, worried Luke would now start yelling at her.

But instead of joyously being able to leisurely plan her wedding and all that goes with this time Lisa had to deal with two huge crises – How am I ever to leave the past when it won't let me go? Will it ever end LORD?

December 18. About 15 years after becoming pregnant with Tyler I have agreed to 'abandon' – the legal term used – him and place in foster care.

Lisa and Luke talked and talked, defining what behaviour was acceptable and what was not from both children. Luke did not want Tyler especially to speak to his wife in their home the way he had been with no penalty. Lisa though does not hear the abuse till it passes a level that deafens Luke! He questions her about why this is, as well as asking very pointed questions about her relationship with Joe – I got a flashback while sitting with Luke on the sofa, of rubbing Joe's back, picking his pimples and the feelings associated with his attitude and speech. I could not bear it, so black, so confining, could not stay inside, almost ran outside and held on to Luke's car. I tried to come back inside but could not; it was closing in on me. Luke wanted me to talk, I could not. I felt frightened, crazy, how could I explain what I don't understand myself, feelings too complex, and fear, claustrophobic. I wanted to run. I wanted Luke to hold me so I could hide.

Flashbacks for Lisa were full on, more real than what was real. All five senses could be involved if fitted the context. This time it was sound, smell, touch and as always vivid coloured sight.

After some time Lisa and Luke agreed on what they both would accept and not accept from the children and had an around the table meeting and discussion with them. Tyler and Alyssa were told of these rules and the consequences if they were broken clearly explained Bodily harm of another or abusive speech was not going to be tolerated. And Luke was going to be head of the home. Tyler and Alyssa were promised new beds and décor of their choice for their new rooms if these rules were shown to be accepted by a good effort on their part to follow them.

A few days later, Tyler lost his temper when he was unable to do a task Lisa had asked him to attempt. Refusing help from Alyssa or his Mum, Tyler ended up throwing the furniture around yet again, marking walls and screaming abuse – LORD how can I truly want to subject Luke to this? How can I bear to disturb the peace of his -- my home, with this violent hate? I asked him if he still wants to marry me. Yes despite concern about Ty, causing a lack of sleep as unwilling to wait any longer.

Tyler however cannot understand why he won't be able to have the role in the wedding he wants and becomes angry over this as well!

Lisa gets pneumonia and spends part of a day in emergency. Her hair begins to fall out.

When she does not listen and hand over more money than what she has already at Tyler's demand one school morning, he throws the vacuum cleaner at her, breaking it. That evening the Reverend Hankey came around at Lisa's request, again because of more violent behaviour from Tyler after coming home from school. Lisa was scared and at her wits end.

Tyler and Daniel sat outside, talking for over two hours. It was a lovely summer evening, full of fragrance. Lisa sat on her bed inside watching through her window curtains, she could not hear what was being said. She prayed – Tyler sees nothing wrong with his behaviour, no need to change unless I let him go and live with Joe. After discussion with me Daniel rang Joe. He will not have Tyler in the foreseeable future. Very blunt and in no uncertain terms, 'upset' that Daniel had rang him. I was in the lounge yet could hear the anger in his voice speaking over the phone to Daniel who was in my kitchen! (These rooms are almost the same room.) Tyler is saying that if I was not so mean there would be no problem. He wants to live in a 'normal' family and home – not a Christian one. He would be happy if the police were involved when his behaviour warranted this as could tell them how mean I was. He wants to live with Joe as he gives treats and lets watch him MA+15 movies. I don't know what to.

I decided to go to the Department of Human Services (DHS) tomorrow and see where Tyler could go. Daniel took Tyler home with him. Tyler was only concerned about taking stuff in case he is unable to come back. Daniel had to prompt him to say good night to me.

Oh LORD the price of my mistakes is very high. I rang every relevant call service in the phone book to see if I was doing the only thing or was there some other answer. Parent Line and Woman's Domestic line answered and counselled – 'I should have called the police the very first time Tyler threatened me, being his Mum is no excuse.' More guilt, but how could I have? Oh LORD get me through tomorrow. Let what is best be done, no matter what. Luke held me and let me sob.

Much later, years later, Reverend Hankey was to tell Lisa that he had removed Ty from home that night because what he heard made him truly fearful that Lisa and Ally would not have been alive the next morning. Dorothy was not surprised. She had often refused to come over because she had become too fearful of what Tyler may do since the custard issue.

December 19. I was at DHS from 0930hrs-1550hrs with Ty and Daniel. Tyler is left in voluntary foster care because 'I could not guarantee to provide him with a safe place to live.'

Apparently there is no legal form that is worded for this situation that the removal of a child from their home is being done for the mum or sibling's protection and safety not for the child's. My body is aching. I have chest pain and nausea. Tyler showed no emotion except concern about his stuff.

December 23. Ally to DHS for interviews. Tyler will not be coming home. It will go through the courts. Placement for a year will be requested, with intensive support then a review. Ally is suffering from 'chronic fear.' Tyler with his 'intellectual disability and living with the grief and rejection of his parent's separation and the controlling emotional manipulation by Joe needs more help than can be given by me. The cycle has to be broken'.

December 25. Christmas Day. A strange disjointed day. No cake. No pudding. No fancy table, no preparations. No Tyler. Ally with Joe to girlfriend's place between 4 and 8pm and is allowed to bring her gifts home for the first time ever. Luke and I to my Mum's. She talks NOW! Why Joe, why cause me and the kids so much pain for so long, why did you not just leave?

Not long after Lisa's separation from Joe, she had run into some of his coworkers who had questioned why she had stayed so long with him. Had she not known, not realized about the affair?

But tonight, Lisa sat hearing her Mum tell Luke that they and Murray, on leaving the hospital that first evening after Tyler's birth, had watched Joe with Carol in the car park and known. They 'had said nothing as did not want to be prevented from knowing their grandson.'

Lisa sat there at the table, silently giving thanks that Luke could carry on the conversation and engage with her parents. She ate mechanically, past feeling, only speaking if spoken to directly, eyes downwards, terrified that the seething rage building within would spew forth as her memory flashed past scenes, past conversations, across her vision – of Murray's anger at her leaving 'such a great guy for what! Look at you, get a life, drop this church****', of her Dad's silence, then anger when information of 'secret' finances and provisions documented in family wills had to be provided to the court and become public knowledge during the property settlement case, and her Mum's, 'I don't want to know. You've made your bed, lie in it', comment when Lisa had summoned enough courage years later, after Ty's birth, to try and speak about her and the kids' lives with Joe.

But Irene was still talking, something about Bill, her Dad, having overheard Joe about a year before the separation commenting to a mate at a funeral, 'guess she's an okay mum for my kids but she is lousy in bed'. Oh this is embarrassing! What is Luke thinking? Is this why they would not visit if Joe was home, all those years ago?

Lisa's Mum also informed Luke that 'they were glad he was around to ensure that their daughter did not go and do such foolish things again, like taking their grandchildren on long interstate holidays by herself. With him around they would not have to worry about her anymore.'

Luke was worried about Lisa and how he could get her away, leave without appearing rude or offended, making it worse for her. He did very well.

Luke again takes Lisa and Jean to the Tree Tops Summer Convention – Feel as though I'm only partly here. Weepy, finding it hard to function. Notes from a message – '1Cor.13:47 'Love suffers long......bears all things, believes all things, hopes all things, endures all things.' 'God's patient Love, all powerful, can turn anything into good. Sometimes we need to 'take our hands off' and let Him. Don't keep the hurt inside. Battle with God, till the joy returns.' Help me do this Father, please.

December 31. Again I cry myself to sleep New Year's Eve, this time because of Tyler. How you loved staying up with me this time of year especially. I love you and hurt so much for you. I am so afraid LORD. How do I clean out his room, wash his sheets knowing I will never have him, his smell around again? I lay in his bed holding his favourite ted, Ted, (ironically the one Carol had given him) and sobbed. Tyler had packed and boxed most of his room, ready to move into Luke's home.

January 1. Tonight's reading Joel 2:12-27. '....So I will restore to you the years that the swarming locust has eaten...My people shall never be put to shame'. And comment – 'How many years have you lost to sin? Perhaps you feel discouraged when you think of all the time that seems to have been wasted, never to be reclaimed? When we confess our sin to the LORD He is quick to forgive our past and fill our future with hope. He can bring good out of our wasted years... What we have learned from the past can now result in productive service for Him.' D. Roper.

God must have wanted to make sure Lisa grasped this passage for a while later over the radio she was to hear – 'God having to repay? What amazing generosity to pay back for the years they forfeited to the judgement of God. Lost years when served in sin or wasted years as a Christian, God may not repay for but he will be generous, He will not withhold grace because of demerits.' Consider Lisa!

January 2. Ally does not want to go to Joe's. I rang him, he is angry with me as he could not contact 'that woman you've put him with' –referring to Tyler and his first fostercarer – and got abusive. I said it was not my fault he could not get them to answer their phone. I was told to 'shut up' then as he proceeded to say what he thought of the situation, I hung up.

January 3. Finished packing Tyler's room and clothes. Looks bare, no posters, too quiet, too still. I miss him LORD – him, not the violence, not the loudness, just Ty, his smile, his presence. Remember when he felt sad as too big for me to lift and cuddle – a couple of years ago now – so I got him to stand on the top step and wrap his legs around me. He was so pleased to have that 'last' cuddle. I wish I could hold him now.

January 6. It's nearly midnight. Steady, gentle rain has been falling the last couple of hours. I've packed three boxes.

Ally is sleeping soundly. Oh God it hurts – too much. I want the comfort of Luke's arms holding me tight and yet it would all still be there waiting. All the hurt and rejection of Joe, all the blame and guilt, doing what I hated yet knew had to happen. Ty won't be coming home. I'm tired of accommodating Joe's wants. He's been organising with the fostercarer and the department when he will be having Ty on the weekends and when I will be, not hearing that I won't be. That I can't. DHS won't allow Ally and Ty to be together for the present. They affirmed me saying I'd 'been a persistent and caring mum but Tyler does not want to come home to me.' Oh I pray that the placement will not break down, that he won't be shuffled from place to place. It hurts LORD. I love him. He is my son who I loved before he existed. Help me. Help him.

Tyler had six placements just in this first year. The first one only lasted about a month, the second not quite a fortnight. Tyler had started to set fires. His DHS worker told Lisa that 'Tyler's feelings of being totally rejected by her were being expressed in either outward anger causing violence or damage or selfhating anger which caused selfharm.' God are You there in all this? Will You stop Tyler from destroying himself, how many times can a heart break? Making wedding cakes and having last fitting for dress. Crazy! Tyler cannot commit suicide without God allowing it. And God would have His perfect, just and loving reason and I would have to trust and accept this just as I have to with this present trial.

Almost three months after being in care Tyler appears at church, he had 'a sore throat and wanted Lisa to ring the Doctor.' The Reverend Hankey spoke to him for a long time. Tyler gave scores out of 10, (10 being a hundred percent at fault and 0 not having any responsibility for his position or problems) to whom he saw was responsible for his current situation – Luke 10, Daniel 9, Lisa 7, Ally 4, Tyler 0. Tyler claimed it was his 'right to behave as he did as it was his right to threaten and hurt Lisa and Alyssa, as they deserved it'. So no change, no hope...for now.

January 12. Ally talking. Afraid to go to Joe's, still picking the pimples on his back, unsure if he has his pants on, worried that she thought it was 'cool' when he first undid his pants and dropped them like on video hits, afraid Joe will be angry, really angry if he knows she is telling.

January 13. Ally now unsure if what she said yesterday really happened.

January 16. Ally sobbing. VERY fearful 'Dads should not be like this with their kids should they Mum?...How did you handle it for so long Mum, were you scared...why won't you help me Mum?' Why am I still concerned about Joe, protecting him? If there is nothing in what Ally is saying it won't matter what I do.

January 18. Daniel's Sermon was on what happens if we die before Christ comes. As a nonbeliever it is hell for eternity, as a believer it is heaven for eternity. Ally was sitting with Ruth, Daniel's wife. Ruth asked Ally what her decision would be. Tonight Ally prayed for 'God to forgive her sins and to come into her heart and to help her live right and not go to hell'. LORD thank You, You have her, never let her go.

January 22. I went to the Centre Against Sexual Assault (CASA) and talked. There is a 'real area of concern, 'true' sexual abuse may not have occurred but they are worried about the degree of emotional and physical'. DHS intake contacted and concern for Ally reported, for 'there is a protection issue'. Ally was referred back to CASA for a six week assessment program. I am to get legal advice on stopping access with her father.

Please let me be heard and believed this time. Help me to protect her from anymore. Help me not to hate. If this is real, forgive me for being blind, for not seeing, not wanting to as had too much else to deal with and previous solicitor had not encourage this path. I wonder how much Tyler's presence protected Ally. How much did he take on? Remember how he would not let her hear Joe go off? It was allright if Ty did but noone else was allowed to hurt her. Thank You that I can cuddle and comfort her. Oh my heart breaks for Tyler though. Ally is worried we will 'get rid of her like Tyler.' Oh LORD, help me to fight the blackness.

January 26. I rang Joe about Ally's unwillingness to have access. He pointed out that he 'has gone from no sleeping, to just a day, to a few hours for him to see his daughter, and I am still unwilling to let her go.' I said when Ally was willing I'd contact him again even if just for an hour or so during the week. 'Yep, Yep, don't want her to hate me but want to keep in contact, even if just going to McDonald's or shopping, don't want you to push her.' This was easier than I had hoped for.

January 27. DHS notifying police about Joe!

January 29. Counselling. She tells me that 'My not liking self because of extra weight and being worried about kids is not letting God be right. He likes me even with extra weight and He knows better that I what is best for the kids.'

C.Swindoll – 'Worry is taking responsibility for stuff that is God's responsibility.' Consider Lisa!

January 30. Joe rang in the evening, wanting to know if I 'knew anything about DHS ringing him and asking questions about Ally'.

Yes.

Were you the one who put in the complaint?

Guess so, they are acting on concerns I raised...

In hindsight after all these years, I have no idea why I continued with this conversation, why I felt I had to answer his questions at all....

Come on! We were married for 15 years! You know I never did anything to hurt anyone of you. I would never do such a mean thing to you or say such stuff about you. Why did you not talk to me first before discussing stuff with them?

I told him I did not want to discuss the matter anymore with him. He hung up, or so I thought. Several minutes later he rang again.

Sorry, lost the connection. How would you like it if a complete stranger started throwing accusations at you for no reason? You should have talked to me first; I would have been able to clear it all up. Where did you come up with these ideas? Who would tell you such stuff, how could you believe them? They would have no idea what goes on!

Joe stop, think where I would have heard such things.

Ally? Well who believes a 10 year old girl! You should know better, have you not learnt anything! I am going to get some advice, will be taking you to court over these lies. You cannot go around saying such things about people and get away with it, you will be sorry.

I hung up. His tone was not loud or abusive, just insistent and threatening. It's strange I can remember him saying I should not believe what my child says about four years ago when a similar situation arose and I did speak to him first! How stupid can I be!!

February 2. Been reading, wanting information on how to 'do' married life as a Christian. I have no idea, too many ghosts, scary ones. I was getting afraid about that first night that Luke would be like Joe. I talk to Luke, 'Okay, so how about we both get undressed to our underwear and get into bed and see what happens.' LORD I do believe I have nothing to fear.

February 3. Visit Tyler at new carers, third lot. Started off okay till – 'Dad says you have to stop telling lies about me doing rude things Mum.' I tried to explain that Ally was not seeing Joe because of what Joe had done, that her reasons had nothing to do with Tyler but he just would not hear me. I'm not to visit him again here as carer cannot handle the agro I cause.

February 7. Two weeks to go. I'm on a guilt trip. Remembering how I used to hit Tyler. I'm tired of this guilt, this selfhate over what I've done to my kids, why can't I forgive myself? You have, haven't You LORD? Why do I keep feeling I have to belt myself up over and over again? It's done. I can't change it. Luke is saying I'll be better in bed than him – how can he be so sure Lord? For 14-15 years I was no good, I was 'frigid'.

Safe – what every mum wants for their child. Would Mary have been any different? Would you call being crucified safe? But look at what it achieved!

February 8. Listening to a sermon on the radio '...run to win race...huge cost...can question if it is worth it...have to trust and pray.' I can only run my race, no one else's, including Tyler and Ally's. 'Grace new each morning, day.' So, today is almost over. I cannot get through tomorrow by myself LORD.

February 9. Court. My son is now in custody of the

Secretary of the Courts for the next year. It took less than an hour.

February 10. I sit, mostly silently, through a couple of hours of listening to Tyler, with his counsellor and the Melbourne Psychiatrist at CAMHS, aggressively, angrily, endlessly listing all the issues he has with me, Luke and Daniel and what he wants as a result. The counsellor feels 'Ty is unable to express his need for assurance and love any other way than by asking for stuff. With their help I have to reestablish a relationship without fights'. Hmmm....

I get home, there is a letter from my solicitor, Joe's has been in touch, please contact them....Oh God, NO. Not a demand to continue access please no. Oh LORD I can't do this, fight again.... Look up! Here is so short, look up, look up, Look at **ME** not at the mud!

I drive to Luke's despite the fact he is at work, I wanted to be in the peace of his home and rang the solicitor. They 'could not send the letter out to someone they did not know as not at all nice'....so this is it LORD.

She read it out to me... 'I've got rid of one child as unable to care for him...my psychological health and abilities were brought into question' Okay, so he's going to fight for full custody like before – '...and as a result of the untruths told against him he is unable to have any form of access with Ally.'

I spoke out aloud, 'Thank God' and started sobbing. The lady on the other end thought I wanted to pursue the matter – 'Oh no, I had been so terrified he wanted to continue access. Oh no this is good!' Oh my LORD You have flung me into hell then into heaven in less than 30 minutes! What an answer to prayer! The power of God when seen, is felt, in action is swift, surprising, breathtaking, bringing one to their knees.

Then tonight's reading spoke into my pain and confusion from this morning.

2 Samuel 16:5-14. '...and he threw stones at David and at all the servants of King David...said thus when he cursed...then Abishai ...said to the king, 'why should this dead dog curse my lord the king? Please let me go and take off his head!'....

And David said... '..Let him alone, and let him curse, for so the LORD has ordered him. It may be that the LORD will look on my affliction and that the LORD will repay me with good for his cursing this day.' The comment followed --

'Unlike David we often want to silence our critics – (Tyler) – insisting on fairness and defend ourselves. But as we grow in our awareness of God's protective love, we become less concerned with what others say about us and more willing to entrust ourselves to our Father...we can wait patiently until God vindicates us. It is good to look beyond those who oppose us and look to the One who loves us with infinite love. It is good to be able to believe that whatever God permits is for our ultimate good – good though we're exposed to the curses of a Shimei; good, though our hearts break and we shed bitter tears. You are in God's hands no matter what others are saying about you. He has seen your distress and in time He'll repay you for the cursing you have received. So trust Him and abide in His love.' D. Roper.

We can endure life's wrongs because we know that God will make all things right.

1Peter2:20-23. 'For what credit is it if, when you are beaten for your faults, you take it patiently? But when you do good and suffer, if you take it patiently, this is commendable before God. For to this you were called, because Christ also suffered for us, leaving us an example, that you should follow His steps: 'Who committed no sin, Nor was deceit found in His mouth' who, when He was reviled, did not revile in return; when He suffered, He did not threaten, but committed Himself to Him who judges righteously..' How did Jesus respond? So how does God want me to?

February 15. Six days to go. Feeling disjointed, isolated, alone, feeling incomplete doing this without Ty, unsure of Luke, unsure if I can be right for him. He keeps 'assuring' me he will 'be a disappointment that I'll get sick of him', I'm scared LORD. At church tonight You seemed to be asking me if I still wanted to 'go all the way', if I don't LORD all that has happened is wasted. Just hold me and keep me so I can go all the way. Without You I am nothing, I have nothing.

I don't feel I have the right to get too excited about our wedding with all that is happening with Ty and Ally. I don't deserve to, I don't deserve to be happy, safe, secure, loved – but what of Luke, does he not deserve to?

February 17. Trouble sleeping, nightmares. Luke changed from friend to husband and I was afraid this distance would remain, afraid I would never feel free to talk freely, afraid I would do or say or think the wrong thing, afraid he would be as Joe.

February 20. Mark – Luke's son – rang ME, asking if I was nervous! 'Good. Being nervous is not bad', he said.

February 21. Arty 'minded' Tyler. Mark, Jo his wife and John their son 'minded' Ally. I started to get the shakes but only till the first Hymn – then it was great, for both of us, even fun and plenty of laughter.

And though there have been some dark times to work through, this was the beginning of the best times for us both.

And that first night, for Luke and I as husband and wife?

Well I had no reason to be fearful and neither did Luke. It was perfect. It was fun. And that dear Reader is all you need to know!

# Part Three

## Facets of Being. Is it worth it?

1 Peter 1:67 *In this you greatly rejoice.....that the genuineness of your faith being much more precious than gold that persists though it be tested by fire may be found to praise, honour and glorify at the revelation of Jesus Christ.*

It has been over ten years since I have been able to sleep every night with my bestest of earthly friends, embraced in his love, warmth and laughter. We are greyer, saggy and baggier, me more so though Luke would not agree, but that's the privilege of being allowed to grow old, along with the aches, pains, and deepening smile creases and lost glasses!

More Grandchildren have joined John to enliven our days and raise the noise levels in our home and yard even if just briefly. We have been blessed beyond our imaginations.

But we have been torn.

And we have learnt to be still and wait, trusting our LORD.

What follows, my dear Reader, is a collection of edited diary entries to bring you up to the present. Yes, my dear Reader, you are only getting a selection, hopefully enough to get a picture rather than a drowning!

But could you have a cuppa first my dear Reader?

I have to find my keys!!!

## Chapter 1

March 12. At DHS, Tyler does not want to go to Joe's, they've had a disagreement. DHS wants to know if I am having any contact, can Ty come here. Can't they understand LORD; it is more up to Tyler than us; that it all depends on his attitude and behaviour. I don't want the high drama, stress and violence in my face ever again. It is bad enough hearing from the latest carer of his selfdestructive behaviour, throwing stuff on the floor, then self and kicking his heels up and down and yelling, not to mention the ongoing hygiene issues. Oh God it hurts, where is my happy cuddly loving boy gone, will he ever be back?

March 15. Is my trust in God greater than my anxiety?

March 23. LORD, thank You SO MUCH for Luke's faithfulness, for family devotions. It does my heart so much good to hear, watch and join in with Ally reading and Luke asking her questions and discussing stuff. We finished the gospel of Luke tonight – just over a month. LORD You have blessed me so much. Luke was telling his brother Bruce, that he looks forward to coming home to me each night. Luke and this home are like a cleft in a rock for me – yes a lesser degree than You my LORD for Luke is unable to meet all my needs, he is unable to understand me fully but it is there, a picture of You and Your order here and I thank You. Oh that Ty and our other family could know this as well.

March 29. CAMHS counselling with Luke, Tyler and I. Oh LORD I wish I could walk away, it is so hard to be around Ty, to hear his wants, needs and rights then to be asked to fulfil them when I feel like screaming out, 'what about mine, Luke's and Ally's, don't we matter – remember it was us who were unsafe!' We are expected to have access at set times, a couple of times a week, phone contact and visits to the home, I can't do it, I don't want to. To have that hate here oh LORD! Luke slept a little, I could not. Ally said she has 'not got second hand arms now, they are new, as no bruises now'. Oh GOD, help me to bear this, this great sadness that is chewing away inside.

April 2. I fear I'm grieving You as I keep looking back and wondering 'what if's'.

April 15. First case plan meeting tomorrow, have a lot to read through today and consider. I 'have Joe's encouragement to see Tyler if I'm allowed'!

April 21. Ally started talking, she has an appointment at CASA coming up, about how 'yucky things pop into her mind and she gets muddled.' Apparently she 'used to go into Tyler's room and he'd have his legs up and apart on his bed playing and she'd have to lick' she 'thinks but does not know.' Has 'licked Dad's yucky too but not sure, does not know', by now she is crying and holding me, 'maybe thought of this because of the movies we watched at Dad's', then says 'Tyler did not get her to do this but mind thinks that Dad did but don't know'. I'd been lying on the bed with her, she 'thought I wanted to do yuckies with her', I sat up quickly. She 'needs to tell me as then the worries don't seem so bad.'

April 22. CASA. Ally is telling them her approximate age, and the time for events, but then saying they never happened. I am being told that 'NO kid imagines such stuff then projects it on to their father.' Ally thinks other kids think the same stuff yet she is horrified when asked if her two closest friends do, and so a series of interviews at CASA begin.

May 27. School meeting: Tyler, his DHS worker and current carer, four female teachers and me. Carer is very protective and defensive of Ty, more believing of his innocence than I, she is asked 'to talk to him and teach him how to talk to and act with girls and answer his questions that arise from Sex-Education.' It was not easy sitting, watching, I am a stranger, an outsider, the carer is the mum with the answers and trust. God I was a lousy parent, You have forgiven me, will I ever? Will Tyler or Ally, what will their memories be?

June 3. DHS worker is 'feeling encouraged as Tyler for the

first time has admitted some responsibility for where he is now' but also concerned as Ty handed over a pocket knife as 'feeling unsafe with it in his room as yesterday he felt like not living, and wants to see me more often and at this home. Luke is not confident Ty is trustworthy enough yet, I feel torn.

June 10. DHS worker brought Ty here for lunch, Luke was at work. Ty seemed to become more hunched over and withdrawn the longer here. He stood in Ally's doorway for a long time just looking, wanted me 'to put up his posters and get him a new bed in 'his' room' – why Ty you are not here, you did not want to be. I felt a bit upset when they left; LORD this is hard and confusing.

June 27. I sit in this lounge room, Luke's. I've sent him to bed; I needed to be alone with You, just the noise of the heater and the dog barking. It seems so unreal, so nice, where is my son? He is somewhere in the darkness, I am in the light, but I can feel the darkness. I want more than life itself to bring him into my light, into Ally and Luke's light but I can't. I don't know how to reach him, I am not strong enough and I am so afraid as I know only You can LORD, but why would You? None of us deserve Your favour, Your grace; You give it to whom You wish and to whom responds in kind. I want Tyler to because I know what happens if he does not, even in this life for it becomes hell on earth as well as into eternity but again I know I cannot. LORD I cannot carry this pain, it is even deeper than I can understand, Help me please but first help Tyler, there is no hope for him aside from the hope You give, please LORD.

June 28. Respite-carer believes Tyler damaged his property because he is not getting his own way; he had not wanted to be there. Well it worked yet again did it not Lord as they moved him again. I am so afraid, how long does he have to hurt himself and others for LORD? How will it end? Will the consequences of my sin end in complete disaster for Ty? Now is bad enough but his torment will continue in hell. I don't see me coping at all well with this LORD, forgive me LORD but in a way being Christian when loved ones aren't is not that pleasant! I see their end, they do not. I fear; they don't. I'm not that comfortable that my skin is saved and theirs is not. Oh God help me, help him. How ungrateful I sound my Saviour, my Healer, I do not mean to be.

June 29. Why would You – because You desire none to be lost. Ally's favourite memory verse, 'Is there nothing too hard for the LORD?' Tyler has to choose – it has to be his choice out of his need not mine. I'm sorry LORD. You love him far more than I ever can. You must hurt more than I ever can.

June 30. Comment on John 8:1-11. From *He Still Moves Stones*[12] – 'The woman has nowhere to turn. v.10-11. I (Jesus) also don't judge you guilty. You may go now, but don't sin anymore. If you have ever wondered how God reacts when you fall frame these words and hang them on the wall. Read them. Ponder them. Stand below them and let them wash over your soul. Or better still take Him with you to your cannon of shame. Let Him stand beside you as you retell the events of the darkest nights of your soul. Listen carefully – *'I don't judge you guilty'*. And watch, He's writing. He's leaving a message. Not in the sand, but on a cross. Not with His hand, but with His blood. His message has two words: ***Not guilty.'*** (Highlighting by me)

As I was reading this I suddenly realised, **not guilty**, everything paid for, no one need pay anymore. Tyler or Alyssa or I are not paying for my past sins. Yes, there are consequences but not paying for in misery and blackness and a hard life – all paid for, no need to flog self/selves, free, free to be new, whole. So the guilt I've felt, believing Ty was paying in his current circumstances for my sin of sleeping with then marrying Joe, wanting children when he did not, of staying so long, of doing so much damage to them, is false, unnecessary, not happening. Consequences, Tyler and Alyssa have split parents, Ty has some problems that may or may not have resulted from being in such a negative family environment but he is not paying for my bad choices – they have been forgotten, forgiven, wiped away by the most important One, so why have not I? No more guilt over past stuff – that's going to take a bit of getting used to. I'm sorry LORD it has taken me so long to see. Diary entries have been wrong. Help me to live without this guilt, thank You for showing me.

---

12   Max Lucado He still moves Stones. Thomas Nelson 1992, 1993, 1999.

And if no guilt; **no** blame – If GOD does not blame me, should I continue to blame me? Perhaps by GOD's grace over time to absorb these truths I will be able to see Ty differently and relate to him better.

'Faith – A conviction that He (the triune God) can and a hope that He will.' (Have no memory of where this quote came from) That is what I need. What I want to have for our children and their salvation.

Sometime later I was to come across a comment of Chuck Swindoll's which I will quote here for you my dear Reader – 'Where did we pick up the idea that God is mad or irritated (with us)? Knowing that *all* of God's wrath was poured out on His Son at His death on the cross, how can we think like that? As a matter of fact, the reason He brought Jesus back from the grave is that He was satisfied with His Son. Ponder this: If the Father is satisfied with His Son's full payment for sin and we are in His Son by grace through faith, then *He is satisfied with you and me.* How long must we Christians live before we finally believe that?'[13]

July 2. Joseph forgave his brothers as GOD had used what they did for good. Help me to totally forgive my parents – remember I wanted to pull out of the wedding that morning but Mum said 'No, think of the presents, the money, the preparation, the people, it is just nerves' – no, it was not Mum, I knew that. Then that they told me I had made my bed and to lie in it even though they knew he was having affairs, and Joe for my life with him, for the 'pit' – it has all worked for good, look at where I am today, two years later. Look at Ally believing in You, look at me believing in You, at Luke and this home and life he has given us by Your grace. Oh LORD thank You so much.

July 3. What did it cost GOD to love us? Which does He get more of, love returned or rejection? The cost of love is great – only the cost of not loving is greater. How You must hurt LORD when I doubt, question and not feel, think, speak or live as though You have all power and love over and for me. How great my pain

---

13    Charles R. Swindoll. The Grace Awakening. Believing in grace is one thing. Living it is another. Word publishing 1990. Pgs. 6162.

over Tyler, how insignificant when compared to Yours! Why do I focus on what I do not have? Why do I spend more time grieving and being anxious and depressed and less in giving thanks and being joyful? Tyler's emotional future is in Your hands and his heart – not in mine. Help me to love You and give You thanks as I ought. Enable me to return Your love, to give You joy and pleasure and not heartache. All the way LORD. All the way. Long term is much more worthwhile in the end than anything short term. In Mathew's gospel, the broken reed and almost snuffed out candle – remember the picture I had? It was so vivid of me being a candle that was all burnt out, almost out, hardly a flicker, nearly dead – as good as, till – till I looked at You. The candle exploded into brilliant light and warmth. It glowed and warmed me from within, enabling me, bringing peace, quietness, stillness and hope. You do not snuff out life LORD, You give it. Thank You.

July 30. Flashbacks causing problems.

The July copy of the *Challenge* paper contained an article by Rob Furlong about *'Building better marriages'* which dealt with how a wife should be treated 'When a man models and practices love and respect toward his wife, he is also passing on a lasting legacy...especially his sons. If he treats his wife disrespectfully – physically, verbally or otherwise – then he can expect his son to follow his lead later in life.....Real men appreciate the hard work and sacrifice that their wives put in that enables them to raise a successful family <u>together</u>. A real man does not think that only his work is worthwhile and important. A real man does not put his wife down in public or private. He <u>does not</u> make her feel stupid or worthless. A real man will stand up for and defend his wife. He will never allow <u>anybody</u> to "have a go" at her...ever! A real man does not abuse his wife. A real man does not regard his wife as his sexual plaything. He values and honours her own needs and seeks to build true intimacy with her. A real man does not lie to his wife. A real man does not cheat on his wife.' (Highlighting by me.) A real man – the first wasn't the second is. I feel slightly affirmed.

During this first year of marriage to Luke Lisa found time to read quite a few books, some of which she made notes from and

## THE MAKING OF A JEWEL

commented on. Because they formed a good part of the refining process I have included some of these notes in the hope that they may befit you also, my dear Reader.

From *Elijah* by C. Swindoll[14] 'When tempted to be defensive and provoked to retaliate verbally these lines can help –

> *Gentle Spirit, dwell with me,*
> *I myself would gentle be;*
> *And with words that help and heal,*
> *Would Thy like in mine reveal.*

Elijah does not attack the grieving mother, he is silent. It is before God he raises the tough questions. All alone in the shadow of God...that's where we fight such battles. Elijah is able to be completely candid with his God because he's developed such familiarity over time in his own place of struggle – in his own spiritual haven. Elijah asked the impossible there was no precedence for the miracle of raising one from the dead. He asked. He then waited. Everything at that epochal moment of faith rested in the Lord's hands. Some of you may be in the process of placing your own life before the LORD in this way. Things are critical and only a miracle can breathe new life into your situation. Circumstances are totally out of your control. So you take it to your special place and standing in the shadow of your God, you lay it out before Him, pleading for His intervention, trusting completely in His miraculous power, leaning not on own understanding.'

Dr. R. Edman in *In Quietness and Confidence* writes – How a man faced such a trial – 'This is how he met it: He was quiet for a while with his LORD, then he wrote these words for himself: First, He brought me here, it is by His will I am in this strait place: in that fact I will rest. Next, He will keep me here in His love, and give me grace to behave as His child. Then, He will make the trial a blessing, teaching me the lessons He intends me to learn, and

---

14 Charles R. Swindoll. Elijah: A Man of Heroism and Humility. Profiles in Character. The W Publishing group. I do not have book now.

working in me the grace He means to bestow. Last, in His time He can bring me out again – how and when He knows.'

Can you say these 4 statements...will you?

1. I am here by God's appointment.
2. I am in His keeping.
3. I am under His training.
4. He will show me His purposes in His time.

A summary of what it means to trust with all your heart. God keeps His promises. It's a major part of His immutable nature. He doesn't hold out hope with nice sounding words, and then renege on what He said He would do. God is neither fickle nor moody. And He never lies.

No games!

God keeps His promises. Agree with it or not, His word is final. God's agenda continues to unfold right on schedule, even when there is not a shred of evidence that He remembers. Even when the most extreme events transpire and 'life just doesn't seem fair', God is there carrying out His providential plan exactly as He prearranged it. And to complicate matters, He doesn't feel the need to clear any part of that plan with any earthling. Why should He? Chances are good we'd not agree anyway. And so we wait. And wait. Our faith is stretched because, I repeat, there is absolutely nothing that makes us think He even remembers the promise He made. Then suddenly without warning He keeps His word. He decides it's time to step back into time as we recon it (which is not at all the realm in which He exists) to make good on His promise. It's the right moment. Enough waiting. As He said He would, He acts. It's happened like that ever since our Creator has been dealing with us. Yet we still doubt. We still worry. We still wonder if He will remember.'(End of Quote from C. Swindoll)

Now my dear Reader I need to interrupt here with a warning. I am going to step on many toes with what I say next, probably even making some rage. I apologise in advance if you are one, yet I'd ask you to keep reading for you are allowed to be disapproving of my personal thoughts on this as debate over this issue has raged down the centuries, even splitting churches. Just know that this topic appears again in my diary entries and so in this book that you my dear Reader are hopefully still ploughing through. So take a deep breath and continue if you can.

The next book Lisa reads had been lent to her by Mrs. Ruth Hankey who wanted her to see that she had to believe in a God who elects, chooses those blessed ones He desires to be in heaven with Him while the remaining humanity get what we all deserve, eternity in hell. Lisa was told that some salvation, faith issues were not as important as others, like the mode of baptism – a dunking or a sprinkling. However believing in a God who so chose was one of the nonnegotiables of the Christian faith, it was necessary for salvation. If Lisa did not believe this of God she was not saved. In the future Lisa would be told this several times, mostly by people who would become rather angry and forceful and end the conversation with a promise to pray lots for her when she would not agree with them.

I will say in advance my dear Reader that I did not find that this book proved I was unsaved. However my warring mind and the respect I had for this lady caused painful and confusing doubts that I agonised over for a long time.

I am trying to read *The Joy of Fearing God*.[15] Stumbling and struggling with that word 'fear'. How can I love and trust God if I fear Him as I did and do my earthly Father or Joe? So I have been making myself read this book. I picked it up this morning after several days break, grimly determined to read a bit more.

'Chapter4 ... crossing the Red Sea, the people feared the LORD but not with the same fear or dread they felt seeing the fast approaching army, but a reverential awe produced by an awesome display of God's might. They rejoiced that this power had been exercised on their behalf, they could not escape the sober realization that this God was not only an almighty deliverer but also a righteous Judge of those who opposed Him – realized that God plays for keeps.' – The light went on; I eagerly continued to read – 'Able to trust God because they (Israelites) experienced

---

15     Jerry Bridges. The Joy of Fearing God. Navpress

firsthand His awesome power to deliver them. It was not just the display of raw power – the Egyptians also saw that – but the exercise of it on their behalf that caused the Hebrews to trust God. God's aims in the events of Exodus were not only to gain glory for Himself but also to stimulate and increase the faith of Israelites. He deliberately manoeuvred them into a situation where they could be saved only by His mighty power and through that experience come to trust Him.

Ps.33:16-19 – encouraged to fear God and hope in His unfailing love that is to trust Him. Why?

Look at preceding verses, 'By the word of the LORD were the heavens made...But the plans of the LORD stand firm forever the purposes of His heart through all generations'. What will cause us to fear God – recognise His greatness as displayed in His mighty power in creation and absolute sovereignty over nations. As we become convinced of His greatness we will fear Him – stand in awe of Him – and also trust Him. We cannot separate trust in God from the fear of God. We will trust Him only to the extent that we genuinely stand in awe of Him. The same God of the OT and psalms who performed those mighty acts still reigns and rules over His creation and is still working on behalf of His people.' (Did I not experience firsthand God's power to deliver? Did it not become very personal? Had He not manoeuvred me into a corner with no way out except by His power and gentleness? Has He not continually shown me He is worthy to trust? – He is safe to trust? Psalm 50:21 God is nothing like my father or Joe, no shadows, no turning, true perfect judgement and discipline, pure love, unconditional, full of forgiveness, mercy, grace not confusion. I can and do fear God this way but not the way I am used to fearing, for where there is love fear is cast out. Oh LORD the wonder that You love me! That You even see me let alone care. Yes, I know the joy of fearing the LORD – it is the joy of being truly alive with peace, joy and hope abounding. I read on --) 'The person who fears God rejoices in the fact that we actually are not dependant on other people. We are dependent on God. The Bible consistently affirms that God is able to and does in fact carry out His plans through the decisions of people – they/we are all subject to His control. This truth does not nullify the freedom people have in their choices, nor does it reduce our responsibility to act prudently and discreetly when we are humanly dependant on the decisions and actions of others. God works through people's wills, <u>not against</u> them, so that they freely make the choices He wants them to make.

How God does this is of course a mystery. This is a part of God that he has not revealed to us, but it is a facet taught throughout the Bible. Ex.12:35-36, Ezra.1:1, Ish.45:13, Dan.1:9, 2Cor.8:16-17. What is our responsibility to influence the decisions or actions of others? One way is to assume God is not in control so that we rely totally on our efforts and ability to influence others. The other extreme is to think that as God is in control we need do nothing. The wise course is to take all the steps we can take in a biblical manner then to trust God for whatever the outcome. The extent we fear God will largely determine how well we're able to steer the proper course between these two extremes.

Ps.27:4, 63:14. David earnestly seeks God; his soul thirsts for Him and his body longs for Him. Why use such intense words? David had beheld God's power and glory and had experienced His love. He had experienced and enjoyed the fear of the LORD. As a result he wanted even more to enjoy God and praise Him. An underlying principle: You grow in the fear of the LORD by gazing upon the beauty of His attributes and by seeking an ever deepening relationship with Him.' (Oh! That sort of fear is easy, I like doing this!) 'Does God always provide? E.g. Food Rather than questioning God's faithfulness to His promises we might better question our own faithfulness as stewards of the resources He has given us.

The importance of trusting God when we don't understand what He is doing – this trait of <u>trusting God in adversity is one of the marks of a God fearing person.</u>' (Would a God fearing <u>person=a 'saved' person? I wonder to myself</u>) 'Christians often talk about 'finding' or 'knowing' God's will, thrust of Scripture though is not on our finding God's will but upon His guiding us. Sometimes it seems as if He leaves us on our own to determine what's best but in the end often in surprising ways He guides us in His path for our lives. Ps.139:16. He will sovereignly fulfil His plan in His own way. As those who seek to fear Him we may plead these promises before God but we have to leave it to Him to fulfil them in the way and time He sees best for us. Claim the promises – claim suggests an obligation on God's part – there is none. Pleading acknowledges our helplessness and dependence on God and at the same time recognises that we have no claim upon Him'. (Not even as a child of His??) 'Though these blessings (provision, protection, guidance, compassion) are promised to those who fear God they do not come to us because we fear God. They come to us because of the merit of Christ. So we do not fear God in order to earn His promised blessings. We fear Him because of who He is and what He has done for us.' (Yes! Oh, yes! See Psalm 130:34). 'And then out of the riches of His own grace in Christ He fulfils His promises to those who fear Him.'(Highlighting etc. by me)

August 31. Tyler is asking again to come home; wanting me to 'help him get out of DHS as Dad and Daniel are,' or he will run far away. 'Christians are meant to forgive and help their kids.' He had reported a school mate to police for 'raping' him at school saying there is 'proof on the cameras' Carer is saying 'no way' and told him to go to his room. I told her how he wants to come home and how I cannot let him as I cannot cope. She could not understand how I had managed by myself for so long. There was noone home when I got home. I cried.

September 1. Tyler ran away from carer's last night, she 'feels as though she has been let out of prison and that the only reason he did not hit her was that her son was there'; and she had told me that 'all he needed was a bit of love and understanding!' He turned up at Daniel's who was only home at the time as had the flu. He felt Ty needed to hear the Gospel again and he believed Ty said a 'true gospel prayer of repentance'. LORD have You done it yet again, turned what seemed an end, no hope, no future into a beginning? Does he have the peace, joy and hope like You gave me? He is not going to be living in a Christian environment, hold him tight LORD, let him know Your closeness, let him see You please let his heart be with You.

September 7. Ghosts and flashbacks causing trouble for me with intimacy again. LORD this has to stop, does it not? I don't want Joe here in this bed between us. Get him out of my head, fill it with Luke and his love and care for me.

October 3. Daniel's sermon was on James 1:5b-12, 'Lies of the Tongue'. How about lies of life Daniel? My whole life, which was my marriage and family life, was a lie. Firstly because it was not built on God's way and secondly because while Joe appeared to be the doting new dad at the hospital with Ty he was off having sex regularly with another woman, the first one I knew of but how many others were there? Then I kept up appearances of a happy family life when overall it was anything but. Sometimes it was, but overall it was a sham. Yes lies destroy, the person, the people involved and the life. Oh and yes Daniel I can remember why and how a person can deliberately use the tongue to hurt and bring down another, I can remember doing so. Oh LORD You keep showing me more, more of what You have done for me, saved me from. Luke is so clean, so straight, so true compared with what I had before there is no shadows, no turning. **Thank You LORD.**

October 24. Isaiah: chapter 54. It is okay for me to enjoy the joy You have given me! Mum had given me a serve on how could I possibly show any happiness with all that Ty was going thru.

December 12. These last few days LORD You have shown me I am in no position to question anyone else's motives when my thought life, attitude and behaviour is so out of line. I want my own way, I sulk, get in a bad mood and not all of me wants to fight against it. Doubting a lot of things, not liking myself, so what's new! Far too short of the mark, all I see is my sin increasing. Help me or I can't be the wife Luke wants or needs. I am too capable of hurting him with my moods, help me to fight myself LORD, let the good win please.

December 31. Tree Tops Convention. Speaker today said that 'forgive and forget is stupid and unbiblical'! 'You are not called to forget but to forgive. But you don't payback. That's God's job.' Thank You, I no longer have to struggle with the guilt that I cannot have forgiven as I cannot forget what Joe did to me.

January 4. Ephesians 2:1-10. My thoughts -- God does not

just cook a meal. He takes care with the preparation, making it good and just right for us. He then serves it with all the trimmings, nice atmosphere, cloth, cutlery, crockery, serviettes, flowers, company, conversation etc. the WORKS, nothing too good or too hard. Yes, He even serves us in a strange way; all we have to do is choose to sit – He will even help with this! give thanks and gorge ourselves, showing our delight and enjoyment, giving praise to the Cook. What a GOD! Oh that everyone would stuff themselves at His table!

January 20. Tyler has been given a disability for life label. I feel vindicated, he did need help, it was not just me and it was **not** me being lazy or crazy, things **were** hard and confusing. He has had a go at Daniel recently saying everything should be reversed back, ditch Daniel and church – it does not stop LORD, Joe is still trying to hurt and control me also...let all that is twisted and black including Joe leave Ty alone. The latest carer told me I 'was not a very caring or involved mum' here we go again!

January 28. DHS meeting, a lot got mentioned, nothing got discussed except Joe's letter which was an attack on 'religion'. The counsellor -- Hugh from primary school years! -- said that 'in his experience no kid gets over the amount of rejection Tyler has had'. Grief then anger. I am tired of being seen in the wrong. Lord he is the one who did not want what I could offer, who threatened to kill, who did not want to live with me. And yet there is no point in trying to explain what it was like, no one would believe me.

January 29. Flashbacks. Remembering the holidays where Tyler threatened to harm us and when we were asked to leave the park. God is in control, no fear, trust, keep focused.

January 31. Ty lost placement again. This time because he ran away after leaving a suicide note as he was cross that he was not given a lift to school and had not been happy with the way the last DHS meeting had gone. God will he ever experience peace?

February 11. Letter from Joe's solicitor, he wants 'access forthwith with Alyssa, including half of all school holidays' – more than he ever had or used. I can't stop shaking.

February 15. We get legal advice. Ally is of age where she

can have a choice. Ally 'shrank' as telling her, she took some convincing that Joe could not just come and take her against her will. Letter to Joe from our Lawyer saying if he pursues this, the CASA reports will be involved. The matter ended.

March 18. Luke takes us and Tyler to the Franklin Graham crusade. Tyler broke down weeping and wanting to go down after the message, Luke went with him; Tyler said he 'gave his life to Christ'.

To this present day my dear Reader Luke honestly believes what he witnessed and heard that night as Tyler went down and talked to one of the many counsellors there was genuine despite the absence of any lasting evidence – yet.

March 23. Tyler's eagerly participating in devotions. Oh LORD I pray this continues that his behaviour and attitude towards us can remain good even if he does not get his wish to live here. I would like to be able to take him to Tree Tops after Christmas.

April 3. Lynette has been out of remission since January but she's now in last stages. Church problems are escalating. No breath between trials this time LORD?

April 4. No more hugs, Lord. Oh forgive me, I do not cry for her but me, for my loss. My body showing signs of stress, tired, nauseated, headaches, achy. Ty had tea with us. It has been great to have these times with him LORD but it's okay to take him back to the carer. I don't feel able to handle him 24/7. I'm scared in case he goes off. I don't feel as though I could handle that hurt again.

Thoughts – Jesus said, 'What is it to you. You follow Me.' (Jn.21:22) I follow, as He convicts I obey. I lay aside the drinking of alcohol, swearing, wrong attitudes, refusal to submit etc. If I do not lay aside what He has shown me or led me to believe is sinful, I am sinning. I am not to worry about another – God has to convict him/her and they have to individually personally choose to follow. I do not have to endorse their behaviour or choice. I have to have an answer as to why I do what I do, not them. Yes, I have to point out in love why I think they may be erring but then it's between them and God, it is not my business.

April 11. Carer mentioning trouble between Joe and Tyler; has letters of complaints about his behaviour from Joe, yet DHS and her putting pressure on me to have him for a couple of nights and some full days!

April 17. Lynette thanked me for letting her be my spiritual mum. Oh LORD I've done nothing to deserve her love.

She died the next day.

Alyssa wrote a note to me – 'How are you? How is Charles? Even if Lynette is dying you know where she will go. 'Is there anything too hard for the LORD?' Even through good and bad times God is with you. I know that when the day comes you will feel very sad but just imagine Lynette will be rejoicing with the Lord. But it is all right to feel down cause I think I will too.'

April 21. Tyler has been missing for over three hours – been drinking whisky at carers, so moving again. I have no contact details so will have to wait for him to ring. LORD I feel so sad. I don't know or understand my son. I'm hearing things about him that makes him a complete stranger. How do I relate to him LORD? How through this pain and him still blaming me for everything?

April 28. I'm having bad nights, hearing Joe namecalling me in my head. Feeling escalating self disgust and hate, mental confusion increasing.

May 11. Picked Tyler up from yet another new carer, he's been suspended from school for selling alcohol. I sat in on counselling session. He has also been selling cigarettes as needs more money, blames everything and everyone except himself; basically Daniel's and my fault as would not be doing this if not in care. Luke is nice, as gave him his jumper when cold, as still has not got clothes from last carer. But I don't care. I don't love or support him. Tyler says he is 'just like his Dad as both are fighting for their lives and it is my fault. It is my job to buy him clothes and supply him with friends etc as Joe is paying me to' – so LORD nothing has changed.

May 12. I had a good day with friends and their children. It seems contradictory; I am happy, content yet so sad and lost as I do not know what if anything I can do. Tyler weighs heavy on my heart yet LORD he is making the choices not me, You are still here for me, I am still forgiven and wrapped in Your love.

May 31. DHS meeting Tyler says visits with me are 'average', wanted to know why 'Luke did not do stuff with him like a dad, like coming to his school interviews'. Luke works like Joe though he took today off to come here with me, to support me. In reply to their question to him Luke said he 'was not comfortable at present with having Ty sleep over.' I was then asked how I felt about his answer – was I meant to disagree with my husband in public? I replied I supported his decision.

June 1. Luke has a possible problem with platelets, blood not clotting. I've never been so happy. I've never been so afraid.

June 2. Rejoice always in any circumstance and give glory to God by the way we live the life He has given us. Luke is worried about me and Ally being alone. I'm grieving, wondering how I will cope without his touch, cuddles and smiles. Oh LORD have I let him mean more than You – need him more? Please no. Help me. Luke has bruising on hip bones from his undies, looked just like Grandmother. Oh God get us through this.

June 4. Luke rang, bloods within normal limits, I cried. I'm glad we could enjoy the sunshine today. Thanks LORD. Yet I am challenged by the thought that God would still have been good if Luke's bloods had not been. Would I still been able to give thanks?

August 3. Bible study, Tyler was there, hardly spoke to me. Paul has told me that he is leaving St. David's because of how Ty says the leaders have treated him. Apparently Ty has accused them of something. Paul asked me if I loved Ty and said that 'all he needs is understanding, yes he is manipulative, could end up in prison or worse' – I don't need to be told stuff I've known and stressed over for years! LORD did I cause Ty this pain and the problems he is now experiencing? It hurts too much LORD, I don't need Paul to tell me I 'will always be Ty's mum and that it is an unbreakable tie!' I am troubled with nightmares.

October 4. Thoughts on tonight's reading Psalm 60:11-12. – 'Give us help from trouble, for the help of man is useless. Through God we will do valiantly, for it is He who shall tread down our enemies.' 'Will' not 'may' or 'might' but 'will', so why not living victoriously, why not living the truth, why do we/I go on feelings and add 'but...'? I checked out Proverbs 1:33. – look at the 'will', Proverbs 3:6, 'shall' is this not the same as will? How about Proverbs 1:23? Why do we/I listen to everyone/everything else instead or even as well as our Lord? Look again at Proverbs 1:33 'whoever listens to me', not me plus....just and only me, then follows the promises, the 'wills'. Why do we add the 'buts'? Moses had uncircumcised lips, I have an uncircumcised brain for an excuse. Why cannot I just accept what my Lord says, do it and claim His glorious promises and be a living reflection of them? Oh how I long to be able to do so – even just a little! Oh Lord remove the hindrances' – ones even I'm unaware of – that I put up so that I can be this – safe, secure fearless. You give all that is needed, power, the Holy Spirit, I get in the way – get me out of the way Lord please I want to fly, I want to go all the way Lord, all the way please.

October 7. Tyler's helping Luke to mow lawns. Luke impressed with his efforts. Bible reading and prayer, Ty 'giving thanks for mowing, families and Alyssa, for being a good sister to play with and talk to and do stuff with'. But later we are told how Ty had stalked a mother and daughter from church during the week and sent emails saying that the daughter had sent him into hell and was saying he was going to commit suicide as a result.

October 9. This scares me Lord. I have no reason now to feel this way. Yesterday I was okay, today I am SO tired, I wondered what would happen if I just curled up and was not. A letter in local paper about parents who reject their kids, what of the other way around, what of parents like me, surely I cannot be the only one? There has been a conference in town this week about family violence and its effect on women and children, article in paper was about a severe case, I have nothing to show, no Xrays, no doctor reports, I wonder what would have happened if I had contacted one of these agencies? I'm the bad one, I'm the one that kicked my husband out who had provided so well, I'm the one that has deserted my son and caused him such depression. God I know things will be set right in eternity, but what if he's right and I'm not? Lord I wish I could feel right now. It should not matter, I have Luke, I have Ally, I have this life yet the other won't let me alone. Who would listen to me Lord – who would believe me – I fear the blame would land on me Lord. I'm just so tired. I just want someone to – I don't know – tell me I'm right to feel all this – that I want people to know what he put me through and the kids, that he is not the 'good' guy. But it's useless.

November 29. Jean has a raised white blood cell count. LORD this is getting to be a 'habit' every couple of years!

Some brief notes from the summer Convention at Tree Tops – What does it mean for us and our life, way of living that the end of the curse has begun?....... Philippians 2:1-11. Read this passage with those you would not choose to be with, say at church's morning tea, in mind. In John 13, Christ understood He was God and in doing so got down and washed the disciples' feet. The One Man who counted others better than HimSelf! So we can instead of squabbling and wanting to be No. 1 within church. This passage is not talking about feelings but an attitude of mind we have. Determine to think lovingly of the one who hurts most. The ones who hurt the most will be brothers and sisters in Christ.' Spot on! But I've gotta to work on **my** attitude!

January 6. DHS meeting, they recommend Ty stays in care another year. Joe had sent a letter critical of me and 'having great concerns as to why I was not having Tyler for sleepovers' and praising up current carers for their care of his son. I sat listening to carers praising Ty for how he makes such a good start in the mornings, thinking of all those mornings that were like a living nightmare for me and Ally and that the eight others in this meeting knew nothing of what it had been really like and how unfair it all was. After the meeting the 'chair lady' spoke to Luke and I saying she 'had several kids herself and knew they could put on the best face for someone else and horrors for mum' – realised tonight LORD that You arranged this to lift my heart, I'd been reading Psalm 5, thank You.

So this is how it ends Lord. Oh please hold me so I don't crack wide open. Tyler rang; it was not a pleasant conversation. Ty ending it by saying, 'I don't want to ever see you again or hear from me again.' I decide to respect his wishes. Relationship, mother and son, husband and wife, it takes two to love and want to work on, it does not work with only one, **ever.** All I see Lord is my beautiful baby with curly hair and gumboots laughing, splashing in puddles, racing around, so full of life and cuddles for me. Now there is so much hate and distance in his voice, he only wants his stuff, not me, not my love. No apology, no remorse, nothing, 'it is his right', what changed Lord? Oh please Lord remember that broken young man sobbing, going forward with Luke to give his life to You. Oh Lord by Your grace I can bare all except the fear of no hope for him ever, please don't let him be hardened so much against You Lord, please let me hope and not be ashamed, I need to know that my love was not a waste, nor my pain. I wonder if I will ever know his wife/family if You so bless him. Oh God it hurts – will it ever end?

January 14. My parents do not agree with my decision to respect Ty's wishes. They, especially Mum, feel that if I really loved him I'd do something. Oh Lord what if I'm wrong...what if it was not Your will but mine...oh the doubts, the sadness. Please help!

January 15. Church  The opening reading was Jeremiah 29:11-14, my verses. Spurgeon said, – 'if there was something better for you, better circumstances, you would be in them instead of where you are.' This includes the situation with Ty. Readings for sermon, Psalm 123 and Nehemiah 4:1-23. 'Sticks and stones may break bones but words never hurt WRONG! Words kill the Spirit and heart, contempt, putdowns, making one feel less than second class, filled to overflowing with such words, first attack on character to undermine and exploit, what said sounded almost true but in such a derogatory manner so to reduce confidence... look to Me, I know the pain you've been thru, Jesus will never say words do not hurt.'

January 22. Did not sleep, sat up in lounge, the madness is back, the darkness. Relationships!!? Reading the book, *Jesus Freaks*,[16] I am going through nothing yet this morning I feel so

---

16  dc Talk and The Voice of the Martyrs. Jesus Freaks. Eagle Publishing 2004.

old, I ached, I was tired to the bone.

Lisa is struggling with the distance between her and her son, he comes to church, he walks past the car when they are picking Ally up from school, she is invisible, beginning to believe it would be easier if he was not around at all, dead physically, than seeing him hate her and look through her and hearing him call out to Ally 'You \*\*\*\*\*\*\* retard' as leaving school – a label from Joe's time. Not that Lisa really wants him dead; she just wants it to be over.

A form from the courts is sent for Lisa to sign if she agrees with an extension of Tyler's care – Lord it seems so unfair that I have to sign something that says I/we are unwilling to have him here except for irregular brief visits. What of him, we were only seeing him when he let us, not when I want. And reunification – what a joke! Noone has brought us together to try and repair our relationship which I thought was going to happen and so desperately wanted to happen. Ty feels rejected but who has done the rejecting? If I feel this pain and frustration of Ty rejecting my love and desire to be involved, how do You God feel when so many of Your children do the same?

February 17. Struggling with Luke casually touching me during the day, I feel invaded, I move away. Confusing, as Luke said I would not have done that a year ago. What's happening Lord? I could almost not bear the idea of intimacy last night the way he does it – a jump on and off yes but not the touching and gazing beforehand. What's wrong with me? It has been so good. Why am I feeling like this now Lord?

February 23. Ally's friends now as concerned as we, about her weight loss and refusal to eat. I was not that keen on a request she made, she went cold, withdrew, not talkative at bedtime like usual, I suddenly saw me losing her like Tyler, being rejected as I get in the way and am no longer wanted. Ally is proud of her weight loss, ribs and hip bones now protruding, saying 'not to worry as if dies I will know where she is'. 'Great', I replied, 'I'll just go out in front of a truck but it will be okay as you'll know where I am!' I don't want to be back here, be like this, my chest hurts, my stomach hurts, I'm losing Ally like Ty. It feels like rejection all over again. Again my love for them is not enough. Don't let this destroy my beautiful girl Lord.

February 25. Forgive me for my lack of trust, for looking more at the mountains, problems and possible outcomes than at You and remembering Your help in the past. Ally like Ty is Yours. You are protecting her as me. I'm sorry I don't trust You as I should, I hurt You as well as myself and Ally and Luke. Fear in, trust out. **I will not fear, my God is for me** – oh help me to live this please Lord.

March 5. Sermon on Psalm 51 and 1Timothy 1 'Saul became Paul. Forgive yourself of all memories, of things in the past life as Christ has done all the dying so you can live'. The words of the closing hymn[17] –'long my imprisoned spirit lay...my chains felloff I rose went forth and followed You.' And the tears of relief, gratitude and joy rolled unstoppable down.

March 7. Mixed up sort of day. Feeling depressed about Tyler, I really am only biologically his mum now. I know nothing of the person he now is, only what he was in the past, and Lord it hurts so much. I feel like running around screaming and going mad, but this would change nothing. Having nightmares of him dying, Joe making all the arrangements and claiming all his stuff, I'm sort of there but only by invitation, not involved, not being consulted – yet how could I as I would now not know what Ty's wishes would be. Please Lord, stop these thoughts, just let me have the comfort of believing that he will be with You and we can be a 'family' there. It's like I'm shattered and scattered. I have this great life that people can see that I'm living and yet I have this terrible one that no one sees or understands where I ache to have Ty and Ally with me as a happy loving family. Help me Lord for You see.

March 28. Still problems within the church. Surely the choice of a minister is Yours not ours Lord, so there should be no need for 'games'. Stop all this hurt, there should be no 'them' and 'us' – I seem to be either, depending on who is talking! We are meant to be one, it really seems as though we are going to destroy each

---

17   And can it be? Charles Wesley, 170788. No.110 in The Hymnary, revised edition. Oxford University Press 1927.

other, please stop us Lord, they are my family, You gave them to me, please stop them from hurting each other, I don't know how.

During the last few months Lisa has had several trips to the doctor and varying investigations for rather severe pain and swelling in her throat, including nuclear scans which finally ruled out cancer. Thyroiditis was the diagnosis given, perhaps a viral cause perhaps an autoimmune cause but the pain should settle.

May 13. Remembering the good times with Tyler, I could cry and cry Lord. I want to be back there, I'm no better than the Israelites in the wilderness wanting the leeks and melons of Egypt. I just feel so tired, part of me just wants to give up, I don't want to keep fighting, and I just want to vanish. Please help me to handle the distance. I keep wondering if there could have been another way, a better way, I have no hope that we will be friends one day other than You are working in us both, but oh Lord it looks so impossible from where I stand.

May 15. Saw a photo in a book of me from my student nursing days – I have a big smile, was I laughing? It seems a lot longer than 25 years. That girl – I had not recognised myself; Luke and Ally picked me out. I had forgotten that day -- is dead in so many ways, her dreams of nursing, being someone, being a wife and mother and happy-ever-after died. I don't know her and I don't know me. I have no idea where I am going or what I am going to do and yet tomorrow if God allows, I will wake and do what is set before me, cooking, cleaning, washing, ironing and if God allows I will lie down to sleep with Luke at the close of the day and I will keep doing that till I go home – then perhaps I will know.

May 17. Talking with Luke tonight and wondering – my stumbling block as a student nurse to the gospel was I did not want to be the cause of another's death, could not accept Christ died for me, I killed Him, I did not ask Him to die. Looking at what I'd underlined in that Gideon's New Testament I understood a lot, so believe I must have had some sort of relationship or I would not have been able to understand as would not have had the Holy Spirit. Luke said 'this is a type of pride; a man he used to work with had said much the same. God had to take me to a place so bad I would not care as long as I could be got out, survive, where the need in me was so great.' 'Get me out, there has to be more to life than this, I'll go back to church' instant quiet, joy and hope. Prayers answered, daily comfort, daily evidence of You in my life and yet I did not fully understand what I had done, did not repent and see that I had killed You till that time You drove me to my knees ages later. You gave me this peace Lord, forgive me when I look away and wonder 'what ifs' – that is my journey not Yours and I want Yours Lord all the way, no more wilderness, grumbling, I don't want to die there.

May 18. Ally asking questions about why she is not seeing Joe, why she had the counselling. I said she had said that she had seen him naked, she did not deny this just said, 'Dads are not meant to be like that, do stuff to their kids' and that the 'pain of all that and lack of family relationships, of being alone was almost too much to live', also 'worried not a virgin because of what he did', wanting to find out, 'wants to be sure as part of her thinks it has happened'. Is it ever going to end Lord?

A physical examination by her Doctor showed that her hymen was intact but the Doctor told us 'this is not conclusive; she is to wait for the memories to come'.

May 28. Cried for ages last night, Luke just held me stroking my head. Can it still be well with my soul Lord and still have this pain, grief over Tyler. You will have to have a big jar! I have all this pain over one beloved son – You, You have it with every generation, lots and lots who reject Your love. You have to be God otherwise You would not survive the pain.

June 7. At the Church prayer meeting the leader was discussing how a marriage cannot survive infidelity, I agreed. He said how some men see it as a 'right'. 'Yep', I returned, 'especially if you are pregnant and fat', another male strongly disagreed. 'Well that is what happened to me and why,' I replied. 'No!' 'Yes and my parents and brother knew but never said till just lately, did not do much for these relationships either'. By now a few are looking slightly shocked and uncomfortable but Lord I'm tired of hiding; this is my reality, why should I pretend it is not?

June 8. Remember Lord all the way, all the way, full on...

oh Lord I want Your praise, Your opinion of me alone to matter. Help me not to 'do' to get man's but Yours. I love You, You have given me life and it IS more abundant, and continues to get more abundant, I can only love, trust and obey, forgive me that they are only shadows of what I wish to give. 2Cor.10:18. 'For it is not the one who commends himself who is approved, but the one whom the Lord commends.' I have been created, formed and redeemed by God. I am approved of, loved everlastingly, considered worthwhile, useful, needed, wanted, cared for, I am 'pleasing, a joy, a delight, a treasure, a jewel, and precious, chosen.' I am accepted, valued, considered, and honoured, worth dying for, worth searching for, worth grieving over.

June 13. I'm preparing Bible Studies for a women's group on 'Intimacy with God' – and look at me! I read less and pray less than ever have, so busy and tired – it needs to stop. Help me to stop Lord, let things get quiet, I must not feel guilty to stop and be with You, this is the most important, not the other stuff that is yelling at and pressing down so hard on me.

July 26. Prayer meeting at church, what a shock to hear that hardly anyone else has one quiet time with You once a day let alone twice! I can't understand this, should we not all be hungry and eager to be with You? As I once heard at Tree Tops 'a Christian should not be a Batman – having lots of tools/nuggets from Your Word for various situations to pull out and use – but a Spiderman, who has been bitten and changed by Your Word. Read the Bible to be changed by it, not to just use it.'

July 29. Watching the sparrows out our front windows and considering Mathew 10:24-31. Fat sparrows, singing, happy, and carefree. God knows I want to be happy also. I like sparrows. Fear lies.

Perhaps this entry about sparrows needs some clarification for you my dear Reader. This section of scripture, this day when Lisa was fearing bodily harm from her son, fearing that noone saw Joe or Tyler as she did but blamed her, fearing how she was judged by friends within and without her church, fear...fear...fear. And then seeing how God saw, knew and valued her and was in control of all things. Yes, those happy carefree nondescript brown fluff balls that were getting on with life and enjoying it despite being despised and mostly overlooked, seen of little value taught Lisa much that morning. And Lisa understood that song *His Eye is on the Sparrow*[18] now and why it was sang with so much passion by Ethel Waters.

August 11. Tonight's reading was by Vernon Grounds, Psalm 94:16-23. '....have you been passing through a time when you are tired of body and sick of heart? Do you find it difficult to focus your mind on biblical promises? Has it become hard for you to pray? Don't write yourself off as a spiritual castaway. You are joining a host of God's people who have experienced the dark night of the soul. When we endure such times, all we can do – indeed, all we need do – is lie still like a child in the arms of our heavenly Father. Words aren't necessary. A comforting father doesn't expect his child to make speeches. Neither does God. He knows we need His soothing care. In times of trouble, His mercy holds us up. We may trust Him to carry us through that dark night of the soul and on into the dawning light. When we have nothing left but God, we'll find that God is enough.' Thank You.

August 19. God the Creator of all loves me so much He died so I could live. Why can't I rest and enjoy this? I stress and get all hurt and upset over the lack of love and rejection from my parents and Ty, why does it seem so necessary to have their love when I have God's just the way I am, why did I cry myself to sleep last night, why did I fear I'd gone against You when married Luke as this has seemingly brought more problems to kids? STOP screwing with my mind Satan. **Christ get him out!**

October 3. The darkness is closing, suffocating. Hope –I see none. Oh Lord that You would give me some, there is no light. I don't want to go through this darkness. I am afraid. You seem distant. The darkness is always there inside. Sometimes it does not bother me, it is just there, a sad darkness. But it has changed, become different. There is a wall. You are not there. My prayers bounce off my ceiling. Your Words blur, making no sense. Stubbornly I refuse to stop opening my Bible, searching

---

18   His Eye is on the Sparrow. Words and music by Chas. H. Gabriel. No. 51 in Alexander's Hymns No.3.

for You, but there seems no point. You have gone and I don't understand.

October 12. I wonder Lord if in some cases that may be easier to pray for some people than being with them and supporting visually. We are told to open up and request prayer, share the burden, why bother? It is words, no follow up, no coming along side, just distance, surely it is not meant to be this way, pray yes, but be there also, a shoulder, a comforting touch, a listening ear, a physical, obvious show of empathy, concern. Lord help me to be able to support others when I know of a need so they do not feel isolated, alone, too much of a bother, not important. Tyler has been missing from care for nearly a week before he was found, off his medication, not going to school, refusing to go back into care, police given warrant to forcibly remove him from friend's who is known to the police as is into alcohol and drugs. I can't bear to think of him going through all that, and so far from You. Lord does he have to? Oh forgive me but if his heart is still towards You at all take him before he goes too far away in such a life style and cannot come back. I can't love him here Lord, I can't see him, I can't have a relationship here, I want one in heaven please. Oh God I need Your comfort and Tyler, oh Ty, Lord save him please. Where is it all going to end?

October 16. I don't understand Lord; he threatened to shoot his caseworker but had no gun, very drunk, very aggressive. Is this darkness always going to be around me? I'm tired of it.

October 17. Got to talk to Tyler on the phone, he is in a secure locked place somewhere. Oh God I don't understand him – I don't even know if I want to. He does not seem to be in the same world as I. What do I feel – horror, despair, a sadness so great I can't even cry, fear for all of us, will it ever end? Does he know what he is saying Lord – if he does it is beyond terrible, if he does not, I don't know how his brain operates. He spoke in detail of how he'd harm us and Daniel. 'Pay back for the last three years, and for Ally telling about how he was going to shoot us, for Luke selling the 'family' home, to sue us, to take us to court to stop us, pay back. How great the high was from the alcohol and what else, what did he mean by 'bun cob' and going to do it all again as felt great, not depressed, could do anything, how he can get $200 a night stealing stuff and doing jobs' – what sort of jobs Lord – not prostitution please! I cannot bear to think of Ty this way Lord. Ally is afraid for her life, saying she 'will be dead tomorrow or next day whenever he goes back to school.' WHAT DO YOU WANT LORD? WHY? I have chest pain, I feel sick, will You get me through this Lord? Will You get Ty through? He no longer believes in You as his Father as Joe 'has explained You're just like witchcraft and that he is going to hell as he deserves to.'

October 18. 'Faith is the bird that feels the light and sings, when the dawn is still dark' Oh Lord, help me to sing please. You think I can handle more than I do Lord. I don't like this chest pain. Should a Christian feel as I do? Is it that I do not trust You enough?

October 19. Reading last night in Luke's book his mum bought him, *Come Ye Apart*[19] -- 'The safest place to weep is on Christ's bosom'. Lord how old is this book, yet it was written for me, for now. Thank You.

October 26. Took Ally to the doctor. He is 'concerned about her attitude and determination to continue losing weight, still within normal limit'. When asked why, her answer is because of 'all Father and Ty had done and were doing, can do nothing else as not as strong as Mum'. Oh God the consequences of my sin are too great, wherever I turn I am being punished over and over for it. Ty and Ally are both trying to selfdestruct, just doing it differently. God will it never end? I might be heaven bound but I leave a trail of destroyed lives behind me – I would give up heaven if I could Lord, if it would make it right for them. Oh God please stop it, undo what I have done by getting involved with Joe. I was wrong but do the kids have to pay? You helped me put a stop to me, please Lord help them find the strength and courage to say enough, no more, it ends now.

Yes, my dear Reader, Lisa has forgotten the lessons she learnt and so be able to write as she did a couple of years ago

---

19    J. R. Miller, D.D. Come Ye Apart Daily Bible Readings in the Life of Christ. Thomas Nelson and Sons. Ltd. There is no date given except for the date of 1964 written in by Luke's parents.

in June and July. Had she taken her eyes of Jesus like Peter and focused instead on the louder more boisterous winds and waves of the storm causing her to reel to and fro and stagger? Becoming occupied with her troubles more than the calm quiet strength of her Christ who was still in full control? (Math.14:28-31)

Lisa feels she is a slow learner. And because I think others may also be I have deliberately included (Have you already noticed my dear Reader?) entries of thoughts and feelings that you will think you have read before. God does not stop teaching a point He wants understood till it is grasped and fully digested, even then He can revisit again! He is patient. Very in Lisa's case I think!!

October 30. I'm not sure why but the darkness is on the edges again Lord, my faith is so weak and small and does so little. I feel as if just hanging on by my fingernails for self, not to mention I'm meant to be 'doing' for others as well. Oh Lord, just get me through, I want all the way but I can't get there.

October 31. Tyler has been with a carer 'who has worked at a juvenile detention centre and can handle far worse than Tyler and is very consistent and unwavering' – till last night that is!! The police woke us at 0500hrs, 'as they had nowhere to take Ty we have to till the case worker picks him up later on. He'd been missing from carer's but had returned, stolen their vehicle and gone for a joy ride. The vehicle had not survived too well! Luckily noone hurt or Ty would be facing manslaughter charges. Carer cannot have him back as she can't handle him!' My husband was amazing; he fed Ty and talked with him till he fell asleep on the couch. Then Luke played scrabble with me as we were too scared to sleep. Ally's in her room crying, terrified. I said little to him did not know what to say till leaving; I then hugged him and asked him to stop hurting himself. God he does not seem to understand or if he does, he does not care. I don't know how I can keep standing. I feel like a punching bag absorbing one shock after the other till I split apart.

Then on a scrap of torn paper Lisa has scrawled -- The darkness is closing, suffocating hope. No point. Just let me sleep forever. It's too painful to be here in the dark. I see no hope.

Oh Lord, that You would give me some! There is no light. This darkness is different than before, it is starting to consume. Where are You? The Psalms – You created the darkness. You are in it. Psalms 139: 11, 12; 39:7. My hope is in You LORD hold me do not let me go. I want to hold on to You but it is so dark in this part of me I cannot see You when I look. There is no light. Just endless darkness – but You created it. You must be there. And if You are it must be okay. Hold tight LORD.

November 1. Yesterday seemed so unreal, so does today – what is happening, where is he? Tonight at Bible study they discussed what faith is, defining it from a dictionary, why not from the Bible? I have to have faith in what I cannot see – You with Ty, directing our lives for good, that with Daniel. then the Franklin Graham festival he was right with You, that You care and love him far more than I, that You have a plan for his life as You have for me and Ally, that You died for him also, for without this there is no hope.

November 20. At another study group (not our church one) we looked at writings by John of the Cross today, discussing 'the dark night of the soul' where You seem distant and withdrawn. Is this not what I was feeling when I could not 'see' You as it was so dark? Where I learnt that Your **presence** was far, far more needed that anything You could give or do? It was not till I 'saw' that You made the dark and so was there also that the fear and panic lessened. See Psalm 18 especially v. 11 'He made darkness His secret place; His canopy around Him was dark..... and v. 28. For You will light my lamp (candle), The LORD my God will enlighten my darkness.'

November 22. A while back I was accused by a leader in the church of being 'legalistic' because I would not lie on the jury selection form to get out of it. Lord I'm struggling, not sure exactly why or what's wrong. I'm tired, lonely. If I was not so 'legalistic' would Tonia still be my friend, would we be able to talk, share and laugh together? I don't understand what has happened. If I stopped being a Christian would things be better with Mum and Dad, would I have contact with my brother, nephews and niece? Would my relationships with my children be better? A lot of people are telling me so. I would not fear as much about where loved ones could be going when they die, would I still have contact with uncles, aunts and cousins? Yet what would my life be like, what would I be – if You were not here? I ache for heaven's rest. Friends go, will Luke? So they are not much help, just You Lord. I know You are here but You seem so far away as if You also are no help, though I know this is not so. I'm tired, my head is sad and tired with the constant fight to be right and yet should this be so when it is meant to be all of You? Am I trying too hard? I don't know how to let go and let God – the fight is in my head, my surroundings are great. Let it stop please Lord.

November 24. Listening to a song on the radio, have no idea of its name but the words, oh the words, *'...who am I that You should die...came from Heaven and die....who am I?'*[20] That was my problem. I felt unloved, and uncared for, unimportant, who was I? I'm just a nothing. Why would He die for me? I did not want to be responsible for His death. I did not ask Him to come and die. No, I did not, but He did come because He loved, because He cared. Because He made me I was worthwhile, I was important. I'm glad that He did, that He saw the sin and knew I could not ask, but He was the only way, the only solution and so he came. Now am I going to accept this most extravagant of all gifts with grateful joy or am I going to treat it as worthless and make it so? For a gift not received, not opened, not used is worthless. Help me to use Your gift to the max Lord, I do not want to waste any of it ever. Forgive me that I do not make enough use of it now, that I do not gaze at it every day and let it give me the joy it should –a joy that spreads to others that they can see. Let it turn the fears into whispers while its hope shouts loud from mountain tops and let its peace whisper 'be still' to my raging, tossing storms, then let me see each day as a gift to explore and use from You and let my joy give You joy as I explore my life with You.

November 28. Preaching to myself – Look at what we have in Christ not at what we have not or what we think we need. The Creator of all looks at me, loves me, I am the apple of His eye. I can talk to Him. He hears and listens. I have a home in heaven.

---

[20]  Who am I? by Casting Crowns, Hall, John Mark. 2003

He helps me. He intercedes for me and fights for me. He lets nothing happen to me that is not okay in the long run. He sees the Big Picture and guides me thru here with that view. He holds me and shelters, protects, and considers. He knows me and still loves and cares without changing. He does not cause misery for fun.

December 4. The wound is ripped wide open Lord, I feel as though I'm pouring out of it. Will there be anything of me left? Will this be the last time, will I survive? I have a huge fear that Joe is right, he's the good guy and I'm the crazy one. I'm afraid for Luke and Alyssa. I've sat through another meeting with Tyler and his case worker.

Tyler has to do this stuff for his Dad as I never did. He is 'going to buy back the 'family' home and its furniture so it will be exactly the same, it is the only reason he's living for, so that Dad can have everything back.' He spoke of using a key and going into the house when we would have been renting it out. The case worker thanked him for telling us this now, all this time later. Ty replied he 'only did so to get revenge on me as Luke has stolen his Dad's place with me. He never wanted to live with me but was too young to go against me'. Yet Tyler is also saying he 'wants to spend more time with me over the New Year but religion gets in the way. Religion is why he is not with me. He believes he will come back as an animal when he dies. He wonders why I wrote stuff in my diary about him' – I wonder how he knew! Worker wanted to know how I felt when the police had left him with us – I said I had not wanted him in the house; he was only there because of Luke. This surprised Ty. Worker then wanted to know where I would trust Tyler – I could not answer this Lord. I don't think I can, the more he spoke and defended Joe the more scared I became. To me it came across that he still wants to pay me back, nothing has changed.

I sat in church thinking. I'd left the meeting quickly when it closed. I needed the quiet peace of this building. My son as I knew him and loved, is dead. This angry, confused man I do not understand or feel safe with. The meeting had brought everything back. I don't want to sleep tonight, scared of dreams and thoughts. Help me to do what I have to do. The case worker wants me to answer Tyler's questions about why Joe and I split after he has checked that I have the same answers as Joe. Good luck with that!! I do not believe that Ty will accept my truth, for it will not be his Father's. I have no hope for a future relationship with my son Lord.

This question and answer meeting, my dear Reader, was ever mentioned again.

December 8. No sky to be seen all day because of a dense smoke cloud that remained till I hung the washing out around 2230hs when the stars were visible. Lord I could not see the blue sky – remember how blue it was that day I laughed out loud, that day I 'saw' You while listening to a song on the radio while driving – does me not seeing the sky mean it is not there, that it is not blue as blue and as wonderful as on that day? No. So when I cannot see You, that does not mean You are not there, just the same as always. I can look thru the smoke cloud with eyes of faith and see the blue sky because I know it is there. Can I not also look thru the darkness with eyes of faith and see You because You are there always? Thank You Lord for this insight on the way back home from delivering a load of wood to Tonia's.

December 13. About a week ago while being intimate, Luke became Joe. I had to concentrate so hard fighting the fear I felt nothing. I've been moving away from Luke's touch for a while now, I don't understand why now, what's wrong with me?

December 14. God sent rain tonight – how can I fight against Him? Mum rings, telling me how much she enjoys Tyler's phone calls, the last one being only a couple of nights ago, a good long talk. She is to take him shopping and a meal out for Christmas'. Tyler was meant to ring me at his case workers request, but he rings Mum instead. I am angry LORD but who do I fight against – You? Why are You allowing this – there is no answer that I can hear is there LORD?

At Tree Tops for Summer Convention. Words of the speakers that 'hit' me and some thoughts follow

'The LORD's compassion/mercy is renewable each day so give all your day over to Him, know that He is leading and you follow even when you have no idea what is going on. Isa. 61.'

'You cannot at the same time convince people how clever you are and how great a Saviour Christ is' – so Lisa stop trying to do the first and achieve the second, who do you want to impress the most, someone in church, Luke or Christ?

'Who am I? The fact I am a 'nobody' in most peoples' eyes does not matter as God is with me. Romans 8:1 – get rid of label 'single parent, wife of an adulterer, basher/abuser of kids, not good enough'.

Jeremiah 1:1-19. 'You are exactly what God wants you to be for what he wants you to do.'

'Build your house, your marriage on the foundation of God, storms will happen but this strong foundation will enable you to have the strength to stand.'

So the year ends Lord. I don't know what You wanted of me. I have not had others ask what You mean to me – does this mean others have not seen You in me? Better wife/mother? -- Hardly! I've been too busy wallowing in my pain to notice them. Better friend? – done even worse here, I've lost my best friend Tonia, she refuses to speak to me and I don't even know why. My ladies Bible Study has ended with the coming of the new Minister, the Rev. Alan Williams and his wife, Marie, as she will be doing this if seen as a need. I have no idea if these studies have helped or hindered. Been more disciplined? – No I came too close to giving up. Know more of You? – YES but I don't live it enough. I know You are there even when the darkness is thick and heavy and suffocating. You are there even when the pain is so great hope is almost gone – for if You were not there I would not be here. I have no idea what You are doing – Ally has to have counselling, Ty faces court and a possible jail term and wants nothing to do with me because of You. I am almost scared to face next year – I could not face it if You were not going to be there. You will be because You promised and so despite the confusion and pain I by Your grace will trust and obey as much as I possibly can. I wanted to do so much more for You than barely doggiepaddling through life I am meant to run. Run! I am barely wriggling let alone crawling, so running for me is a fantasy! You will have to drag me across the finishing line; I won't make it unless You do!

I had a panic attack today because a male sat next to me – so the ghosts hover still.

And so another year starts. Last year I started with lots of grand ideas, hopes and wishes. This year I know I am incapable of anything. You promise You will be with me. Be with me this year LORD. Get me through. I would like to do more than just get through but this will be enough. Get me through in a way that glorifies You, lets others see You in me please.

And so, my dear Reader you start to travel with Lisa into another New Year. This one was to be the year of strange phone calls, of things going bump in the night, of loud rapping on the front door and running footsteps up the road fading into the darkness causing the neighbourhood dogs to start howling and increasingly anxious neighbours to put on their lights as the darkness was disturbed by yelling and demented laughter. The front walls of their home were found to have been decorated with splattered eggs during one such night. An empty carton was found across the road along with several empty cans of alcohol. Lisa writes – Oh Lord please let us see who is doing this so we know for sure, no more guessing, no more blaming Tyler for things he is not doing. I'm going crazy suspecting it is him. Dogs are barking again. Ally is jumpy. Luke is out looking around. Ally voices her fear for him and herself, refusing to go up the passageway past the room that would have been Ty's. I tell her there is noone in there, Ty may be outside but he's not inside. 'Yes he is', she replies, 'he is in my head.' Please let us get past the past Lord. I hate it that we automatically blame Ty because our experiences in the past have taught us to.

Tyler is sentenced to a year's good behaviour bond and fined for last year's joy riding escapade. Lisa is unsure if she should feel relieved or disappointed that yet again he seems to get off lightly for bad choices and behaviour.

As he is to leave foster care by the end of the year there are numerous meetings that Lisa has to attend. These are mostly painful and unproductive from her perspective, where she has to sit silently and listen to her son's angry demands and accusations. Perhaps a sample of diary entries over the year may give you, my dear Reader some idea – Luke has used him to get to me and Ally, he is brainwashing us. Ty is now safe from this but at the time of the Franklin Graham Festival he was not. He only went forward to please me. I am not to pray for him or even mention his name to God. I replied that I may as well be told not to care for him. He and his case worker felt this was a bit harsh....

Met the latest carer, another lady who does not understand, who 'cannot see why I cannot see how much Tyler loves me and wants to be home with us. And how caring he is and how rejected he feels.' Here we go again Lord! Ty 'left' the relationship when he continually made behavioural choices that made it impossible to parent him. He is now demanding amongst other things, that we take him to church, to youth group. Talk about confusing!......

Ty is accusing me of 'not having equal input into his life compared to his Father, but he does not want contact with me as I'm not worth it. He became threatening. Will we be safe when he goes out of care Lord?......

Ty has a new case worker. She questions my unwillingness to have contact with him, why I am not. I said yet again, that contact is not up to me but him. I am as willing as he allows. She is to visit our home and check us out. So it starts again Lord, me having to explain I'm not necessarily the 'bad guy'. She expressed surprise on entering our home. Obviously not what had been expected.......

I take Ty out for Christmas lunch, just the two of us. Ally did not want to go so Luke stayed with her. It was good but I'm exhausted, drained. I don't know this young man......

And Alyssa? Well she is struggling with her own problems this year. Lisa learns from a counsellor that her daughter was so depressed at some stages the previous year that she considered suicide. This year does not seem any better for her. Her eating is more of a concern, or should I say the lack of, now requiring medical help and counselling. Ally also starts cutting her face and arms and questions Luke and Lisa's faith and life style choices. The following are some of the year's entries about Lisa's challenges with her daughter -- Ally says the paediatrician seemed to become upset over hearing what we had both been through and amazed that we had survived.......

Ally talking tonight and asking if we need to use special toothpaste on Sundays since it has to be a special day. I hear her tell Luke, who had not changed his mind about her 'wants' which included being allowed to watch M/M+ movies, that in a few months' time he would be sorry. Payback Lord?......

Ally asked tonight if You are worth losing family for. Luke said yes, though not necessarily in this life. I silently considered – if I join my family and have nothing to do with You it may be easier here but here is so short a time and eternity is, well eternal. If I join them and Ally here there will be no hope for any of us.......

Ally's interest in family devotions is waning. She does not even like simple questions now, so different from when she was so hungry. Is it her time to start questioning, to start choosing? I pray she does not do as I. I refuse to lose hope despite Alan questioning her 'spiritual commitment and therefore her salvation because she did not complete the youth group studies or attend all their events or share like the others.' I was there Lord when she asked You into her life. I have seen the changes. I have read her notes, heard her pray, I will trust You......

Ally acknowledges it is 'good when You answer prayers but wonders sometimes if You exist'. She wants to be 'normal', to go shopping, have unrestricted internet use, go 'clubbing' and is 'not sure if she really wants to be in Your family.' I feel upset. She is opening herself up to being badly hurt and worse – there are eternal issues at stake here. Lord how much do we let go so she can find out how empty the world is and hopefully return quickly without too many consequences, or is this pushing Your love and protection too far?.........

Ally troubled with nausea and chest pains, not wanting to return to counselling since they told her to write a letter to Joe. She is missing a lot of school – great, now it sounds as if she is trying to throw up in the toilet! I am not allowed to ask questions though. What am I meant to do Lord? I am tired of trying to figure things out.......

At her request, Ally and I are watching the DVD, *The Price*

*Tag of Sex.*[21] They talked about the diseases that are worse than pregnancy, including pelvic inflammatory disease. (I had been diagnosed with this in my second year of marriage to Joe. There was lots of scarring but I was told I should still be able to have children. Had Joe already found someone else that soon? Is that why the hurry to leave the city?) They talked about how sex outside of marriage is the only sin that damages the **whole** person, soul, emotions, heart, as well as physically. Love does not equal sex and sex does not equal love. (Remember when I thought it did Lord?) It is just about being used. Love is not about losing your friendships, job, plans, just focusing on each other. It is just a part of the whole of your life.

Yes Lord, You have forgiven me but the consequences, my emotional pain and the ghosts that share our bed sometimes never seem to go. I want better for Ally Lord. She thinks this is boring. It never entered my head either that these things could happen to me but – keep her safe, let her have the beauty without the ugly......

Tonight Ally started talking. I had said nothing the other day, just silently thought a lot. 'How do I know that Dad did not give me anything as he slept with so many other women and what about you, Mum, you could have something and given it to Luke. Was it normal when you can't remember stuff, to get little pictures of things? Don't remember what Dad did to me, but it was disgusting!' My gut response was if Ally had anything I'd kill him, as in Joe. Scary Lord, vengeance is Yours. She seemed eager to see a doctor; can this give her peace of mind Lord, this time?......

> *What do you see when you look at me?*
> *A child who could never please or make mum smile?*
> *A student who worked always within the rules?*
> *A clown with a mask of smiles?*
> *A bowed worn woman grieving the end of dreams?*
> *A single parent without hope, joy or help?*

---

21   The Price Tag of Sex. A DVD produced in Toowoomba Qld.

*A person, angry and prickly who onone loves?*
*A person worth dying for?*
*A person whose tears so precious are bottled?*
*A jewel of immense worth, far above rubies?*
*A woman worthy of praise?*
*What do you see when you look at me?*     L.

So what else happened during this year?

I had a friend who was going to assist me with putting all this together 'nicely', only to have her discover she could not handle reading what I had already put down, so I do wonder how you are going, what you are thinking.

Do you want to keep reading my dear Reader? Will you? I think I need a cuppa, how about you?

January 4. 'Let no man think himself to be holy because he is not tempted, for the holiest and highest in life have the most temptations. How much higher the hill is, so much is the wind there the greater; so, how much higher the life is, so much the stronger is the temptation of the enemy.' John Wycliffe. Satan is not threatened by low lives only those who aim high. Even so LORD by Your grace and strength still All the Way. Yet I do not think my crawling run is aiming high!

January 10. I would have hassles whether a believer or not. Sometimes it seems the only difference is that with You LORD there is a reason, a plan, even if I have no idea, Your promises are there. Help me to hang on please.

January 15. 'God's servants are immortal till their work is done.' First thought – we do not die/leave this earth till what work God has for us is done, we cannot die till God is finished with us here and that makes our death okay and right. Second thought – When we die we go to heaven as God's servants so our work is never done it just changes locations – we truly are immortal. But God I get so tired of fighting mostly against myself. Help me not to, I want to make it, I want to go all the way, I want to see You to be able to say a hugely inadequate thank You face to face, help me to fight now so I can rest then.

January 16. You've done it again LORD – thank You. Reading today from *Surviving the Storms of Stress*[22] – 'Are you satisfied with your current situation? No. Why? Not doing enough for Christ. Who says so? Me. We stand tired of fighting (sound familiar??) and Jesus quietly whispers, 'Come to me all you who are weary and burdened and I will give you rest.' Okay, I have unGod like expectations of what God wants of me. Stop, rest, let Him set the pace and level of achievement not me.

Then tonight's reading Isaiah 50:10-11. '....who walks in darkness and has no light? Let him trust in the name of the LORD and rely upon his God. Look, all you who kindle a fire, who... walk in the light of your fire...you have kindled This you shall have from My hand: you shall lie down in torment.'

Warren Wiersbe says of this passage, 'trust the Lord, wait on Him and He will give you the light you need when you need it.' Trust, wait, and come, to rely upon Him to do for you when you rest in Him.

January 19. I fear for Alyssa, for me, what will she do to herself, put herself through that she could avoid by being close to You? How will I handle it if she goes away, against You, like Ty? I've lost Ty; do I have to lose Ally too? Are the attractions of this world too great and we too unattractive? I can't do this anymore, can feel myself withdrawing.

February 4. Sermon this morning, Mathew 14:22-33 –'Storm and Peter walking on the water. Storms of life, Christ is there even if in the distance You are watching, knowing what is happening. You are in the middle of the 'messes' (as with the darkness Lord?) Reach out to Him, and if no strength just call out.' The words of a hymn we sang 'Holy, holy, holy though the darkness hide thee'[23] You are there. You are in the dark.

February 25. At Luke's request I read Isaiah, Ch.43 and I saw it. This is my God, loving me, grieving when I do not respond. This is my Father, my Abba and like a proud child boasting, my

---

22   Surviving the Storms of Stress by Ron Hutchcraft. Discovery Series. Discovery House Publishers 2005.
23   Holy, Holy, Holy! Words By Reginald Heber, 1788-1826. No.249 Alexander's Hymns No.3.

Abba is also King, Lord and Creator, just look at what my Abba does! Oh LORD, thank You. How I've felt I should but could not, now can call You my Father. Oh the joy – it is as bright and as light – no more so – than the darkness was black and oppressive. Sermon today on Phil.4:11 about contentment. Help me to learn. Yes will probably cost, so help me to pay.

March 18. Not sleeping. Have no idea what to pray for especially re Ty. You are not a God of confusion, confused mind. I cannot go back to living that way, not knowing which way to jump, how do You want me to relate to my son Lord?

March 20. The chemotherapy for Jean has cleared her blood and bone marrow of the chronic leukaemia but the lung nodules are still there.

April 8. Tonight's reading about Joseph telling his brothers not to feel bad about what they did as it was in God's plan; same goes for my past. Stop being angry at myself, focus on what Christ has done, not what I've done. Look at the Light not the darkness. Yet the darkness is there, it helps to show the brightness of the Light but I do not have to focus on or study it. Thank You for my freedom, that I do have hope, joy and peace. I never want to go where I do not, please keep me from that.

April 15. Questions from the evening sermon on Forgiveness – But Lord though I'm to mirror You I am not You. I know that every time I forgive I am open to being hurt again. I'm tired of being a punching bag. I am fed up with the hurt. Ty demands forgiveness for that which I have already forgiven. Only a while ago he got me to recite the Lord's Prayer, stopping me at 'Forgive us as we forgive others' to tell me I 'will be going to hell as I don't do this'. But he never stops hurting. I slept little last night, too many memories stomping around. What am I meant to do Lord? I get so frustrated with myself, the gap between what I read or know and what I do or feel about You and being a Christian just gets bigger. Why do You bother with me? Do something with this hurt Lord please.

April 20. It is good according to Your Word to be a 'nobody' here so a 'somebody' in heaven and Oh Lord I do wish for that as it is forever. But it is so hard to be a 'nobody' and I so much want to be important and have a position, to be a 'somebody'. I was so involved before, so 'in', now I feel very much 'out'. I'm not bringing people to You, doing important stuff, I just play with flowers and cook and clean, invisible, definitely not drawing anyone to a deeper knowledge of You. How full of pride I am, how unloving, ungrateful. Oh Lord, help me to be more than content to be a 'nobody' hidden in the shadows.

May 11. Tonight's reading –'You may fear that circumstances and human caprice have overturned your plans But nothing can frustrate God's loving intention. Tertullian (150-220AD) wrote '(do not regret) anything which has been taken away...by the Lord God without whose will neither does a leaf glide down from a tree nor a sparrow of one farthing's worth fall to the earth' 'Here I am, let Him do to me as seems good to Him.' 2Samuel, 15:25-26.'

Personal thoughts – 'Do not regret' – anything taken away, anything includes my son. The Lord gives, the Lord takes away. It is His right, He is Lord, He owns and controls everything, blessed be the Lord. It is not always well with me – I hurt, I bleed, I grieve, a lot, but it is well with my soul and this is what lasts, the rest does not, there is no pain or tears in Heaven.

May 20. 'If Jesus Christ be God and died for me then there is no sacrifice too great for me to make.' C.T. Stud. Some at church believe, tell me that I think the church could not manage without me doing stuff. NO! Wrongly judged again! I go to church to worship You and give thanks. I 'do' in gratitude for what You have done for me and as such I can never do enough. I live to serve not St. David's, not to get their thanks for it is very fickle and oft comes with a backhander – but You. I live because of You, help me to serve rightly.

Statement by visiting minister today – 'We have persecution and suffering in the amount and type that is sufficient for us individually to reach God's individual purpose for us.'

May 29. I go to a female counsellor that my doctor recommended. She tells me I'm to be more assertive.

May 30. No sleep, just more nightmares and memories, Murray trying to run me over with tractor, hitting me with hay bales, uncle calling me fat and parents not speaking up for me

– should I not have been able to feel loved, cared for, important, safe, heard? Tyler rang, moving, new carers again.

June 1. Confused and down, feeling it was all because of me that Joe changed and did what he did, that I caused it all, and made Tyler worse also. Have a huge fear that I'm doing it again but this time with Luke and Ally. I am giving myself too much power with this thinking. Others still have a choice, and what of God, does He have no say?! Help me to keep a stable mind please Lord.

June 3. Feeling very sore and achy today. Luke said I was thrashing around while asleep for ages last night. I remember that the pain of everything, Ty, parents, Joe was too much and wanting to give it to God and fighting, not sure who just that the pain was overwhelming. Jean to have the lung nodules checked in case cancerous.

June 10. A good sermon Lord but hard after the other day. 'What rules do we live by, Yours or man's?.....Discernment is needed; it's okay to break man's but not Yours....God does not make heavy burdens; just love Him with all your heart, mind and soul and strength. Trust Him....'

What has Ally done but this Lord, who is anyone, what right has anyone to know, to question what she prayed to You (and Tyler for that matter), what was in their hearts, was not right or correct – that is Your business! You will grow them Your way in Your time and show the fruit You desire. Considering the hymn, *How deep the Father's Love*[24] – '...make a wretch Your treasure..' Am I Your treasure? Yes. Treasure, really? Yes, consider this!! I was a wretch, now I'm treasure! What a God You are Lord.

June 12. Counselling. I am am told I did not have a 'validating childhood.' I am uncomfortable that this counsellor also seems to want to place blame on my parents and upbringing. They may be right but I don't want to stay a victim I want to move past that.

Linda Tschirhart Standford and Mary Ellen Donavon in their book, *Women and Selfesteem*[25] wrote – '...probably the most

---

24   How deep the Father's Love. Words and music by Stuart Towend. Kingsway's Thankyou Music. 1995.

25   Linda Tschirhart Stanford and Mary Ellen Donovan. Wom-

important factor in determining our level of selfesteem were our parent's motives for having us. Were we wanted children? If so, why were we wanted? What did our parents expect of us? These questions need to be asked if we are to understand how we came to see ourselves as we do....but an important task of adulthood is sorting out the negative and inaccurate selfperceptions we were taught and replacing them with something more accurate and positive. After all we are adults now and have power and the potential for insight, judgement and personal change that we never had before. We are no longer dependant on our parents for our survival and no longer have to rely on them to define who we are and what we're worth.'

June 15. Luke and Ally are mock fighting. I had an extreme reaction, fearful wanting to run, disappear, flashbacks; keeping brother quiet in the sleepout while fearing Dad and Grandfather would kill each other, being taken away thinking I'd never be able to come back. Chest pain +++.

June 17. Luke is home sick. I still go to church with his encouragement but my motives are questioned by some. Lord I did not go to church to ensure all went smoothly, that all was tidied up and put away, I went as I always have because I needed to worship You, I needed to go. Because I am me, I just feel 'safer', more comfortable hiding in the kitchen working, than out in the hall socializing. I thank You that Luke understands these quirks of mine.

This year the family took a friend, a single female friend who had been away with them before, on the interstate holiday. But – Ally's saying that she is telling her that marriages do not last…that she is bagging me and twisting what I say… that her relationship with Luke is stronger than mine as family/blood connection…what dress to wear to church, would Luke consider this one 'sexy'?...Ally worried Luke and I will divorce as she is like a shadow with Luke…Lord this is not a good witness for Ally of how a Christian woman behaves…I'm not either as having trouble even being polite… she will only talk to Luke now, stays

---

en & SelfEsteem. Understanding and improving the way we think and feel about ourselves. Penguin Books. 1984. Pg. 31 & 96.

in her room if he's not around.... so I lose another friend...Luke silences my fears by words and actions while remaining polite to her...

July 16. Evening beach walk, we are on holidays. There washed up in a wave in front of my foot was a big cowrie, unbroken, not shiny but whole and noone inside unlike the other day. I wonder – I found a smaller shell but it had 'someone' home so I put it back. I was faithful in a little; You have given me a bigger. If You can do that for something so 'unnecessary', a wish, can't I trust You for the real 'necessaries' the 'big' things; say like keeping Tyler and Alyssa safe as they rebel and bring them back, to do for them as You did for me?

During this time away Tyler had been texting Lisa multiple times a day for several days. The following are a brief sample just as they were sent, except there are *'s instead of the actual obscenity Ty used.

Lisa only responded to the one about him being in a car accident. They had not informed him of being away as fearful of what he may have done to their home in their absence

0839hrs  and u did rapped rev dan mum your sick as a dog doing that 2 him! Get a ******* life!

0844hrs  and had a 3 way with Luke to! Sick!

1257hrs  and if u don't respond I will go over to your house! Then look out!

1259hrs  and I will use my granddads gun if I have 2 mum! Like what I said 2 u in past years!

1506hrs  where's my stuff mum?

1524hrs  and I no where u live mum!

1547hrs  wheres my stuff mum? Or do I need 2 get my dad 2 punch and take luke out stone cold!

1618hrs  I thourt u and luke love me mum?

1828hrs  Mum **** off!

The next day –

1116hrs  Mum iv just bein in a car crash!

2013hrs  mum why didn't u tell me your not home?

Then a couple of days later when we had come home

2103hrs  its a bit rude u not talk 2 me mum and i no where u live so don't make me have 2 go over there with my mates car!

2118hrs we should do one big burn in ur drive way if u don't talk 2 me!

Then the following day –

1954hrs c u 2morr mum at church with rev dan then we talk then haha!

July 22. Elijah's depression was because he saw that the show of God's power was not able to turn Israel back, so gave up. The pain was too much. Last year the pain of knowing what awaits my parents, other family and Tyler if they keep going away from You was too much, I wanted out. Help me to bear this Lord.

August 5. Sermon – 'Christ is not only an example to follow but our restitution paid in full. Do you know what it means, what it is like to have all your sins paid for? Peter denied and followed Jesus at a distance. Then at the beach Christ said he was now to follow closely.'

And I remembered. Thank You Lord, I'm sorry I had forgotten yet again – all the way no matter what, all the way just don't leave me when things get dark or hard for there is no other way that is worth it.

Mark 5:36. Do not be afraid; only believe.

Believe In **ME**. Look at what **I**'ve done including the cross, look at how much **I** love and do not fear. -- The words flowed out of my pen -- I have no idea where You are taking me but neither did Abraham. I just have to follow You in loving trust, help me to stay focused, to declare Your loving kindness in the morning (I have another day), and Your faithfulness every night. (I got thru the day) Psalm 92:2

September 7. Collecting photos to do an album for Tyler's 18th. It is strange going thru the photos, I feel sort of distant, as if looking at a past belonging to someone else. This sort of saddens me, there were bad times but there were also ones of great joy like when I first held Ty, but these have a dream like quality to them now.

September 30. Jonah 2 – sounds so much like my experiences Lord!

October 16. Jean has multiple myelomas on her lungs. She

has been given 6-9mths to live. Some at church are talking of bulldozing, relocating or renting rather than maintaining a very old building, being grateful for the building You have given us.

December 18. I seem to be less sure and more confused the older I get. I am more aware of how I do not look good, if I thought about how I look I don't think I'd let Luke into bed at all!

December 22. Micah 6:8. 'He has shown you, O man, what is good; and what does the LORD require of you but to do justly, to love mercy, and to walk humbly with your God?' Freedom is found in walking obediently.

While at the Tree Tops Summer convention Lisa writes what made an impact – Philippians 1:1-19. I stood with tears running down my face after the first speaker. Why do I still live as though You are not all sufficient for every need Lord? What is my prison? I seem to have a few – life is not supposed to be this way, unfilled dreams, resentments, disappointments, ageing for starters! But why Lord, I should be free, should I not? Speaker went on to say, 'examine, test yourself, is there evidence of Him doing in and through you, do you see Him in your life?'

Oh, yes! How blessed I am and I should be showing this in the way I live. Why do I 'forget' You Lord? And yet have I not been shown this year how really sufficient You are? Yet I want more Lord, I want to rest more and stop thrashing around, trying to 'do'. I only see how little and how much more there can be but how much more is there compared to 6-8 years ago? Thank You for this incredible journey Lord.

Reading my diary entry for the beginning of this year while considering something one of the Speakers said today about being like an empty glove. 'Stop writing your own story. Stop doing. Trust and obey. Get on with life. Do what you have to but trust Him to write your real life story. Let Him be your source of energy, of doing. Like an empty glove, I can look right but cannot do anything unless filled with Christ and then it is He that does, even though I, the glove move. Being in God's will is not my business but His responsibility as I trust and acknowledge Him in all my ways. We are never told to pray for His will as we can assume we are doing it if trusting Him. We are told to pray for wisdom.'

I want to live Lord, all the way, not just exist. Don't stop helping me.

'Come and abide, it is that simple. Philippians 1:20-30 but especially v.21 'For me, to live is Christ, and to die is gain.' The Christian life is Personal, Practical and Possible – it is Christ. God gives us Christ when we are saved by repenting and believing, everything we need is in Him. He is in you and permanently so, death is only gain. The gift of God is eternal life not God's gift is eternal life. Psalm 23, He refreshes your soul, when you meet with God you are refreshed.'

It happens every time down here Lord. I cry partly in relief I think why not at St. David's? Have I got that busy there I don't stop to see You? A fear of being judged? Help me to change.

Philippians 4:47, 10-20. 'Peace that passes all understanding is not rational; you may even feel guilty about having such peace.' Have I not felt this Lord? Remember when Mum questioned me because I was not as distressed over what was happening to Tyler as I should have been, causing me to wonder what sort of mother I was?

Reading for the day by A. LeTissier – Mark 4:35-41. 'God's comforting presence calms the storm of the soul. The clouds may not pass but His perfect love deflates all fear. 'Who is this?" v.41. It is the Son of God who has the power to take authority over any situation as and when He knows best. Jesus does not promise a life free from difficulties but He has promised to accompany us through every storm. (Hebrews 13:5) It is an awesome experience to engage with God's peace that passes all understanding, guarding our hearts and minds from tremendous anxiety (Philippians 4:67)'

Personal thoughts I think the 'world' will try and rob us of the full impact of this peace, will try to make us feel guilty –'how can you be so cold and unfeeling, uncaring; how can it have no effect on you, how can you not do something, you cannot just let it be'. Why can't I just trust God with it all? Do what I can then stop. Stop scheming, struggling. Accept it. Accept God is in control, working, even when you cannot. And just stop, be and enjoy Him and what you do have because of Him and leave the rest with Him. This is peace. A cessation of the struggle against things in and outward. A rest, a stillness that comes from just trusting Him and letting Him 'do'.

'For this I have Jesus. When the lights go off in your life is when you discover the reality of Christ being sufficient.'

Personal thoughts --Yes have I not started to see this? For this I have Jesus. Isaiah 49:13-23. Refuse to be defeated. For every regret, missed opportunity – especially with raising the kids and what I missed out on – what 'ifs', for every sadness, for every pain my children have gone thru and have, for my inability to help them, for Joe's parent's and family's treatment of me. For every fear, for every hurt and rejection I have Jesus. Jesus, Saviour, and Creator what can He not know, understand and do? my Forever Friend, Counsellor, Guide, Lover. Can I still wobble with the blows? How much more can my body take – yet not mine but Christ's! Can I tire and find comfort in Him, will He treat me as He did Elijah?

So here's to another new year of adventure with You Lord, may my hand never leave Yours, then I will be safe in the dark on a path I have not trod. May I show interest and care to others, may I make them feel significant. May I make people important and not the stuff I 'have' to get done. May I love Luke more and be a better wife and mother. May I love You more, heed You more and rest more trustingly and childlike in Your incredible love for me.

## Chapter 2

So another year has begun.

Irene, Lisa's mum rings. She complains to Lisa that she is having difficulty in contacting Tyler and has not seen him for ages. Lisa got that ruffled she forgot till later that Irene had seen him the last time she had.

Luke wonders why Lisa feels so unfulfilled, restless and discontented when she was content and happy when they first married. So does Lisa! She is struggling with 'enjoying' things (holidays, clothes, sex), feeling she is unworthy, and wonders where the line is between unselfish, constant joyful service to others and caring for herself when tired and unwell. She is also still troubled by resentment towards Luke because of Ally only talking to him, refusing to talk to her; having to make the home nice for Luke's grandchildren, John and Kari, to accommodate Luke and their needs yet Tyler not being allowed into the house until Luke knows his attitude has changed.

Lord I wish I could rip myself apart and pull it all out. I'm tired of the battles inside. Hate my fat that is increasing again and yet I am so tired of watching and being careful with what I eat. I 'have' to do the right thing (whatever that is) with Tyler, groceries shopping etc. and back to church stuff (our holiday is about to end), appear in control when I feel mad, insane inside. I have sex when I feel no desire to even touch or kiss Luke at all. I'm tired of doing and yet Lord I have no problems compared with others, please help me to get a handle on living this life and pleasing You, Luke and Ally. Cleaned church set up for morning tea and did the flowers. The flower cupboard was messy only one week after I had tidied it! The kitchen cupboards were also messy and the floor filthy, I got stressed, tired of feeling responsible and 'having to do it' as noone else seems to. Got home all upset and walked into another mess all over the kitchen and lounge with food and toys, it was the last straw. I'm tired and what does it matter Lord in the end where things are in the cupboards, or if fresh of artificial flowers are used, or how the cups are set out or having nice home cooked food or bought plain biscuits – none of what I stress over seems involved in advancing Your Kingdom. Compared to those working in the schools or university or overseas to bring Your Word to others, I do nothing. How will cooking and cleaning bring someone to You? I wish I could do big things for You as You have done big things for me. Yet Lord just let me be faithful in the little things, I struggle so much sometimes (probably why You won't let me do the bigger) I just want to finish well, to do Your work that You have set me even though I have no idea what this is, I just do what is in front of me each day let this please You. All the Way Lord.

During this year there were again sermons and messages including those from Convention that struck a chord within Lisa giving rise to personal reflections. A selection follows – Sermon on having a free mind; the verses from Romans 8:56 and 2Corithians 10:46 struck me. I wonder Lord – physical violence in marriage or in persecution of a Christian is visible. Easy to act on but emotional or Satan's mind games along with the flesh and the world's are not, they are an invisible, silent battle that for me is wearing, becomes too hard, too much, the effort to turn off or stop wrong thoughts to keep alert. Oh Lord not only give me the ability to fight but the strength to choose to do so time after time after time, especially with all the selfhate voices.

Message from Jeremiah, Ch.15 and 20 – 'Are you experiencing bitterness, resentment, selfpity? Repent for you have not come to terms with the situation.'

Oh how I've fought for so long against this Lord, not to come to terms with opposition, family, not honestly facing my emotions. I don't even recognise some they have been so squashed down for so long. Help me to be honest and face them in a way that is not destructive to self or others, to know them and call them for what they are.

One of the Speakers spoke about 'the dark night of the soul, when all we know about God does not match up with what we feel, but is actually denied by feelings. God is gone'.

So what I felt others have. He went on to say 'that only great saints like Job experience this', well Lord I ain't no Job, I am not a great anything but thank You that others do know what I am describing.

Sermon at another church was based on a song called *The Desert Song*,[26] 'God is my victory and He is here (inside) in the dessert or dry times, in the battle, our spiritual battles, in fire or testing times, harvest or times of abundance, whatever season of life God is there. Worship Him and sow the seeds you have been given. Challenge was could we say this' – thanks Lord that I can, that experience has shown me the truth of this, though I forget. Lord I lay down my life, You take it up, it is Yours. Use it as You would, make me willing and able to all the days I have, do not let me take it back up.

March 5. Ally is refusing to go to Church; we reluctantly let her stay home. Luke has to repair and replace her bedroom window flywire again, the clips keep breaking. She is still cutting herself, refusing help, I feel so helpless, letting her make her own choices is not easy! It was not for You either was it? It cost You more than I.

April 15. Romans 8:28. '...for good...' Ally said 'that if You were the God I think so much of, were as good as I thought, how come You allowed what happened to her, me and Ty and what of the people who die of cancer'. Oh LORD I was so much older when the struggle with this question came....she will have to find her own answer and decide for herself...like Joseph and his brothers as she will not listen to me.

During the month of May Lisa has to have a Colonoscopy --- Terrified I'd be awake and flashback to Joe and the pain he caused. The anaesthetist missed seeing me despite being first on the list but gave me a light anaesthetic after I spoke to him while on the table in theatre, thanks Lord. I'm free of cancer but Jean's melanoma is aggressive and fast.

---

26    The Desert Song. Brooke Ligertwood. Hilsong United. From album This is our God 2008.

May 15. Ally told Luke tonight she 'has been sneaking out to see a boy, which is why the flywire has been broken but she stopped when he wanted more than kisses despite him saying he would kill himself. She is not liking what she is becoming' (neither am I) and wants to be home schooled (not a good idea, I don't think I'm that sort of person and I don't think she would listen to me.)

May 21. Tyler is here for meals as Ally 'felt sorry for him' when she saw him sobbing uncontrollably because Joe had told him that 'if he showed his face at his grandparents again they would all beat him to a pulp'. I'm taking him for driving lessons.

June 11. Ally decides to go to a Christian school despite me making sure she knows how Christcentred all the syllabus is.

July 3. I dreamt last night that a thing of great evil was nearly upon me. I spoke Psalm 23 – I remembered all of it! When I woke I realised there is nothing between me and evil but You Lord. Don't let me move from Your shadow ever, it's too horrible.

By the beginning of August the melanoma had spread into Jean's brain. She is hospitalised, has a massive bleed and dies within several hours. The day Jean dies Tyler is at the Police Station making them find Lisa as he has an urgent matter to discuss with her – He is going to put an AVO (Apprehended Violence Order) out against Luke for taking me away from him – I can't cope with this yoyo relationship, abusive then demanding hugs. Too much like Joe.

About a week before this Tyler had sent a text threatening to kill Luke if he did not apologise for taking Lisa away from him. There were multiple abusive and threatening messages left on the home phone, including one where Ty threatens selfharm if he cannot see Lisa. She writes -- I can't live like this, never knowing if he is trustworthy or not. I had started to trust him again but there is no way I can help him get up his hours for getting his driving licence, at present anyway. I'm scared for all of us. What do I do Lord, is he ever going to settle down and not flare up?

During Jean's funeral the now exprincipal of Tyler and Alyssa's Primary School came up and talked to Lisa, remarking on how different she was from that time, younger, beautiful, and peaceful Really Lord? Can she see it is because of You?

Ally cannot come to terms with a God who would allow such a good person as Jean to die. She had got very close to Jean with their love for animals, shoes and handbags.

August 7. I found an article in the local paper upsetting. It stated that 'Women are increasingly being threatened and attacked by their young sons – sometimes with weapons.....a common but taboo form of family violence...sons who abuse their mothers crossed all walks of life and had severe and lasting effects on mothers...exploding into fits of rage, (the) 13yearold would not only assault her, but at times threaten her with knives...the violence could stem from something as simple as telling her son to go to bed ...you'll get the times where he'll go to bed but other times if there's something there he'll grab it and throw it…Police responded to more than 30,000 reports of family violence...with more than 3500 directly related to attacks by adolescents ...'

I remembered how I was made to feel guiltier; if possible, by DHS when they had no 'box' to put me into other than the one where Tyler had to be removed from my care for his safety when it was Ally and I who were being threatened by him, who wore the bruises.

Lisa's dad, Bill has health issues during this month. He is diagnosed with aggressive prostate cancer, but gets the all clear after the prescribed treatments. She had hoped this wake up call, as she saw it would have been a turning to God time for Bill but if anything he was even more closed to her timid efforts. Lisa writes – Dad's having radiotherapy for aggressive cancer, he 'took Murray with him to the Doctor as wanted someone who could understand what the Doctor was saying.' They do not need my help, my medical knowledge, with anything. Murray's helping; I got angry with myself. Why should it have hurt, surprised me, why should Dad having cancer change anything? I have done nothing to them unlike Murray and his wife yet I'm out and he's in. I will always be out – it really feels like once my existence allowed them to marry I was no longer needed except to work, just the way it seems LORD and You have used it to make me, me, suitable for whatever You need me to do. Joseph had no bitterness after all those years towards his brothers but he also did not jump into a close renewal of relationship till he knew where their hearts were. I will just be. Jesus did not try and clear up misunderstandings his family had of Him thinking He was insane – He just kept on doing Your work and let them figure things out, or not, themselves.

Lisa has developed a mutual friendship with a new family at church; June is around the same age and has children of similar ages as well. As Marie, says 'June seems to get' Lisa. But June, who has had cancer a few years ago, finds she has it again and this time it is not good.

During the September holidays Luke, Lisa and Ally go interstate for a holiday. Ally assures them that they can trust her and leave her in the unit and park by herself while they go walking or swimming. One night though, Ally is behaving strangely so Lisa goes into her room to check on her, the bed was stuffed with clothes to look as if she was in it and the window was broken. As they were dressing, stressing over what could be happening Ally returned with an explanation that made no sense. Luke decides Ally is to not have access to the internet for two weeks and they will not be coming back here as they had previously discussed Luke says that 'Ally's dishonesty to him was the worst disappointment he'd ever had', I just felt violated and rejected. Ally is asking 'to go to Mark's for a sleepover with the kids when we return home'. In a way it was a relief not to have her around but it haunts me how she left, sitting in the front seat not looking anywhere but straight ahead holding on to her packed bag, no goodbye to me, which surprised Luke, not even when I went out and said bye and hoped she had fun with the kids.

October 1. Mark, Luke's son rings, 'Alyssa does not want to come home. She has been cutting herself because of our oppressive, excessive religious attitudes, and about 6mths ago she was going to have a baby or facial tattoo to get back at us'. Jo, Mark's wife, said 'they both strongly believed it was not over us disciplining her but over our beliefs and that was why they were giving her a safe place to stay, where she would be listened to and not judged.'

I rang the Christian school counsellor who had been seeing Ally about her 'cutting'; 'it is up to me to open up communication'. Why is it always up to me? He 'thought this house was full of do's and don'ts because of our excessive involvement in church, Bible studies etc!!'

I am given permission to visit Ally and 'hear' her talk, if Jo can be present. Luke however is not to come with me. Ally 'is afraid we would choose religion rather than her. She wants to stop going to church, no youth group, no daily family devotions, no grace with meals. I'm to stop doing so much for the church and to remove all the religious books in our lounge room as she is ashamed to have her friends over, will keep climbing out of her window if we do not agree.'

Jo wanted to know how Luke would feel about these needs of Ally; I said I could not speak for him. I had to leave. Alyssa was a stranger demanding to be able to be 'true to herself' whatever that means, while expecting us to be what we are not.

'None of her problems are because of Joe, or Jean dying but us. She wants contact with Joe, would prefer to be with him than us. School is okay as she is not expected to believe what they teach, where as we do.'

I was so upset I got the shakes. I did not feel I could tell Luke she expected us to choose between God and her, so waited for our minister to come – I had rang him.

Cost is great Lord. I was told if I gave You up I'd have Tyler back, well here I go again. Does she not see or understand everything she has and gets now is because of You and our faith in You?

I became very depressed; looking at the pain I thought I was going to have to go thru again. Suicidal thoughts kept me awake, I was scared to sleep, could not stop crying, pain in chest crushing. Luke hurting too, crying also but I was unable to help him. He held me and we both sobbed.

October 2. Madge, an older friend from church came and helped me move Jean's stuff that we had been given, from the spare room wardrobe into the kitchen cupboards so the offensive 'religious' books could go from the lounge into a bookcase we bought and 'hid' in the wardrobe . She was shocked when the reason why I needed to do this was given.

October 3. Ally back, acting as if nothing has happened, as if just had a sleepover, getting Luke to take her shopping and talking about the things she wants. I found it very stressful.

October 4. Tyler came over for tea. He brought 2 DVDs of sermons he wanted us to watch. Ally's not interested and Ty's bringing church messages to share with us – crazy!

October 8. Ally has a boy visit and they go for a long walk.

October 19. Had a nightmare where I had to 'prove' my ability and worth to be Ally's mum over Mark and Jo's claim to be the better parents, noone stood up for me. I was just a monster, useless, nothing but an embarrassment and Ally did not want me so why fight?

Lord help me to fix my eyes on You, to consider You and those who think well of me, who challenge and encourage me, not those who hurt and make me feel bad about myself and question myself so that I do stop being wary and sad and so pain filled – I'm no good to You when this way I feel.

October 26. Ally asking, no demanding, us to take her to church today!

November 2. Ally is again wanting to go to church.

December 14. She has another 'boyfriend' and again we discover from a school parent that she is lying to us about her whereabouts and who she is with. I feel like I'm in a game, where nothing is real all is pretend like it was with Joe in a way but different. Christ, You could love without trust because You trusted Your Father, help me to do so too. How can life be the same, our relationship the same when I will always be wondering what she really is doing? It hurts. Ally who once could never lie to me now does it so easily, so convincingly, what to do Lord?

Yes, my dear Reader it is Summer Convention and what follows are a sample of the many notes and thoughts from this period – Thank You that You see each person individually and answer our needs. I needed You to 'prove' You, make Yourself real to me. You answered prayers, some not even formulated into words. You 'proved' Yourself to be trustworthy, dependable, strong enough to lean on. You were not just words in a story, or a history book, but here and now and for me. You heard. You cared about me and what I was facing and still do. Thank You for being real.

The Speaker said 'that if we understood that the Lion is the Lamb and that they are the Christ it is only because of the working of the Holy Spirit, we must never forget this or take it for granted.'

Okay, but I have known this for a long time (though not to the depth of now) even back as a student nurse. I thought it was something any reader with school taught comprehension skills would conclude but then the Jews and Pharisees did not, so have I given myself credit for something the Spirit has done? And if I knew this, and so had the Spirit, why was it impossible for me to accept responsibility for Christ's death, why did God seem distant and uninterested – how did this happen, did I who prided self for not following the crowd, being able to be different, actually decide to follow crowd away from Christ, was my foundation okay but I chose to move off it and not build on it because I had decided God did not care, could I have chosen to understand unconditional love? Was it me that became distant and disinterested and uncaring, me that moved? Oh my Father, how I have hurt You! What an insult to the Holy Spirit and how I discredited Christ's blood! Thank You – how pitiful those words seem, how inadequate! – for waking me up, for the pain before it was too late. Oh God help me to fight and not get tired, help me to now have patient endurance to see You, to love You and follow You all the way Home.

January 9. It's hard when Luke is really interested and I am not and cannot or will not make myself. Once I could not get enough of touching him, now I'm almost disinterested – what's happening Lord?

I was too tired to take Tyler for a driving lesson when he rang, so our phone conversation deteriorated rapidly 'why won't I take him on family holidays, why care more for Luke and Ally, will kill himself then it will be too late for me,' I turned the phone off. Oh my Father I don't know what to do, I hate it that he can drag me back there, why can't I stop him, what if he does kill himself, could I actually live with the guilt that would bring? I was considering taking him to the beach, just the two of us but scared now. I could not handle it if he was like this face to face. I don't want any more bad memories; I want ones like the other night. I really enjoyed taking him driving and teaching him how to reverse for parallel parking. What has set him off again?

January 10. Tyler kept texting and ringing till around 0130hrs. One voice message said he 'knows I still have feelings for Joe and am just waiting for Luke to die so I can marry Joe again' – oh boy did I want to reply to that one!! But I was reminded by Ann that I cannot go to his level, it was a gentle but firm reminder, a rebalance, thanks Lord.

January 13. Reading tonight – 'best thermometer of your Spiritual temperature is the intensity of your prayers.' Ha! I desire to read, study and think slowly but I rush, cram it in as quick as I can, usually around 22-2300hrs, a quick think on You, hardly what I'd call a prayer compared to how it used to be and fall into bed only to get up and repeat it all again, no time to breathe and rest in You, just go from one demand to another. It needs to stop Lord. I need to enjoy a stroll with You, help me to get rid of what is not important, what You don't want me to be doing so I can see You.

January 14. Ty here early in the morning with new support carer asking what happened to Jean's tools. Luke and I took him out for lunch; grocery shopping then I helped him cook meals for the next four nights while Luke read the paper at his unit. There was no talk of being raped (he had left a message to this effect a few days ago, I only got message bank when tried to contact him at the time), holidays, nothing, amazing! I've got a headache!!

January 20. Hebrews 11:6 – 'But without faith it is impossible to please Him, for he who comes to God must believe that He is, and that He is a rewarded of those who diligently seek Him.'' Do you see the 'and'? Consider.

Well I have not even since a child had trouble believing

in God, just seeing the sky, clouds grass lambs, rainbows seas sunsets, I knew. My problem was with the second half of the verse. Believe this great God who could do and make all that would be interested in ME, see and hear ME and THEN reward ME, I was invisible to my family, how, why would this God see me? He had much more important stuff to worry about than me! So if this was so, why seek Him? Oh boy was I wrong! How I've hurt my loving Father who just wanted me to rest safely in His arms and yet He did not give up on me, what love! And back to the Spirit – so if He was working in me so I could see and understand, why was I not listening as a 'Christian', whose definition is one having the Spirit – perhaps it should be more correct in saying one obeying the Spirit within.

January 28. We are home from holiday and looking after John and Kari. Ally told Jo that she 'has to wear her school jumper despite the heat as I'm too busy with church stuff to fix her dress's torn armpit', and the kids mess up the van after I'd finished cleaning it. I think I committed 'murder' at least four times today if not more!

January 31. The neighbours' dogs are barking and growling. They are putting lights on. It's after midnight again.

February 1. Ally wanting us to meet another new boyfriend.

February 2. Eight threatening texts from Tyler today.

February 3. 25 texts between 0925 and 2353hrs including these – why not invite me and girlfriend over cos that's a bit rude mum…if u want $ back should invite over 4 tea….should call a lawyer and take this 2 court so cu 2morr so we can have a talkLuke not welcome 2 come over…I wnt my stuff back by 2nite mum!.... mum I can't breth iv got th fright on top of me pls help me!

This after he spoke to Luke on the home phone threatening to 'kill self and bash Luke's brows in with a baseball bat and sending Joe around to sort me out and get a lawyer so can live with us' and goodness knows what else as Luke only told me this much but he was very upset and shaken. Despite this he went around to Tyler's. Support carer was there, having lifted fridge off Ty's legs, kitchen knives and scissors were scattered around

Ty on the floor. Carer took him to Emergency. Luke said that the fridge was empty and light enough for Ty to lift himself. The texts continued all night accusing us of not caring, I did not answer, no point.

February 4. I rang DHS for advice. They had shut his file when he turned 18. I was told to ring Psychiatric triage services. I did. They 'would not have sent anyone around there as too risky'. Sorry Luke. They 'knew Ty well,' and instructed me 'to tell him I do not love him when he is making such threats, but will be happy to be involved in his life if and when he chooses to treat us as human beings and stop this antisocial behaviour.'

So I told my son today I did not love him and I did not want to be around him when he is like this. He rang and talked to Luke sobbing. Luke could hear someone prompting him as to what to say. I've heard it all before Lord, nothing changes, the last text after all this was 'mum whers my fishing rod my pa gave me yrs ago?' No nothing changes.

It is now 0030hrs, a new day. I'm scared to sleep. Oh Lord help me and keep him. A total of 13 texts yesterday including – 'mum u may be a granprient in 9nouths tie and Ally maybe an anti…want my stuff.'

I texted back that Luke had returned it all the other night. Reply – 'not my matchbox car' – so I posted it.

He then visited with Max, the support carer, asking for more money for driving lessons among a lot of other wants telling me he 'thought its Christian to forgive and forget', Max brought in mercy and grace, saying he is a Christian. Tyler went on to tell me 'I only do stuff for him because of God but I should love the son,' as in Tyler. I shut the door and let him bang till they decided to leave. Were they only dreams Lord of having a relationship with him, a good one? Can I hope for this in eternity? I feel numb and yet everything hurts.

February 5. I don't know how You did it Lord but thank You. I woke abruptly everything rushing in at 0600hrs. First shock – I slept! But then everything flooded in. I can't do this again. What have I done? Others before have told me 'I had to hang in there as I was the only one, as Ty had been deserted by everyone else' and now for the second time I have 'abandoned him, such a hurt confused boy', tonight seemed a long way away and yet night is scary. I thought Luke and Ally had left for school, I started sobbing and shaking uncontrollably, Luke rushed in holding me tight. Oh Ally you were not meant to hear your Mum sound like a wounded animal, I can't do this again Lord, I remember the last time. Get out of bed place one foot in front of the other – move!

Rang our doctor, can't get in for four days, so far away, how am I going to cope?

While doing the reading for the day I thought of calling Daniel. Daniel, who knew, who had seen and heard Ty, who could understand. He did and the advice was good. Lord I could move again.

He said I 'was a good mother, I'd held out the olive branch more that he'd thought possible yet was still bitten. He did not understand why a person who was given such a great capacity to love had been given such a burden.' His voice was so soothing; telling me 'to give Ty to my Lord, not to let him consume me, to live in the square God had drawn around me not the one Tyler has drawn.' Daniel said 'as much as I want to I cannot get inside Ty's head and change or fix it, only God and Ty can do that, he's at the age and ability to choose. If Ty chooses to harm himself HE chooses NOT me, like a pendulum swinging will not stop unless stopped, I had to do this.'

Daniel went on to say 'he'd often thought about what he had done and wondered if it had been the right thing to do but could never see another way; he'd gone into a bad place to be and was spiritually, emotionally and physically exhausted'; I said I'd been there too. He said 'not to let the devil get into my mind and cause guilt and doubt, but to read, listen to music, keep mind occupied.'

February 6. 'Due 2 how much hurt im in atm im going 2 step down as your son.' So Lord, one day at a time, lived to the full of what You give me with an eye to being with You at the end – my choice. TY has to make his as does Ally.

February 7. Mum rings, 'had a lovely visit from Tyler for a cuppa.' I told her a bit about his threats to us, 'silly boy, but boys will be boys' was her comment.

February 16. Tyler wants to visit with Max to 'talk'. Conflicting feelings, I want to know how he is doing as he has not come to any of the arranged meetings. Yet I don't feel up to facing him and Max to 'talk', knowing how Ty's 'talking' goes from experience.

February 23. 16 texts – 'including maybe dad needs a talk 2u mum and my grandad …andu cant keep on runin 2 Luke al th time with your troulbes and your problmes cos when hes gets older and past away one day who r u goin 2 run 2 then mum? cos luke wont be hear and he pasts away one day so u will have no one 2 run 2 anymore. Besides my dad cos hes a bit younger that Luke so yea…. and I want dad's weddg photos by 2nite ….or do u want me 2 go over 2 your house and pick them up 2nite mum ……cos u said that u will give it 2 Ally and me when u past wasy remember ……um whats goin on u don't want me is this u want 2 stop contat with ur son for good……' Lord how much longer? How will it end?

February 24. Thoughts after yesterday – God as Creator loves all humanity. God as the Father can only have a relationship as such with those who acknowledge and respond to Him rightly on His terms. I will always be Tyler's mum, I will always love him but there can be no relationship the way things are currently. I am responsible for some things, for these I am accountable and answerable, but I am not for those that are another's responsibility. This includes another's choices; I cannot make anyone choose to do something such as love me or to change. I can only advise and encourage, I can only be responsible for my choices, and so I am not responsible for the consequences another experiences because of their choices, I am only responsible for my consequences. This covers choices for salvation to being 'nice'. I cannot make anyone else do either, only suggest they consider carefully and choose wisely. Ezekiel 18. The pain and grief of a loved one's bad choices will always be there. But that is okay; God has this pain also so He knows and understands mine and lifts some of the weight so it is bearable. It is okay.

February 26. I visited Mum. She wanted to show me a new

bedspread she had just got. I was admiring it, she turned it back to show me the matching new sheets but as she fluffed the pillows I saw the bed. Flashback out of nowhere, I struggled for breath. I needed to run. It was the bed Joe and I had shared. I had to get out of that room. I could not hide my need to do so, to escape. Mum had no idea, no understanding. I felt a fool. She thought I was being one. She had 'thought they were doing me a favour keeping the bed!'

March 1. Max rings asking for a recipe that Tyler wanted, Ty also wanted to talk, 'Hi Mum, love you, see you around some time Mum.' So we go to love bit, no apology, and move on till next time. I am tired Lord. I don't want to face a next time.

March 4. June's MRI has shown the cancer is now in her brain, we both cried. I don't want to lose her Lord, be kind to her as You were with Jean please, strengthen me so I can offer whatever You desire for her especially now. We discuss funeral arrangements.

March 8. We are at the beach. There are a lot of single grains of sand Lord, if one represents my time or June's time here and all the rest represent our time in heaven with You, our time here is truly insignificant, over and gone before even began and yet it is Your training ground for us.

March 22. Marie tells me 'the church can run very nicely without me'. I had been stressing about a clash of social events – a catering function at church which previously I'd been very heavily involved in with – organising, setting up, cooking and cleaning up -- and a craft day so I had asked her advice. I felt hurt. Do people really think that I believe the church cannot run without me being present? I am a 'nobody' Lord, yes I'd like to be a 'somebody' but I know I'm not so I guess my prayer last night is answered, I can go to my craft day knowing I'm not letting anyone down, making things harder for others by doing for myself, what I'd like to do.

March 24. Ally is saying she is leaving home next year. This Christmas will be the last one she wakes up here for. I wonder how Luke and I will be. We have never had her not around. I'm missing her noise, perfume and laughter already as she is with

# THE MAKING OF A JEWEL

David every spare moment.

April 9. Ally telling us she 'does not have to do what I say or think is right but as she wants.' Luke is upset by her choice of words and tone.

April 10. What happens in me is more important than what happens to me a speaker at Easter Convention said.

April 19. Ty appears at church, aggressive and threatening towards us demanding we 'move his stuff from his unit or he will lose it tomorrow, I'm your son don't you care.' A church member tells us how impressed she is that he ran all the way from another church to see us; he'd been speaking to her as we drove in.

April 20. Police visit us, they 'have a paper to give Tyler, he is not in trouble from them they are just acting as glorified posties but becoming frustrated as unable to find him. They keep going to his unit but there is no answer and now the neighbours are telling them he has gone today.' As they cannot even contact him on the phone, I am asked to text him. Much later Ty replies – I've moved! Goodbye

April 21. Ty texting – 'stop trying 2 get the cops involve with me if u do that again I b getting a new number and goin 2 th usa for good and live their full time.' Had several very weird calls on the home phone with just sounds and breathing noises. Much later here were loud thumps outside.

June texts, 'Hi Lisa just letting you know that I'm missing you ☺'. Oh Lord this hurts, she is having radiotherapy each day just to be able to swallow. There are more lesions on her brain.

April 22. The Minister of another church that we had taken Tyler and friends to for Youth Group rings wanting to know what is happening with Ty as he visited today, then the police did, asking questions.

April 29. A lady notifies us that she 'has taken Tyler in since we won't give him a home, such a nice kid'. So this one has all the answers and knowhow, good!

April 30. Daniel phones, 'has had trouble with Tyler over the last four months, texting, commenting on Face book, threatening and nasty'. He 'believes the legal stuff is over a restraining order from past girlfriend as Ty has told him about following her.'

May 1. Daniel rings again. 'Tyler is now threatening to kill Ruth and/or him, the face book messages have also got obscene. He has sought advice, showing the police what Ty has been sending but is unsure if he could testify against him, feels so sad, so confusing, has no idea who he is dealing with.' I cried and cried. Could I have done anything differently Lord?

May 4. Should not have turned the phones on today! He is homeless and threatening us again. This has been going on for months this time; I'm tired of feeling controlled by him, being worried about making him angry. I wanted to text back 'get lost' but that's not nice, so confusing, he's my son and so I do love him and yet I want nothing to do with him. Oh Lord, help me to know what to do and to get out of this way of living. Luke was running late to pick Ally up from the school bus stop; she thought Tyler had kidnapped us or worse. I am too scared to answer the phone, and become fearful when the dogs bark at night or when there are noises out front, this is crazy Lord. We are having multiple calls and messages being left on both land and mobile phones. Luke is dealing with them, he does not want me to hear or see them.

May 6. I have an appointment with our doctor. If he decides I need antidepressants, let it be from You Lord. I have also organised to see a Christian counsellor, with June's encouragement. Alan and Marie visit to counsel and pray. Marie tells me that 'Tyler needs help and I am not to abandon him, he is not really meaning what he is doing or saying.' I no longer know Lord what is true but I don't think I can 'support' him anymore.

May 8. Doctor tells me I 'have reactional stress causing me to be depressed. If Tyler was removed I'd be okay so medication is not needed. If another person on the street was sending such messages etc. what would I do? Yes blood ties make it more difficult but do I see him changing in the near future, has the way I've been handling what he's been doing changed things for the better, perhaps I should treat him as I would anyone else?'

May 9. Mother's Day and Tyler wants to meet me. Luke and I meet with him at a cafe for coffee. He hands over a lovely card and gift box of chocolates. Oh that he really meant the words in that card, that his behaviour towards me reflected them! I felt numb, distant and confused.

May 11. Daniel phones, 'things are very bad his end. Tyler had rang him last week and talked. Result was that now among other things he is saying that Daniel had raped me and that he and his wife Ruth deserved everything Ty does to them including killing them as they have let him down. Daniel could get a restraining order if Ty was there, would face criminal charges and possible jail. He felt the need to tell me as I understood what they are going thru.' Oh Lord I wish he had not, how much more do You think I can take?

May 12. Luke comes with me to see the Christian counsellor, Martin, as he is a male. But he heard me and addressed my, our immediate problem of Tyler and the safety issues for me, Ally and Luke. 'Yes Ty needs help but doubts I can do much about that now. I need 'girlfriend' support to help get thru, with letting go without guilt.' He is taking the danger more seriously than I, so perhaps it is not me just being a 'scaredy cat' and Ty not being a typical boy, he is 'wondering if an intervention order would be best for my safety or not.' He asked about 'Ty's conception context, how I was being treated during the pregnancy as research is apparently showing this can impact on the baby, 'shrinking' his brain the same as a neglected child's;' this takes out some of being all my responsibility as all my fault, interesting thought Lord.

May 13. Feeling really tired. Woke unable to remember Tyler ever hitting me yet clearly seeing me hitting him lots so worried I gave Martin the wrong impressions; got upset till the memory of the park manager having to step in between us to stop Ty came. Oh Lord if You want me to go thru this remembering stuff and talking, help me with the pain and guilt, I don't want to face it again, want to run and hide.

May 17. June is now confined to bed. It was a shock to see her, less than a week ago she had us all there for Bible Study, sitting up in her chair, praying loudly, clearly and long. The tent is collapsing, oh God I'm going to miss her. Have to go to Martin's tomorrow, there has been nothing bad from Tyler, I could 'forget it all' again – till the next time. Should I go or is it 'petty' in the light of eternity? I don't feel as though anything is not petty in this light, but I have to live here and now, and I'm meant to be joyful and attractive to others – Ha!

May 18. Luke and I to Martin, questions for me to consider and answer Do I, can I go thru the pain to be 'better' or do I just want to get by? What do I want out of life? Once I would not accept it as it was with Joe, do I want to fight again? Can I? Do I want to survive? Do I see that as a priority? It has to be if I want Luke and I to survive.

May 19. Survive. I am doing that now. If I have to go thru pain and things getting worse as Martin say they will, I want to do more than survive. I want life like it was when we first married, when I first knew You; the brightness, abundance of life, of desire, full of energy otherwise it is not worth it. Is it okay Lord to not want to settle for survival only? I want to live, to be alive for me, for You.

Ps.141:7 Bring my soul out of prison, (the prison of my mind) that I may praise Your name.

May 20. June's face is cold; the colour of death is marching across her face. Oh my forever friend...

I ring Mum, Dad is in remission. Will he make good, real good use of the time You are giving him Lord? June will be at home with You, I doubt if it was Dad I was watching die that he would be. Perhaps there is hope yet, thank You that You are giving him more time, please let it be worth it.

May 21. Ally informs Luke tonight she 'will be gone by the end of the year to live with David, no more school.' Oh Lord I am so scared she will tie herself emotionally and sexually though she again 'promises that has not happened and that we can trust them.' Please Lord if that is what has to happen to turn her back to You so be it but hold me together.

May 22. June is so much worse today. Her face is now icy and dusky. I stayed a couple of hours till felt I was taking up time and intruding. I held her right hand; I believed she held mine as her thumb was pressing into mine. Resting my face against hers I told her I loved her and would see her around soon. It seemed like with each drawn breath she was saying 'I...luv...you' over and over.

She passed over around an hour after I'd gone home. My forever friend, so full of life and love, I got good at texting because of you. I'm really going to miss you.

May 25. Martin put me on edge though affirming me. Affirming makes it 'real' and I'm not sure how to handle that and all the feelings that goes with this. Unlike previous counsellors he does not want me to blame my parents or upbringing. He wants me to look back, to see with the understanding of an adult, to realise why I 'tick' as I do. By understanding, I can begin to change with God's help. He said I'd 'been abused from an early age, possibly inutero as I was a 'tool' rather than a desired child. To sleep, if and when I need to, as getting out of this cycle will reduce my adrenaline levels which will make me very tired.'

June 3. Should I trust You Lord to such an extent that I never feel the need to know if Ty's safe? Is it wrong to want to know this? Is it just my need to keep in the cycle of high stress? I don't know Lord. All I do know is that inside hurts, my body hurts and I am fed up with hurting.

June 12. Martin is suggesting that I am pulling away from Luke as he has got too close.

June 13. Dogs barking, late night phone calls with just breathing and sounds. Luke answering calls. A lady phones to tell us that she has taken Ty in and 'where's the mum?' So here we go again, I'm the baddie, why do I care? David staying here again to save on travel, lots of extra work and cooking.

June 14. Dark thoughts, dark places inside. See the 'other' journal, the 'other' me.

How much more of Lisa do I want to expose to you my dear Reader, a stranger?

In this 'other' journal, Lisa sat and let the feelings, thoughts flow out of her pen, a rambling jumble of questions seeking, finding rest, and conclusion in her Lord.

So here goes, this is a sketch of what she wrote in that single night – I have come a long way – at least I thought I had. Things are not so good, I'm unravelling. I cannot say 'No'. I cannot stand my own ground, state my own opinion as I could before, too scared of hurting Luke, upsetting things, of him not liking me, of me being too selfish, selfcentred. I don't want to be this way, it is not freedom, it is oppression. But to change..... Have been reading *Restoring the pleasure*[27] by Penners and *Hiding from Love*[28] by Towensend, books lent to me by Martin.

So much wrong with me, so much to fix, so much to face. Pain.

Seems like I'd be ripping myself apart.

Can't I just hide? Can't I be the guy on the cross? The one that got to be in paradise that day?

Don't think I can face all that is wrong with me; there'd be no good left and other than You who could love or want me then? Oh they might say they do but would they really or just out of duty?

There is always pain, it overshadows anything that was not so. But I must be and do as expected, selfcontained.

Who am I? What do I want? What meaning, use am I, to myself and others, to You?

You have shown me; let me feel what intimacy can be like but now I hate it. I want it all, my mind, soul and body engaged, not just being a compliant 'thing'.

Now yet another woman believes me to be a bad mother. I am tired of trying to show, prove otherwise, to explain. No one believes me.

I can't afford to be wrong, I need to be justified, validated, what I've done with Joe and Ty. Is this why I've not told my story, scared I will be told its 'usual, normal', should have put up with it, it was not bad after all?

Can't I go into a hole and never come out?

Relationships – I disappoint You too; You who gave me life again.

How much do I really trust You with me?

How much do I really believe You are capable of? –

---

27   Restoring the Pleasure. Clifford L. Penner PhD. Joyce J. Penner RN. MN. Thomas Nelson 1993.
28   Hiding from Love. How to change the withdrawal patterns that isol and imprison you. Dr. John Townsend. Harper Collins, 1996.

answering needs I don't even have the ability to find words to explain as I'm barely aware of them?

How safe are You really?

Can I find out? Can I afford to?

Can I afford not to?

Can I risk what I think I have now?

What did Jim Elliot say – give up what cannot keep to gain what cannot lose?

Can I survive yet more pain?

Can I trust You to hold me together so I don't scatter everywhere?

I should have let sleeping dogs lie, accepted things, instead of wanting more.

Do I deserve to feel such great feelings? To be dependent on Luke for them, therefore he controls, he has power over me? Is this one reason why I kept on shutting off, not letting 'go'?

Do I deserve such love?

Can I trust it?

Why are some things okay one time and not at other times? Why can I like more intimate things sometimes and yet be repelled by just the thought other times? Why do I feel as though I have to givein regardless of what I feel, why does it feel like I'm doing this?

Why do I really dislike him cuddling into my back at night? Because of Joe?

Why is there this tension now?

Am I making too much of a 'nothing'? Why does it feel claustrophobic sometimes now when before it was never enough? Perhaps I should just accept, give thanks and leave alone.

You do not snuff out life, You give it. You died for me before I **knew** You.

**I** don't judge you guilty.

No guilt. No blame. No shame.

You fashioned my days before time – You know who I am, where I'm going. You walk before me making it safe. Oh God, do not forget I am the worst sort of dust. Help my lack of trust, my unbelief. I can't do this. I have no answers. I cannot see the path ahead. You want me to grow, to be whole, help me not to work against You. I know – still that You gave me Luke, let me find safety in that. Help me to open up not close, shut down. You taught me gently to trust, showed me I could; forgive me for forgetting, now teach me, show me it is safe to keep going, that this is part of 'all the way'.

Let me see me as You do, the good and the bad, let me like – No, love me as You do. Help me to believe Luke and trust him too.

Yes, well I did say a 'sketch'; perhaps I should have found a different word! How about 'magnum opus'? Hmm.....

June 15. What happens if counselling finds or decides that it is all my fault, that I am really bad, that all this now is just a dream that I don't deserve, that there is no rationale for my actions, that I was never close to being good at anything, just my wishful thinking and pride, what then Lord? Will You still have forgiven me, will I be able to?

June 16. I'm in a dangerous place to be. I'm doubting my memories, perceptions of past events – what is really reality? Luke bought me a lovely floral arrangement but my first thought was what a waste of money– how far I have sunk! I don't want to be like this.

June 17. Tyler rang around tea time, I could hear STD pips and loud car noises, 'just needed to tell you I love you Mum, never forget that,' I kept him talking for a bit, I was fearful for him. Later we found a phone message from Daniel, Ty was on his way up there. Luke rang him and talked. Pray – What? Safety for Ty and others, where is he in mind as well as body – broken needing help, or revenge?

June 18. I rang Ty's school. He 'had failed the year as missed too many classes, they had had trouble managing him, girlfriend and her parents had taken out two intervention orders against him, they insisted I ring Daniel and get him to notify the police where he lives ASAP (as soon as possible) in view of what they have had to handle.' I'm shaken, feel sick and have chest pains. Ty's texting, Luke's talking to Daniel.

June 24. Tyler's landlady rang Luke. 'Ty has emailed very

rude stuff about her to all her friends and owes her rent.' Ty texting us, Luke checking his replies as usual said he became angry and abusive, bad enough for him to consider going to the police.

These texts continued and escalated despite Luke requesting me to reply telling Tyler that until he could communicate decently we would not respond regardless of what he was asking for. I begin to wonder if my body will always react to stress by experiencing chest pain, bodily aches and migraines.

June 29. Luke interested, I have no desire at all, he does not deserve this, he is such a good man, I am hurting him and myself. Why? What can I learn from this Lord other than I am a complete failure as a woman. Luke says 'it is only **a** problem that **we** can work thru'. The **'we'** is different, used to it being a 'me' with Joe but I am so tired, there is always a problem and none of my working has ever done anything for the better. Was I wrong? Oh please NO Lord, don't let me doubt that it was Your will for us to be together. My mind feels so screwed, unsure even of my understanding of You.

July 17. Luke goes to the police following yesterday's calls and texts, the worst yet, taking the mobile phone. They 'suggest a restraining order; if Ty breaks it he will go to jail.' Could I handle feeling responsible for sending him there over a phone call and yet I would not be it would be Tyler's choice, his behaviour.

July 30. Ally informs us she 'has no intention of returning to school,' we were floored. Luke talked and listened, I watched. I got really upset again. I'm crying myself to sleep again. Last night over Ty, tonight over Ally, and her attitude and how I let her make me feel. Why could I not have had a 'normal' family? Answer: s I n.

July 31. Still upset, and upsetting Luke with what I'm saying. I feel totally rejected by Ally. I feel that dreams and hopes are useless, she may as well go right now so I do not have to keep going thru this over and over again, felt just like last year when she went to Mark's. My Mum resented my education, she felt as though I was above her. It's now reversed; Ally resents my desire for her to be educated. I feel beneath her 'superior' understanding of what is best. Tyler is texting 'nicely', 'I'm sorry mum that I let u down all the time. Can I see Luke and u one day?' We organise to meet tomorrow, he has moved again.

August 1. We had a 'normal and nice' meeting with Tyler. He talked openly about stuff and answered all our questions. David is up here every week night till after midnight since Ally is not going to school and all weekends. No space to be.

August 2. Oh God I feel so scared, so sad. It feels as though all I have gone thru, all the pain that I cannot even now bare to really look at has been for naught. Yes I am okay, I am with You – I know I should be thankful, I am and yet I care little about me (except perhaps that the pain will not always be with me, heaven looks better each day) when those two I love more than life itself are hurting themselves so much. Ty – I can't dwell on what he must feel like to act, like he does and that statistically the end is usually suicide...if that happens will it be an end for his pain or just the beginning – can I really rest on him going forward that night or am I deluding myself?

Then there is Ally, my beautiful, beautiful girl who will not heed my loving concern, who is so stubborn, to her hurt I fear. I am so angry and disappointed. I don't know or understand her at all. Oh she is 'nice' as long as I don't suggest what she should perhaps consider doing. Do I have to watch? I feel so helpless, so frustrated that I can do nothing to stop her. I had such hope Lord that I had broken the cycle over the three of us, that we could all grow as should, that there would be no child produced out of wedlock, that spouses would be carefully and rightly chosen You over all, that there would be a lessening of the pain, that my grandchildren would be blessed with a brighter childhood in families knowing and fearing You. This hope is slippery now Lord, hard to hold. I just fear and my heart breaks again – how many more times can it endure this pain Lord? I am so tired, so tired....

August 4. Reverend Alan visits. I 'have used the wrong tone when speaking to a male from church, two ladies also upset, apologies being demanded, they will not be attending church unless I do.'

I sat there listening to how much they are hurting,

wondering if You could hear me screaming in pain, I felt like a trapped wounded animal. I am glad You can hear as noone else can. (Ps. 94:16-19). It's ironic that men have nearly destroyed me and I have to apologise 'for my tone of voice has caused terrible misery' to a tough man's-man. Me a 'nobody' having such power, interesting thought but so very ridiculous! I have to wait till it is convenient for them to all meet together with Alan to hear me give it though.

Jn.13:15. 'Jesus knowing You had given Him all things and that He had come from You and was returning to You....' Can I not know the same and so do what is being asked, even though for me it will cost more than I have left inside?

August 5. Feeling very tired and chest is again hurting. I tried not to think too much about yesterday.

August 6. Thank You for what I am still drawing from that verse You gave the other day from John's gospel. I'm still thinking on it.

August 7. I stop doing Ally and David's washing, tired of doing this while they are out and about having fun. I left them to get their own meals also. She was not happy. It is difficult when she wants to make adult decisions yet expects to be looked after, e.g. pocket money but no rent. She states, 'anyone can get a ring'. Oh Ally that is not marriage, you think you so knowing and I am so stupid. Do I have to watch Lord?

August 9. Martin begins to look at my family tree. How screwed up was Joe, why did I think I could handle it, change him, that my love would be enough? What a price I've paid for my foolishness!

August 10. Some of the ladies including Madge from the Ladies Group at church publically speak of their desire for me to leave this group; the nastiness took some of the others by surprise. Hurt, but Lord I've got to see it as either coming from You, being allowed by You and not to get into their games, not care about being a 'somebody' with a voice and ability to organise, just let go, or become a bitter game player again. What are You going to have me do instead?

August 13. I started yesterday in tears missing Grandmother,

Lynette and June. I am now older than June and wasting my life as not enjoying living or living it to the full like she was. She wanted to live and after tonight I am only half hearted. Madge, who seems to be the spokesperson for the Ladies Group now, verbally attacked me out of the blue tonight at Bible study, on how I 'hate her' – I replied that I had been hurt over the other day and what was said about me and how I was 'removed' but not about losing the position I had held and I did not hate. But she kept 'pounding' me about how I'd hurt her. I had to turn my attention away from her to the smiling others who had brought out a birthday cake for me but she followed now accusing me of 'not letting her finish what she had been saying and that I obviously did not want to resolve anything and that she'd pray for me as a result.' Thelma looked stunned. I went outside to the cold to 'breath'; Marie came out with Madge and Thelma, making us all hug as they talked and prayed. Madge went 'home as happy that she could sleep tonight as had been so distressed over the hurt I had caused her.' I did not sleep, chest pain and sick again.

August 15. I'm still not sleeping. Still waiting to give my apology to the gentleman and two ladies who demanded one, looks may not be doing this till after September as Alan is away till then. Madge 'no longer feels safe at church because of me.' Ally and David taking up all my space, so there's no 'rest' in this house, and yet I fear what it will be like with just Luke and I and the silence, the lack of activity. Intimacy again resulting in flashbacks, wanting to run but to where, how? Just not wanting to be here, too much hurt. Does anyone see me? Mum phoned, she is staying away as heard I was sick and she did not want to catch anything. So that's why she did not do her usual birthday visit. (It's one of the few times Lisa's mum does visit her.)

August 23. Why do I feel so useless inside Lord, so unneeded, unwanted? Why am I here Lord? All my life I seem to have put my dreams on hold, my wants so much that I'm not even sure what they are now, to look after others, Joe and the kids, yes time goes and they grow, no longer needing mum but time also goes for me too – I feel old, too late, wasted, nothing achieved.

September 15. Martin. 'When I get panicky or busy to avoid

feelings or flashbacks I'm not to isolate self, push Luke away. To hold hands, sit with it, tell him how I feel, what I'm thinking, to give him attention and time that is nonsexual.' Then he fires questions at me – Surface intimacy, why not going further? -- Never did with Joe. -- Why not? -- Not safe. -- Luke is, is he not? God is. Do I want to go on, through? -- What is in there? What sort of person will I find, will I be? Is it worth it? -- Is what I am, have now in my relationship with Luke good enough, all I want us, me to be? -- Can I risk me? -- Would God want me to stay in the shadow, on the surface? Is this the sort of marriage I want for the rest of my life? -- NO...but I'm scared and I'm tired, scattered, disjointed, and warring with an invisible me.

September 29. I did not sleep last night. I felt like destroying everything. I imagined wrecking the lounge room, books, photos, wanted to rip my insides out. I'm too scared to work on my craft stuff as this involved using a knife. The extent and strength of these feelings terrified me. Ally and David's conversation the other night about budgets and what they had to plan for triggered something inside me that I don't understand and yet struggle to contain. There's a lot of selfhate and loathing. I sat up with lights on, did crosswords, and had a cuppa, too scared of myself in the dark. Went back to bed around 0500hrs, been up for over four hours. Talked to Luke when he woke, the little I could as still too scared of these feelings.

October 1. I feel that Luke's cousin and wife's prayers are enabling me to hold together and even get me thru the other night.

October 10. Ally and David keep changing their minds as to when Ally will be moving out. I had a dream where I fronted them and told them that they are under God's judgement as He exists whatever they think. What they are doing is illegal, and that they have violated and abused our trust as she is pregnant. We love them though and now it has happened and they have to face the consequences we will still love and support them – I was glad to wake up!

Ally is still asking us 'to trust her that nothing has happened.' But my 'nursing mind' suspects… my mother's heart cries NO.

NO not my beautiful Ally. I say nothing to Luke, he is already very upset about her behaviour and not wanting the church congregation to know of this struggle, as if they prayed publically or asked questions, he would cry.

October 13. Ally packing her room but out at present. I went and sat on her bed, just to remember. An open condom packet was sitting there by her clothes. 'Trust me', she had said, 'you can trust me.' How they have violated and abused our trust! I would lay down my life for you, to save you, swap my position in Christ with yours in Satan but would you take and use my offer or spit on it as they spat on Christ? He died for all – but not all will take His offer. So I can only do what I have to, what I can do to please my Father, you have to choose to do for yourself. He knows this pain. Oh Lord He knows yet He still loves, does not shrink back and protect Himself. Hold Luke and I tight, cover our hearts and do whatever must be done to bring Ally back, whatever as the only thing that matters, really matters is where she is in eternity.

October 14. Ally's gone. I spoke to her and David saying that we loved them both and had trusted them as they asked us to and how this and our hospitality had been abused. I told her again that I loved her dearly but at present did not like what they had been doing and that it may be best if she finished her packing today. Ally snorted and told me off for being in her room. Luke and I had to be at a church meeting, we reluctantly left. When we came back they'd gone. All of Ally's things were gone.

I finished cleaning the room, finding more empty condom packets. It does not seem that long ago that I did Tyler's room. Luke and I both cried. Bathroom looks terrible, all neat and clean, no stuff. A big black gaping emptiness, what now Lord?

October 15. Martin. 'I got principles correct, I was right to be angry and hurt, right to cry. Not to get busy, put responsibility of first contact on to Ally, not to allow her to make me feel guilty.' Wish I could see Joe's face when he receives the letter stating maintenance payments are ceased he'd been trying to do so since we separated, now I have!!

October 16. Both of us are weepy and struggling. I decide to return all the Christian literature into the loungeroom bookcases.

I won't have Madge's help this time though.

October 24. Went into Ally's room; it still smells of her scent, she always smelt so good. I realised how much I missed this and that it would fade, that I would probably never smell it again and I cried and cried. Please let her be safe Lord, watch over her please. Neither of my kids left home safely did they?

October 28. We have not heard from Ally yet. I don't know where she is. I wish I could know that she is safe. Yet what could I do other than what I'm doing now – praying? I have never in 16 years been so isolated from her. I miss her so much, she has been my sunshine, my joy, my reason to get up and keep going sometimes, now there is just a big empty black hole, full of pain and confusion.

October 29. *'It is well'*[29] – it does not look well for Alyssa. It does not seem You are doing a very good job of caring for her, protecting and keeping her safe. But surely one teenage girl is no match for the One who keeps all things going? It does not feel as though You are struggling to juggle the Universe as there are no bumpy crashing drops or jerky off time events, all goes as it should. It is well – it should be. I should be able to say this and know it inside, deep. Ally was Yours before she was mine – You planned her and who was going to (attempt to) parent her, You (should) care more than I. You have her life in Your hand, it should be well. Who am I that I should think or feel it is not? Am I bigger, better than You? Help me to see that it is well even though it does not seem to be. You have been teaching me to trust – that You are trustworthy. Why can I not fully trust You with my beautiful girl and cease to be fearful for her future and the now? It is well with my soul, please let it be well with hers – let me trust You in this also.

November 1. I wish I could hate You but I can't, You gave me life. I remember all too well what it was like without You and

---

29    It is Well with my Soul! Penned by Horatio Spafford, a lawyer and business man as his ship passed near to where his four daughters had died when their ship sank. His wife, Anna had sent a telegram 'Saved alone..' Music by Philip Bliss. First published in Gospel Songs No.2 by Sankey & Bliss 1876.

what it was like in the beginning with You but at the moment it just hurts. I hurt. There is a pain in my chest that crushes. I needed You to protect Ally, to give her a start that I did not have, a perfect good start, a relationship that would last and be good – it looks bad, very bad, full of pain and heartache, more than I had. Why did Ally have to be hurt, why could she not have had it like it should be? – Because she chose a different path. Why could You not have stopped her, I prayed that You would, what was wrong with wanting all that is good and right for her so she would not have to go through what I did, including watching my kids hurt? Why could You not have answered? I can't see the big picture. No, I don't want to, it may contain more hurt that I want to know about. I have this voice warning me that worse is to come because I am determined to stay with You, why does it have to be this way? I don't want to hurt anymore, have I not hurt enough already, apparently not. I'm sorry, You have done all for me, so much and yet all I can feel at present is pain with hope of more. Hold me, don't leave Ally, don't lose her.

*A path ye have chosen*
*A path I neither'd wish for yea*
    *But your soft*
    *Sunshine childishness*
    *Is gone.*

*Gone all too soon*
*Believing you have all the answers*
*Yea chose with deafness and new hardness*
*A path I neither'd wish for yea.*
    *Oh my LORD*
    *Be a light for when she*
    *Awakens.*
*Shine on a path*
*I'd have wished for*
*I pray.*
                                               *L.*

November 3. Thoughts following us seeing Martin and statements he said: 'I am not abnormal, just a lady struggling with a lot of bad stuff.'

I have NO reason to be ashamed or guilty for even if I have done something wrong (can loving too much be counted as such?) God who alone I am accountable to has already forgiven, wiped the guilt away with His blood and promised no shame – my thinking when I realised that feelings of shame and guilt over my children's choices and behaviour were one reason why I'm not ringing Mum yet, as I believe she will only increase these feelings.

After tonight's reading I wondered if I could claim Jer.31:15b-17 '...Lamentation and bitter weeping,..weeping for her children, because they are no more. Thus says the LORD: Refrain your voice from weeping, and your eyes from tears; for your work shall be rewarded, says the LORD, and they shall come back from the ...enemy. There is hope in your future, says the LORD, that your children shall come back.....', or am I taking it too much out of context for both my kids.

Then later 1Jn.3:20 – '...For if our heart condemns us, God is greater than our heart, and knows all things..', just popped into my mind and I wondered. So checked the *Nelson's Study Bible,*[30] 'Our heart condemns us in that we recognise that we do not measure up to the standard of love and feel insecure, In approaching God our conscience may not acknowledge the loving deeds we have done in the power of the Spirit but God does and He is superior to our hearts. Unlike our conscience God takes everything into account including Christ's atoning work for us. God is more compassionate and understanding towards us that we sometimes are toward self.'

November 7. Bit hard singing *'my heart is full of thankfulness'*[31] as I feel so empty, so ungrateful. One night Tyler and Ally are sleeping in their beds after a day with me and the next gone, everything gone, changed, lost and I am left, still wanting, needing them. Why could I not have had more time with them?

---

30   The Nelson Study Bible NKJV Earl D. Radmacher, Th.D. General Editor. Thomas Nelson Publishers 1997. Pg. 2145.
31   My heart is filled with Thankfulness. Keith Getty and Stuart Towend. Thankyou music, 2003.

November 13. Sermon on Psalm 18 – 'Life is like a maze, you don't know what is coming up ahead. Nothing is working out as you thought – trust God.'

Luke talking about the book he's currently reading, *Where is God when it Hurts*,[32] says it sounds like what Martin has been saying, 'stuff comes at you, what matters is your response to it. Look at Job, 'Though He slays me yet will I trust Him!' God throws us in deep waters not to drown us but to teach us to swim, someone once said.' I'm floundering again Lord, I'm not a fast learner I guess. How I want to trust You! I just don't like the lessons needed!!

November 15. Not sleeping much. Christ is or should be my fulfilment, not relationship with Ally; that like any other only leaves emptiness. Thinking a lot during the night with You when can't sleep. You Lord give me the right to make choices – should I not do the same for Ally? I get to experience the results of these and yet You love me and are good. You caused Ally to be born again, You will not let go without fighting for her. You love and care more than I. Trust. My grumbling about how You are doing things is a sin. Me wishing for something different, my ideas of better for Ally a sin, doubting Your goodness, care and provision. Forgive me.

November 23. Our home phone is again ringing, just single rings then stopping, but multiple times, day and night.

It seems to me that love when unaccepted, unreceived, unneeded becomes useless, worthless, and pointless even. How does God feel then if I feel this so deeply and with only two errant children?!

November 25. We have a taxi waiting outside, horn blaring. Driver says he had been called to pick up a Luke Denny. He had the correct spelling of name and address, only we had not called it. He was nice about it and we were not charged. Tyler? This was kinda of funny though.

December 7. Who am I? A child of God snaps back. Well

---

32   Philip Yancey Where Is God When It Hurts? A comforting, Healing Guide for Coping with Hard Times. ZondervanPublishingHouse 1977

what does that mean? Pain. Tiredness, a desire to just lie down and yet a force that will not allow me to do so, that 'powers' me on in a fashion. On to what? The knowing that there is more than this though I will have to wait till God allows me to leave this life hopefully without more pain. Considered the on-coming car while waiting to cross a road, it would hurt a lot and no guarantees and I am not my own, Christ bought me, I cannot do that. Oh but Lord I sit here and wonder is this how I'm going to feel till then? How can I do it? One day, one hour at a time? But I want more, I want to rejoice and please You, to be content and grateful, to be real, not a mask hiding emptiness, nothingness.

December 8. Listening to Focus on the Family on the radio. The speakers were talking about how girls especially can get hooked on casual sex; their brain is literally rewired making it more difficult to maintain a long term relationship. They discussed what the parents should be doing. Exactly what I've/we've done! Especially the bit where they said because I had done the wrong thing I have 'credentials' to say why it was wrong and what is better. This is not being hypocritical as Ally said I was. No details need to be given, just the consequences showing that it is not worth it. Discuss the possibility of diseases; how it affects emotionally, that there is more to sex especially for girls than just physical contact. Thanks Lord for reinforcing that I/we did everything as right as we could, gave Ally all the information, she just chose not to listen, I/we are not at fault as did all we reasonably could.

December 12. More trouble with the women of the Ladies Group at church. I am accused of things I have no memory of (which they consider very convenient!) but my diary entries do not back up these allegations when I check back. I try to explain my feelings but am not heard rightly, not even by Marie who seems to agree with them. My friend Madge is doing most of the accusing to the church leaders. It has become so bad these ladies will no longer help in the kitchen if I'm present. Am I really this awful Lord? If so I need to fix things with You and them…but am I….I never set out to be …I just cannot see how it was right to get so angry and go against the shepherd You'd put over us when there was no heresy being taught…but yes I don't know how things are supposed to work within the Church.

I am not sleeping. We do not get to see Ally over Christmas, had not seen for her sixteenth birthday either, she is going to my Mum's. I felt very hurt and sorry for myself and angry that Mum has 'won' again. I don't not understand this as there is no competition yet I don't know how else to describe the feeling.

December 24. We took Tyler to look at the Christmas lights and Carols; it was a good night, Thank You Lord. He has moved accommodation again.

December 26. Ally visited but 'only to see the family pet'. I wondered if she was pregnant looking at her.

December 28. Watched DVD, *How Great is Our God,* by L. Giglio at Tree Tops. What hope! 'The word 'wait' in Isaiah 40:31, is about being renewed, resting, riding on the power of eagles wings. It is standing still in the midst of chaos and pain and declaring your trust in God to hold on to you and carry you through it, to keep you together, to keep you going when you have nothing to keep going with, breath by breath.'

YES! I know this but I am sorry I so easily forget it, that I am so quick to take my eyes off You and cease to see You fully and clearly yet see surrounding stuff very clearly and fully and so get caught up and hurt by the chaos and pain of life. Thank You for refocusing me. Oh please help me to remember and see You clearly all the time. (Yes, my dear Reader, I used some of these words, ideas right at the beginning of this book towards the ending of the Introduction, pg.5)

December 29. This is the first time since Ally was old enough I have never received a card, homemade or bought. Oh how I miss her little notes as well! Did she mean what she used to write? I miss hearing her talk and share about her day. Feeling lost, disjointed, fragmented, scattered. What is the purpose of my existence? I do things that fill in time but feel these are meaningless as lacking eternal value in my view. What could possibly be left when burnt? Why am I not fulfilled, satisfied? Am I wrong to want to feel my life has meaning, purpose, a reason? What do You want of me Lord? Why is eating, sleeping or being married not enough?

## Chapter 3

Many of the messages we heard this summer at Tree Tops spoke directly to our sad and wounded hearts. What follows are notes I took and some of my thoughts as a result.

1Pt.1:1-12. 'Needed – Contagious Christians. We die on time, shielded by God's power. In the meantime we are as safe as houses so LIVE. Do not be a custard Christian getting upset over trifles. Nothing is more important than having a relationship with Jesus.'

Thoughts – It's okay to grieve over lost dreams, relationships, over what might have been. It is NOT okay to feel guilty for enjoying life when those you love have made choices that make it hard for them to enjoy life. God your Father has given you life to enjoy as well as all things, so lift up your heart, look at Him full in His face, be warmed and grateful, praise Him and let the sadness evaporate like the morning mist in its time under the Son.

'Gen. 38. Living with disgrace. Gospel is gospel for failures. No one needs to stay the way they are. Suffer a big pain, grief, loss, heartbreak, when you start to feel better thank God. Do not think that you should remain feeling terrible, do not feel bad about feeling good. It is all right to recover, it is correct, God honouring. Sin can be superseded. Prov.28:13 –'He who covers his sins will not prosper, but whoever confesses and forsakes them will have mercy.' Jn.8:11 –'...Neither do I condemn you (no full stop here!) go and sin no more.'

'Are you going to be bitter or faithful? Joseph. Gen. 39, 46:41-50. Holy desperation is a great piece of ammunition in God's arsenal 'Help Lord"

Fractured family? Reconciliation takes two. Some situations have to be left to soak, rinsing will not work. Consider the Prodigal of Luke 15:11-32. The Father did not drive the kid away but let him walk. If he wanted to live like that he could not do it at home.

Then came the famine. Be a watching father, not an older brother. Jacob had 17 years without his son Joseph, believing him to be dead but he had 17 years with Joseph in Egypt. God gave back the lost years, the years the locusts had eaten (Joel 2:25). Stay God centred come what may.'

What could I say? – As a friend said, this morning's message was written for me. The tears would not stop flowing, Luke was having difficulty and so were a lot of others. You Lord were very busy!

I had never considered the locusts of Joel 2:25, in regards to the kids. Jacob had Joseph for 17yrs. at the beginning of his life and again at his end – before Jacob died. Also spoke how the Father let the prodigal go as could not stay if not accepting the values of home but waited for the famine to come, as Joseph did, and then loved like God to take back if a repentant/heart change. Joseph checked for this first, and then reconciliation was possible.

Lord in regards to marriage and that pain You have given back what locusts took – I did not deserve or merit this. I cannot believe and yet I dare to hope that though I again do not deserve but Oh that it would be possible for both of us with our children, Oh the joy of hope, thank You.

All the way Lord, all the way no matter what, just keep Your promise and don't let go, I cannot do it myself. Forgive me for my ingratitude and for fighting against Your sculpting and refining. Help me not to resist Your moulding. Help me not to see the pain so big but the end goal bigger. What would I be if really trusted and let go? It scares me and I resist, help me not to.

January 7. Tonight's reading Col.3:8-17. 'Pleasing God does not mean that we must busy ourselves with 'spiritual activities'... Any human activity may constitute an offering to God...we spend much of our time immersed in the mundane 'But we have the mind of Christ'...The world crowns success; God crowns faithfulness.'

January 10. At 2345hrs we got a phone call from Tyler's house mate, 'wanting advice on how to handle him, also Ty had asked him to ring us as the fridge had fallen on him and he was crying, hurt but okay. They had asked him to leave several weeks ago but despite several offers of accommodation elsewhere he has refused to go. His behaviour is escalating; the two girls there are frightened as he is aggressive.' I told him to ring the police. Ty had rang me a few days ago asking 'if we could help with somewhere to stay'; part of me wanted to say yes, come home till you find somewhere but I knew I could not do that with Ty. I could not handle having him refusing to go and going back to the fear and always having to be on guard waiting for him to blow, having him go thru our stuff, never knowing if he is telling the truth or not. I got upset. I felt angry and ungrateful at God. This is not the reality I want. I don't want to be a 'super' Christian, just let me be ordinary, normal like other mums. Not to be my reality though, is it Lord? Ally and David have to move, needing money so asking Joe. They had contacted Tyler for Joe's number but now Tyler won't stop texting them and his messages are not nice.

January 11. Feel like I've been hit by a bus this morning. Tyler rang to let me know he has accommodation, would never have known from his conversation that last night had happened.

January 13. Tyler, Ally says is threatening to kill her on Face book and name calling. I've been talking to Mum. She is talking as if she knew nothing of Ally leaving home. But Ally has told me she told her all about it, all what I'd done. I am sick and tired of the family games of silence!

January 14. What do I write? I visited Mum. How You reverse things Lord! My family would most likely see me as the black sheep – broken marriage, problem kids big time whereas Murray is all success and yet in Your view I am possibly the only white sheep in this room full of people I don't even know. Mixed feelings handling things I knew Grandmother wanted me to have...Stuff! It's not the 'things', it's what I rightly or wrongly consider to be behind it. Injustice, me not mattering, games but it's always been this way in many ways. The hurt is there the sadness more, the why's, yet does it matter? NO. Why not? YOU. You have given me back all and more. You gave me, me. You gave me Yourself – a Father, a Brother and a Husband – men who love and see me as the apple of their eyes. I am important, every part of me. You have given me family church and Luke's, I belong, I have a hiding place here and a Home to go after I leave here and things to do while I wait that make me feel useful but most of all let me focus on the love You surround me with and no longer see or look for it where it is not, especially stuff.

January 15. Reading tonight: Laminations 3:22-33. 'In times of crisis we grasp the importance of every hour. During our ordinary routine however we often forget that each day is a second chance. We can choose to live with thankfulness for God's mercy and grace with confidence in His faithful care and with hope because He is with us forever. Today God offers us a second chance in life. Let's make the most of it'. Ally texed – 'I love you too mum.' Thanks Lord.

January 20. Reading tonight: Genesis 39:1-10 'When our dreams are shattered how do we react?.....Do we love God more than our own dreams? Although Joseph must have grieved the loss of his past and what his life could have been the Lord led him to a calling he had never imagined. Today the Lord longs to lead us. Are we willing to be redirected by Him?'

> *My cherished plans may go astray*
> *My hopes may fade away*
> *But still I'll trust my Lord to lead*
> *For He doth know the way.*
> *Overton.*

January 23. Reading tonight: 1Kings 19:11-18. 'Are you despairing at the circumstances in your life? Let God speak to you. Instead of allowing you to quit, He will show you what you can do through His strength.'

January 24. Ally is pregnant. I could not sleep, past was too close. Joe did not smile when I told him. She says David was still smiling. I feel so alone Lord. I guess I am in a way; noone else has my desires or fears. I feel so sad. I had wanted so much for Ally – what I did not have I guess and now I have no kids that I can walk with as grown and gone. I have to let go, this is right and good, and they make own choices. Am I still important?

## THE MAKING OF A JEWEL

Luke cannot understand how I can feel stressed seeing Ally and being involved (she wants me present at the birth!) as it was what I hoped for. I mostly don't either, perhaps as in my face more, what she is exposing herself too and seeing problems easier and my inability to do anything. Oh Lord I wanted to see her dressed in white and being married in a church and settled in a nice home with a husband who knew how to treat her rightly and not look at other women and raise kids lovingly, fearing You. Not reality right?

> *Look away, look away*
> *Away from the groaning people*
> *Their blackness and pain*
> *Their tears, anger, hate, cruelty and death.*
> > *Look away, look away*
> > *To YHWH Lord over all*
> > *Who holds your breath in His hand*
> > *To YHWH who died that you might live*
> > *Look away, look away, look away.*
>
> *Look away, look away*
> *Away from the 'all'*
> *as 'tis pointless futility*
> *Emptiness rushing ever onwards to nowhere.*
> > *Look away, look away*
> > *To YHWH Lord over all*
> > *Who holds eternity in His hand*
> > *To YHWH who died that you could hope*
> > *Look away, look away, look away.*
>
> *Look away, look away*
> *Away from the groaning Earth*
> *Its cyclones, quakes, droughts, locusts and floods*
> *Heaving and gasping in labour.*
> > *Look away, look away*
> > *To YHWH Lord over all*
> > *Who holds the Universe in His hand*
> > *To YHWH who died that all would be rightened*
> > *Look away, look away, look away look away.*
> > > *L.*

February 8. More nightmares involving Joe and Tyler.

February 14. I'm walking the beach, thinking. Consequences I just wanted kids. I wanted someone who would love me because I was me. Is Ally doing the same? Oh Lord I did not want her to have consequences like I have to live with. Love is not enough, at least mine is not. I could not stop her, how I wanted to, did I try hard enough? What if...NO! Not to go that path.

Could she not see how much I loved her, how I just wanted to keep her safe – much the same could be said for Ty. Could she not trust me, my love and listen and do as I requested?

You are love. You did not stop Eve and You could have if anyone could have. Why did You not stop Ally? Why did You not stop Eve? You loved more than I ever could. And You love perfectly! You taught and instructed perfectly. You provided all that ever could have ever been wanted and it was not enough to stop Eve. You are God, You would not feel guilt, failure. Did Christ when He walked here, at not being able to stop others He loved? Love does not seem to be enough does it and yet in the very end it is, for You win. The consequences of our sin are used and changed to our good instead of our pain.

February 15. Reading tonight Hebrews 11:24-34. '...What if we remembered Abraham only as a deceiver, Genesis 12:10-20; Moses as disobedient to God, Numbers 20:1-13; or David as a murderer, 2Samuel 11? Despite their sins these men (and women) are remembered for their persevering faith...Our life is not a failure if we've repented of our sins.'

February 17. Thinking while I was floating on the mirror flat sea before my breakfast – In heaven we work, we do not float around on clouds as no rest required. Here we cannot be sanctified sitting on a rock watching the waves. It is hard work, really hard work battling self and others who do not do as should. God knows this, so occasionally we get to float around for a while, we get a breath(er) before we have to dive back into the madness of this world and battle old natures. Here we do need a rest. Thank You for this breather Lord. I need to trust You more, You are not as my father, You are safe, caring, unchanging and do all things for my best, knowing me better that I ever will. Help me to live this please.

# THE MAKING OF A JEWEL

February 19. Readings tonight: James 1:1-11. 'Real trials in life are not 'ifs' – they are 'whens'. Life's most profound lessons cannot simply be observed they must be experienced. It is here in actual seasons of heartache and loss that we gain greater insights into life, faith and our need of God...Trials come because we live in a broken world but we decide if we will learn the lessons taught...Tough times can teach us to trust..'

A comment on Psalm 62 by J. Scriven – '...while there is great comfort in sharing our difficulties with a friend we miss the greatest help if we fail to bring them to the Lord...what a friend we have in Jesus...Oh what peace we often forfeit, what needless pain we bear all because we do not carry everything to God in prayer'.

February 23. After seeking advice from and being encouraged by a trusted church leader to apologise for the hurt I'd seemingly and unwittingly caused the ladies I arrange to visit Madge. She would not accept it. I was told I had never been and will never be part of the Ladies Group at church as I do not act as a team player. I have only ever caused them trouble and pain. She realises this is painful for me to hear but it is about time someone told me the facts honestly and that I faced them. There is no need for further discussion, no point as there is no trust left between us. I gave her a hug and told her I loved her and left. I was devastated.

I scribbled on a bit of paper – I do want to belong. Do I have to have both my families reject me Lord? Am I only suitable or acceptable because of the 'work' I do? What of me? 'Consider Him who endured such hostility against Himself' (Heb.12:34) – I've not yet shed blood but it hurts so much it feels as though I am. Is she right, is it a truth about me I need to face and correct, do something about? Not a group/team player -- did this go back to the day a while back when at the last minute I'd realized as 'hostess' for that day I'd not organised a gift for the speaker so just got one on my way to meeting without consulting anyone from the group or was it when I felt I had to refuse a 'position' because of a prevailing attitude within the group I considered wrong and said so – all of life has constantly taught me that other people are usually a source of confusion and pain, they are untrustworthy and undependable so I guess I'm not a team player.

I know the truth of Ps. 69:20 'reproach has broken my heart, and I am full of heaviness; I looked for someone to take pity, but there was none; and for comforters, but I found none.' and Ps.109:15, sadly described my feelings. Yet God calls me to trust as He is trustworthy. To love as He does. To love myself and others as we belong to Him and are guided by His Spirit and made in His image. I also know I cannot rely on myself – my heart is also untrustworthy and deceitful. This is not easy. It is confusing and scary.

Is God really big enough to handle my unknown and keep me intact and sane? I don't know. But do I have a choice? No, because I do know who I owe my life to and I have found noone else who comes anywhere near worthy. I have proven Him to be so, so far anyway. I wish things were black and white. Afraid for self. I want to be with You, pleasing You but I am so unsure how to handle things down here sometimes, most times.

I love these women. I want them all with me and You. I am worried how far is too far off the track of submitting and following You and Your shepherd You have placed over us?. Does the attitude behind all this Ladies Group stuff really matter in the light of eternity? If it does not, great! If it does...oh my!

And what of me, what do You want of me? Give me a backbone and yet love. Why do I have to be so different, so separate? I want to be involved, not picked on. I know 'me' colours things, how much is it this time and how wrongly? Let me see clearly and truthfully. They hurt so I withdraw. Is this trusting You? NO. So I am doing as they, hypocrite! Help me to not withdraw, to keep loving, keep being there, serving, vulnerable and open to hurt, trusting You, if this is right in Your sight.

Just an aside, dear Reader, I never did the apology demanded by the gentleman and two ladies, as apparently the opportunity to do so never eventuated. They have now left my Church.

March 11. Nightmares and flashbacks of Ty and Grandmother and my fear he would hurt her when we were on holiday, then of custard incident and threats to kill me. Nightmares leave me unsettled. Lord will the ghosts and the sadness they bring always continue?

March 23. Luke and I were exploring an old cemetery. One family tomb, which had cherubim on its top, contained two very young children, the husband, then a seventeen year old buried in it. On the cherubim were the words 'God's will be done.' She, the wife and mother could say that! Lord life is a gift. My life is a gift. I'm sorry I don't always appreciate this or make the most of it. Help me to do so regardless of the circumstances swirling around me.

March 30. We now have a car outside some nights, really late, revving its engine with loud music blaring.

It is Easter Convention and what follows are a sprinkling of notes I took as well as some thoughts -- 'When we cannot see God's hands because of our tears caused by life here, trust in His heart'.

If I can hope that those – good and bad – who have touched my life would turn and have You for eternity can God be any less – surely I cannot have more compassion than Him?

'...Do you have enough confidence, or faith to suffer, risk all? Is your faith sufficiently strong from God's point of view for now? Have you the certainty that it is worth it to endure whatever? The Gospel is free but may cost everything to receive it and to live.' – What happened Lord to 'all the way no matter what'? When did I start to fear pain and withdraw back and stop taking risks?

Psalm 77 'God is the source of pain and distress. (Well He is in charge of all! I think to self.) That God has lost the power to help is bad but worse is has He lost His love for me? Then there is a slow shift to God's PAST behaviour, this helps me to understand present plight. It is not escapism to remember. Feelings are not reality. God is never absent or forgets a believer.'

Psalm 91 'Not to believe that God is but to believe in the Person of God. Keep good company so can hear good things, dangers are NORMAL, must trust in God thru all dangers all the time. Trusting God rescues us from the fear of dangers. Sometimes we cannot sing, need others to do so for us. Satan misquotes the Bible to get us to test instead of trust. Trust God simply for who

He is, not what He does (How do I like being 'needed' or liked just for what I do?!!) Fear is a great enemy of discipleship to all cost.' All the way no matter what? Okay God, so how do WE –You fix this in me? Help me with my fears of more hurt so I can move on and be as You want.

'Psalm 22 is about a righteous believer who is in trouble, and his desperate prayer but a silent God.'

I am not Christ, it was far worse for Him. But Lord I remember how bad it was for me, others were being heard, I was not – why not? Your love and all things for my good, does often hurt and confuse me. I want to please You, help me to know You better, trust You more, lean harder, get that foundation more stable – who I am in You rather than who I am to everyone else.

Feeling concerned and a little upset as I've not heard from Ally for over a week – this has to stop. Ally has her own life, separate and independent as it should be. Help me to find my own life, to let her go, to find this new me. The changes have been too many and too much for me, I am struggling not knowing who I am now and yet I should know – I am Your child, Your princess, Your Jewel.

April 8. Now the car is going past every night late, after 2000hrs usually, then most mornings. Revving and going very fast, with loud music and horn blaring. Neighbours are expressing concern.

April 26. Felt flat today, back to Martin. He says I am to get angry, have good reasons to be so. But, You Lord, are at the root of all, like with Joseph, have You not allowed all this for my good? So then how can I be angry?

April 30. I feel so – I don't know – bewildered, confused, lost – I don't know how to be, what to feel. What Ally and David have done is wrong but then there is this beautiful baby. I loved Ally before she was here, I dreamed 'nice' dreams for her not this, yet You have allowed it. Then there is what is happening between Luke and I. Luke is saying 'it's not good that two married people live as if not' and I agree and yet...Why don't I want to, why am I feeling 'used'? We started counselling for this yet it's getting worse not better. He bought me a beautiful bunch of roses because

I seemed down today – the guilt increases Lord. Tomorrow – get me thru tomorrow then the next tomorrow. I cannot, must not think past tomorrow. I cannot handle my thoughts Lord, my fears or pain or worry about how to be a witness for You. HA! I can't even get thru a day for myself. Selfishly wish You would come or take me – wrong! Should not the joy of a grandchild hinder this? Oh Help Lord!

May 2. Sermon was on how we need to remember and the use of aids like 'stones' to do so as Joshua did. My cowrie? Psalm 33 'Hope waits, stands despite the swirling personal chaos and declares faith in God and His ability to pull us thru'– I needed to remember this again, Thank You.

May 11. Martin. Sex because of my past, we wait till I can initiate. Seems selfish Lord and yet inside I know I will 'kill' self and our relationship if I just 'do'. There is no reason for this to continue but I have to want to go to next 'layer'. Do I? No...Yes... Reach another layer – it does feel as if starting all over again to trust, to not pull back. Oh Lord I'm sorry – yet again I want a relationship with You, one of response and expectancy and with Luke too, not of responsibility and expectations which 'kill' the freedom to grow, love and rest. Help me.

Martin gives us some 'homework' to do in regards to our, or rather my, problem with intimacy. Luke is eager to do this homework. I am not! Wish I'd never started this counselling stuff. Every day? For 30 minutes? I'm going to be too busy. I'm sure I can find stuff to do.

The brick wall that is impossible – I don't want to – why not – I'm scared to find out, I just might find me – whoever that is!

Why do I feel so awkward, stupid, should this feeling of exposure exist between us? 'Lust' has gone, it drowned the fears. Now they are creating mountainous waves! Fears -- what of? — my inadequacy, being really seen and found wanting badly, all a front, a sham – this goes back further than Joe doesn't it, he and Tyler and now Ally just reinforced and 'verified' what I already 'knew' or 'feared'.

I did better than this (with the cuddles and kissing) with being fully dressed when courting. Tried to 'feel' the need, nothing. I did not want to give. Yes I mean give when the homework is all about me receiving. So tired.

Silently cried, tears just ran – to sleep last night. Wishing I could have my 'babies' back. Back in our home. Just the three of us. 'Garlic and onions' (see Num.11:46. Complaining that before God is better than the now with Him) I know and not reality. It was not that rosy except I had self to self. Oh Luke I'm so sorry. I just sat on his lap, curled up, feeling the rise and fall of his steady breathing while he loosely held me.

I try to explain about this 'wall' to Luke – I don't want it (I don't think), I don't like it (and yet it is my friend as stops what I don't want and yet I do want. Very confusing!) But it is like telling a depressed person to snap out of it and get going. I run into it and that is that. I can convince myself to do the 'homework' but the wall finishes anything happening.

I have no trouble in some ways giving Luke what he wants but if I'm asked what I want, I have no idea and I just say 'No' or 'Nothing'. So I miss out. Luke does not and I seem comfortable with that but is this why I feel 'used'?

I wonder how 'sinful' I am being in 'allowing' this behaviour of mine to continue. I'm not even participating in the homework that is the 'program' to fix me! Why do I find it easier to be too busy, not to have the time? Don't I want to have our marriage as a priority?

Back to Martin. He talked about me 'not running but to know it is okay, safe to be vulnerable with Luke, to trust him'.

I talked about the two of me, one wants this, to trust and be safe. The other does not. Like two voices and how exhausting this is. Like Paul battling with the two natures. Martin actually got what I was trying to explain!

Later the homework caused flashbacks again. I buried my head in my hands, wanted to run, to 'do', I stayed still and let the tears fall, stayed silent, could not speak., I was right back and worse, just as with Joe. Luke rocked me, 'Oh Lisa, I'm sorry, I'm sorry', he did not turn over, leave me, or go to sleep like Joe. He never has.

May 16. Last night we had multiple threatening and offensive texts from Tyler, a car going past quite often during the day and late into the night. He seems to be a very angry, hate filled man. A stranger. This morning there were tyre marks across our nature strip and front lawn. The grass was all ripped up. Ty leaving his mark like a dog? What to do? If it was anyone else we would have gone to the police.

May 17. Luke was taking me out for lunch. We're walking down the street. Joe is walking towards us. He looked up and saw us and tried to 'disappear.' I said 'hello Joe'. He replies 'nicely' then almost broke into a run. Lots of thoughts. How short, small and hunched he is! How 'nice' the outside, how foul the inside. A 'white washed tomb', (see Mat.23:27) and how easy it was to be drawn by the outside and trapped, then hurt so badly by the inside.

Why do I feel any contact with Tyler better than none? Why did I let Joe keep treating me like he did? Dependence like a junkie? Break it Lord. It wraps around me, drawing me back inside. I pull it out but never find the end. I want it to stop. I want it to lose its hold on me. Kill it Lord, please.

May 21. Talking during our together quiet time, discussing the day, I told Luke I don't doubt that God can keep us safe, just wonder if He will. Luke wondered when had Ty actually hurt us? He believes God has kept us safe these last six years and feels He has even longer with me. Has even kept Ally safe as wonders if her being pregnant and with one guy not better that what a lot of girls from her sort of background end up being.

May 30. It's evening. Two police cars are parked, one either side of the street, outside our house, looking for Tyler. What now? You know Lord, I don't and part of me does not want to know, yet my imagination may be worse than fact, but I do know I can't 'do'. You can. Please do what is needed, please let me see him in heaven.

Today's sermon -- Joshua Ch.6 'Jericho wall – what is your wall? God is bigger. Keep doing as He asks despite it seeming pointless, illogical.' Your idea, Lord of safety and mine look very different in practice!

June 2. I ring Mum. She 'tells me Tyler has bought a really

good red car, has taken it around to show them, he is really proud of it, and polishes it up really nice, so no way it could have been him in our street doing burnouts on the lawn.' – Yep nothing's changed, I'm still not believed.

June 11. Two more police at our door looking for Tyler at night. I have had no contact with him since his last visit.

June 19. I have withdrawn further from Luke. I am terrified of myself, of losing myself in the feelings Luke causes. Vague chest pains most of the day. Since when was it not okay for me to feel? Forever? There seems to be a line I must not cross in regards to depth of feelings.

Over the month of July we were visiting another church while they ran a course on Sex in the Scriptures. What follows are notes from this series and some thoughts --

They talked about getting the core right first. If it is, is Christ in the centre or competing with a bunch of other stuff for attention? (Luke, kids, church jobs, stress over relationships with ladies at church, my ideals or standards and what I have to do?)

Get house in order! God knows us intimately and decisions needed to be made. He graciously waits to walk with you. (Okay, for some reason I have taken my eyes off the centre and looked around, listened and dwelt on things that had been shaken off, that I was free from, get me free again Lord. Will I ever be free here from shame, guilt, regrets of past sins – Yes! All connected to sex outside of marriage. Let me find myself in You alone – that is the picture, image I can live with and will live with forever).

Back home, listening to the radio, I picked up my cowrie and noted that the tiny little shell that had been stuck in it had gone. I gently shook the shell. It still rattled but then that shell that had been inside just fell out. My shell was now 'whole', no 'intruders' inside or out spoiling it. What are You saying Lord? Can I just as suddenly be whole and free? Oh that whatever is holding me down would be removed, shaken off. I want to fly free Lord, to be whole, real, and contagious to others for You.

Continuing on with Sex in the Scriptures we were asked to consider the Beatitudes, Mathew 5:3-12, as eight attitudes to living, and that they can heal and help you move on from the shame and other stuff of a sexually sinful past. Blessed = favoured by God or empowered by Him to succeed.

1. Humble=poor in spirit. Realize you are not perfect, you have flaws and deficiencies. Face this reality that you cannot do this on your own, you need help.

2. Mourn=emotional honesty. Realise the pathway to healing will be an emotional journey. Shame haunts and burns.

3. Meek=teachability. Drop your defences and embrace the changes needed to move on with your life, be willing to be corrected.

4. Merciful=proactive. Take the initiative; go after what is upright and godly, that which never changes. Embrace godly goals. Are you willing to take whatever action is necessary?

5. Pure in heart= forgiveness. Inappropriate sexual activity often stems out of the pain of life. Wounded people use this pain to justify this sort of activity. Sexuality is used for compensation for unresolved hurt.

6. Hungry=pure motives. What is your motive for moving past all this, where are you heading?

7. Peacemaker=healing love. Instead of sexual love learn to enjoy a loving touch with NO sexual connotations. The male is to learn how to relate to his spouse without getting anything in return. The female has to realise how difficult this is and to connect at a deeper level when her husband tries, affirm him as ego is fragile.

8. Persecuted=courage. It is not an easy decision to wrestle with old ingrained habits; thoughts are hard to lose, to cut free from. You can get discouraged and find yourself drawn back to old ways, thinking it is too hard or painful so not worth it. No one said it was always going to be easy. <u>Do you want to change</u>? Then suck it up, live with the tension of insecurity. Suffering leads to perseverance, leading to hope. Facing things that cause you great grief and pain, you will need courage to persevere. Jesus did not find it easy, He prayed for the reality of the Cross to go yet it did not. God has empowered you, you can succeed, strive to live.

August 10. Martin is 'excited over my writings as open, honest and real. Seeing it the way it is, apparently a rare thing in a person.' I'm not screwy but real? This was an interesting idea for me as I'd always thought everyone else had it all together and I was just weird.

August 23. Our financial situation is not good, I have to find work. Luke retired a few years ago. I am so tired Lord, I don't seem to have time or energy for what is now expected of me – perhaps I'm just lazy and unorganised. What will happen with the added stress of actual work?

Actually Lisa, after three years of cleaning schools every night became declared 'medically unfit to work'. With a diagnosis of fibromyalgia and arthritis, over a year's rehabilitation was needed so she could get up steps, carry the washing out to the line and hang it up, do some light gardening and get off the floor after playing with her grandchildren. God has taken care of their finances though.

August 24. Martin discussing 'lies verses truth'. Luke 'she will leave me'. No because she feels safe and has not left yet and with monthly PMS that is 84 times she has not! – Haha Martin! So Luke she loves you and is committed to the marriage. Me – 'It is not safe to be honest, with PMS and pretending I am not feeling what I feel for other people's sake'. I have to be real for I am safe.

October 15. David's hit Ally. Tyler is suicidal again.

October 18. Considering my 'professional' nursing job vs. toilet/cleaner job, which is the greatest? I had no personal relationship with You as a nurse so is toilet cleaner the highest, the one that can bring You glory even if I can't see how?

October 24. Why are 'perfect' days followed by 'bad'? Ally and David fighting over money, violent, Ally is going for custody, his parents are here in our home with them. They want assurance she won't adopt the child out, demanding to know what she is going to do – she does not know. Ally and baby are staying here. Luke sobbing as brought back his past – help him Lord, not sure I can.

Comment on tonight's reading – 'God has a purpose for each day. We may not like His purpose or understand it but He's using our experiences to make us more like Him. .... I said to the man who stood at the gate of the year, 'give me a light that I may tread safely into the unknown.' He replied, 'Go out into the darkness and put your hand into the hand of God. That shall be to you better than light and safer than a known way.'

Coincidence? I think not!

November 9. After six months of quiet the car is back and now along with all the other sounds we have Tyler loudly yelling obscenities.

> *It's a dark lonely place here*
> *Oh my Lord, hear me cry Hear me.*
> *See me.*
> *If You don't I am undone*
> *For there is no one else*
> *No one sees me.*
> *I am invisible.*
>    *Invisible.*
>       *Invisible.*
> *I cannot fight outside and in.*
> *Put a hedge around me.*
> *Clean my mind.*
> *Break open the bars and let in the light*
> *I want to feel warm and alive again.*
> *Hear my cry,*
> *My Lord hear me.*
>     *L.*

November 15. It is 0030hrs. The swirling, despairing blackness of confusion and doubts, fears is back. Yesterday morning some sunshine, I wrote a poem as of old, (The one just read by you my dear Reader) it just came and I found myself scrambling for paper and pen. Now I cannot sleep for the thoughts and feelings rolling about me. Could I have turned them off, as not all of a sudden, just scattered but now gathered and collecting. The conversation about Calvinism over lunch yesterday caused me to find myself revisiting an older thought – will I find myself at heaven's door only to be told Jesus never knew, elected me, even though I did things in His name, thinking I was saved, His child and so acted as if even though I cannot even evangelise my own family?

Who am I to go against such learned teaching and those raised in good Christian families and the church? Those who in the past have told me I am not saved if cannot believe this, whose voice I can hear tell me because my child is behaving in such a way 'proves' that their confession, profession, repentance is false and as such they are not of the elect. Dooming my children to hell, for both are not behaving 'right'. Hearing Tyler ask, 'so my choice does not matter, my going forward?' after he had heard some church leaders discuss this same topic.

My sin, my consequences, hurting me and destroying my kids. My pain unbearable and now a granddaughter – another daughter caught, doomed. I can do nothing but cry out to You – but what good will that do if I'm not elect, if they are not?

Then say I am, say I am safe, heaven bound – what of my flesh and blood, what of them? I can hear Peter asking 'what of him' and Christ replying 'what about it, you mind your own business.' Saving or not saving is God's business, not mine – but what do I do with my pain? And my stubborn belief that God does not play games? So why allow me to witness Ty going forward and his changed heart, be it for a little while and Ally's fear and changed heart be it for a little longer?

Did Elijah wonder why God killed the widow's son who he had fed to keep alive? (See 2Kings 4) What doubts (if any) did he struggle with that this question raises?

Sermon was on not stealing, not to try and keep what God is taking back. As in my kids? So let them go.

I wonder why God gave me this life why could I not have had one that hurt less. Apparently great pain results in great service to Him, not in my case, just more pain. It never goes and I seem to get less Christ like not more! More proof that I'm not elect?

Yes I know the pat answers – long term view, big picture, be grateful for all that your life holds, do not question God's wisdom and way nor desire what is not yours, what He has not given. Oh how I fail when the darkness gathers and the pain settles and my chest aches and I can see no end in to the pain in this life and how

I desire escape.

But would I be going to a better place?

I can hear Luke's reply but he is not You! Why do my family have to reject me? Why does my son have to hate me and seem to delight in hurting me more and more? Why do I fear how I act with Ally in case I cause her to reject me and I lose yet another child and grandchild? Will I wake up one day and all this has been for nothing – everything just a huge joke and then the shame crashes in.

I wait in fear for Ty to drive past yelling abuse, fear of his hate and fear of his indifference if he does not go past. I fear Ally's texts of more relationship troubles. I fear the pain reawakened of access, of watching these two girls go thru what I went thru – I cannot survive that again! Please don't ask that of me and yet I fear Your answer is 'Yes' because that is what I deserve. Seems my role in life is to carry pain, to have it heaped upon me. Why has it not stayed at the Cross, more evidence that I'm not elect? This is my blackness. Do others have this behind their respectable Sunday church masks or just me? 'How are you Lisa?' 'Fine, good'. Liar! Yet would they care or understand if I said about the 'blackness'? Hypocrite that I am. I wonder what Alan would say. What do You say?

What do I say?

Well here's proof I'm crazy! I will praise Your name and what You have done (or what I think You have done) for me in this life for I am still here and I can still enjoy the flowers, rain, sunshine, my granddaughter's smile, the peace this home wraps me in, the small rays of light that split the darkness for a moment. Whatever happens at heaven's door, I still have now to do this. Don't take this away as well.

November 23. Had to use the other cleaner's, a male, vacuum tonight. I was surrounded by the smell of his sweat. So for the next 30 minutes or so I fought against wanting to throw it off me and run. I could not get in the shower quick enough when home. I can't talk to Luke, he's a bloke. I can't talk to Martin, same problem, he's a bloke or Alan he's a bloke also and he has too many other pressures from others so does not need my stupid ones – and God, well He's a male, a bloke as well! I'm trapped!

November 24. Hot, I'm not enjoying work. Wishing I could be as selfish as some. I'd just walk away from everything, Luke, church, church duties – we are expected to attend a meeting tonight and tomorrow – maybe even God. I'm not sure where I stand, if I'm even right with God. Stood in front of the mirror, had to while filling mop bucket to clean the toilets – yep I'm a 'nobody'. Told Jane how I was feeling, she said I 'can't do that, where would St. David's be without me'. Where God wants it, I think to myself, I don't hold it up!

*Hello again old Friend.*
*This fallen world*
*Groaning, full of pain and woe*
*Tis not always safe*
*To be*
> *Whether with neighbour or brethren.*
> *So help me to hide*
> *Again*
> *Behind curved mouth*
> *And painted face*
> *And smilingly serve.*

*And yet old Friend*
*Let me cast you off*
*To Be*
> *To be true, be real Face to face Heart to heart*
> *Embraced by the Father*
> *For then*
> *It is safe Smiler to be.*
> *To be.*

*L.*

December 1. Feeling a deep sadness tonight, thinking of Ty and how he had loved this time of year; finishing his prep. year and moving up, doing all the Christmas stuff. I don't feel like putting up a tree. Christmas is painful for me, lack of family events, memories, access stresses. What was it like for You to let

Your Son go and enter this place where He would be hated and killed? At least You knew the big picture, that He would be back home. Have pity on us who don't know that for our children.

December 5. Sermon this morning was on Psalm 130. My guilt of not being what others want or expect does not apply to God. This is guilt that others put on me, I put on me, not what God puts and this only is what matters. Not what I feel, not what I see, not what I experience, but what I read in Your Word Lord. This is real, this is truth. Oh let this sink deep within. 'Your Blood has washed away my sin, Jesus thank You. The Father's wrath completely satisfied, Jesus thank You. Once Your enemy, now seated at Your table, Jesus thank You.'

This morning's reading: John Ch.21 -- the restoring of Peter. This reading this morning when I'm feeling as though 'too dirty' from the past to be of any great 'help' in advancing Your Kingdom to be used or wanted by God, as there is no way I and my children will ever be described as 'such a lovely Christian family' as the Anderson's were, up front of all the congregation the other Sunday. I'm in a bad place wanting praise, wanting a position, like the two brothers asking Jesus – I just want to be of use, real use Lord but I feel hampered by the 'failures' that surround me from past bad choices, sin and being female. Help me to get beyond my pride that hangs around wanting to be 'somebody' of importance, to be 'noticed', help me to just be faithful to You to the end. Please don't let me quit or fail this one thing. Let me feel some reassuring joy, not this dark, sad, despair.

December 6. Coffee with Jane, wow! How humbling yet...I don't know Lord...to hear someone say several times, not just once, and in a choked voice full of emotion, 'I love you' and that they are in tears, on their knees praying for me – for me Lord!! – Probably why I'm still going – thanks Lord and thank her for me too.

December 16. This morning's reading included the verse, '... He which hath began a good work in you will perform it until the day of Jesus Christ....' I have claimed that for me but today I looked at it and wondered why I'd never seen it for Tyler and Ally. You have put this verse in front of me a few times lately, is this why? Ty went forward, Ally spoke of fears and prayed, both for that short time gave us the privilege of seeing a marked change, an eager hunger for all You offered, to read, to learn, to be with. But now for a longer period there has been a turning away from You. Yet perhaps I can claim the longer view promise, that You will keep performing what You started in them until Christ's Day.

December 17. Its 2330 hrs – 'Do not fret; do not be anxious, afraid, strong right hand, arm will finish what has begun.' (See Ps 37 & 73, Phil.4:6, Ps.56, A mixture of verses into one idea but see Ps.89:13 and Is. 59:16. Can be good to go thru your bible and underline in red all the 'do not fear's' checking contexts) – Funny how these bits of verse kept popping up the last few days, against all logic Lord I hold You to this one for Ty.

Joe, yes Joe rang (where is my pen?) around 1300hrs this afternoon. I answered the phone but did not recognise his voice, so he had to say who he was! That would have dinted the ego!

He went on to speak of problems with Ty, texts, threats, phone calls with noone there. --Sounds like what we have had for ages -- As a group -- Group. As in all his side of family. Oh what courage and strength in a pack! -- they have taken out an intervention order which is to be served today. Then in 3 weeks' time there will be a hearing in court, and if he does not pull his head in they have all the evidence needed to lock him up and throw away the key. The 'him' is my son, our son!

He wanted to let me know as worried about retaliation, worried about me and Ally.-- Oh yea, since when?! But I did not think quickly enough or clearly when Joe was talking. I was disarmed by his apology for not believing me earlier about problems I'd been having with Ty -- How earlier? Would have to have been before I married Luke, as we have not told Joe of what we have had since. I reminded Joe that was why Ty had been put into care.

He wanted to know what Ty was capable of. I said that Psych Services had said 'anything or nothing'.

Joe said he had not had contact with Tyler for over two years but as I'd know, he could not be trusted – Oh yea, so how did Ty find out about Ally if Joe had not told him? Not trust Ty, like not trust Ally when she started talking about abuse?

Joe said Ty had always and only targeted him – Wrong! -- why he had to change phone numbers so often -- So how did Ty get his new number to do all this threatening texting?

Joe went on to tell me that Ty had been in another hit-and-run, that my Dad had repaired the car after the first one. Joe was protecting his Mum and other female family members, escorting them around if it was dark -- What concern for others, pity Ally and I'd never experienced this! -- He wonders if Ty could be Bipolar as becomes a different person – And this without any contact, amazing! -- He wondered where Ty got the idea that he could treat women like this – I wonder!

Joe's phone is making a noise, is he on a speaker? Great!

Why the sudden concern for our safety and that of my parents and other family members, why asking questions about my last contact with Ty and his relationship with my parents? Is he covering his 'backside', getting in 'first', looking good in case I hear from Ty and get a different story?

After Luke and I spoke to Martin, I wrote a letter to Joe telling him I did not want any further contact from him in regards to his problems with Tyler and that I did not want to be involved in his course of action.

Summer Convention: so what did I learn this Convention – Plod on, trust, trust, trust, trust, lean hard – is this not the lesson from this year my Lord?

Psalm 105:4. 'Look to the Lord and His strength, seek His face always', was a New Year's resolution suggested by one of the speakers at Tree Tops. 'Go to God first, not as a last resort. His strength that created the world, that released Israel from Egypt, took the people thru the Red Sea, that rose Christ from the dead – this strength is ours, is directed to those who look to Him. Seek is active, urgent, not casual, offhanded. When? Always. In ALL circumstances.'

Do I believe in the Second coming of Christ? This was a question put to us at Convention. Yes. Do I believe it will happen in my time? No, not really I don't think. Apparently such an answer diminishes my ability to live rightly. Does it Lord? For You to come while I live would make things too easy for me personally, all my pain, tears etc. finished just like that, too easy! Also if I think of those who I love, who are not walking with You, I'm not sure if I want You to come right now. I would like, want You to continue to have patience for longer as I want them to come too.

How are you going my dear Reader? How I wish I could know, but perhaps it is best I don't. My head may get bigger, or my ego may be squashed more, neither is good.

*I know I've been there.*
    *No!*
    *Your shoes are not mine*
    *Nor the days you've been given*
*Our being*
*Stamped by His image*
*Gives common ground*
    *But*
    *My heart soul and spirit*
    *Cannot be known*
    *By you my friend*
    *Only by Him.*
*So listen*
*Please just listen*
*Stay close*
*Share my tears and joys*
*Be my friend*
*Not my God.*
    *L.*

## Chapter 4

January 5. Phone messages from the police looking for Tyler. Also the weird phone calls at all hours have started again.

February 6. Luke and I on holidays, the minister at this church is the same one who came into my home years ago and told my son that 'he deserved to be stoned to death for the way he was treating me', he said he 'would be keeping an eye on Ty' and then he disappeared. I never heard from him again, no support, just a mess to clean up like with everyone else who knew how to 'fix' my son. I could not go back there to that church again.

February 9. Luke said 'it was because he loves my 'inside' so much that he finds my 'outside' so desirable – whatever, saggy, baggy, very round and yes, as I age.' I heard but not sure if can digest, but I heard. He has answered other times when I ask him 'why? As I'm nothing special, any woman would do'... 'No they are not the love of my life.' What nice things to consider and think on Lord.

February 10. Ally texts – 'don't stress...when home can you take me and help me find some accommodation...I'm getting out, this isn't a life I want for bub....' I went with my cuppa and sat and watched the waves and prayed. Am I wrong to hope, believe that because she made a commitment to You Lord, You will be and are caring for her and only allowing the 'good' to happen? Oh that I may not be ashamed for thinking this!

February 13. We go to a different church. The minister, a stranger, tells me he 'could see the joy of the Lord in my eyes'. Really Lord, really? If that is so, thank You. If he can maybe others can and see You.

February 14. I'm watching the seagulls. There is one that hunts all the others away so that only he is at the front to get food. He puts a lot of effort into keeping others away, even viciously pecking those who get too close to him, drawing blood occasionally. So they left him, ignored him, he was alone. What happens to us when we ignore You, Your image in us? We become like this gull, like an animal, stressed, keeping all at bay as all are perceived as threats. If we do for long enough and nastily enough we are alone, we isolate and become isolated and why? For something that may happen, for what we think is ours by 'right'? What a personal tragedy to turn our backs on You and Your image, we become less human, we become less not more, we lose.

February 20. Forgive me of all my sins that aided Ty and Ally being what they are, for my hand in aiding them to make bad choices, for all the wrong I did and all the good I did not do and remove my guilt and shame of these please.

March 4. Strange phone calls, car driving past with horn blaring late at night several times most nights now.

March 6. Humility= 'acceptance of what God does and where He leads you in life.' Well I am not humble! I grumble, complain and fight a lot of the way against God's ways especially where Ty and Ally are concerned. Why do You put up with me, I just can't get things right, can I? Help me, I owe You everything.

March 19. Rang Mum to have a talk, as I've not heard from her in ages. Dad, who rarely answers the phone and even more rarely talks to me, did so in a rage of palpable anger because of 'your son'. It was like listening to Joe or Tyler in full steam! It is so hard Lord to love let alone respect him in this situation. Don't let me become so bitter and twisted. Apparently Tyler had taken money – 'all their holiday money' -- from Dad's wallet and let down the car's tyres but he would not report him to the police as I asked, for 'what good would that do, besides he's blood, family. But is going to turf out all Tyler's stuff stored there and dump it on the street'. He got angrier at me when I said this was between him and Tyler, not my business, for I have no contact or communication with him now. '... and he won't be getting the money that's been held in trust for him till now, till I decide he deserves it!' And down slammed the phone.

I asked Alan tonight, if when I see God, will He look and speak to me with appreciation and approval? 'Of course He will,

He loves you.' No hesitation, no doubt, just wonderment in his tone that I had to ask. Lord if You looked or spoke to me the way the father You gave me does I could not bear it. Nothing would be worthwhile; all would be pointless, meaningless. I need Your love displayed this way also. I need a Father I matter to, am important to. Oh, that godly men would be aware of how they affect their daughter's lives and how their sons affect the lives of the girls they touch. Could this 'achievement' be any less important than any other for You?

March 21. 'Love is not... '[33] As Luke was praying for us tonight my mind wandered (not good I know!). I've always associated love with what? How those who supposedly loved me treated me, parents, Joe. But we are all sinners and as such we don't get it right. Love is what You are. The way You are not rude, unfeeling etc. and who You are.

April 25. As I'm teaching someone else a skill I'd just mastered, I'm told I 'am an inspiration' – I've never been told this by anyone before! Thank You.

May 4. Over the last few weeks coming home from work I have understood some stuff –

1. God loves me, not my ability to do. He is pleased with me, He is for me.

2. Re stresses and unable to sleep one night because I was upset about Mum not telling me about a close family member dying till it was too late for me to get to the funeral and realizing when Nan dies I will have no information about family happenings. If God wants me to know and be present at funerals and the like He will make sure I find out and can get there.

3. I realized that Ty and Ally have had far more exposure and better teaching of the Gospel and God than I had. Tyler had about 6years before he went into Foster Care and then intermittently, Ally around 11years. If I could make a decision on what I had, they should be even more able to do so. I've not done well with

---

33  See 1Corinthians 13:48. But read it as – 'Love is not impatient...unkind...envious.. showingoff... arrogant... rude... crass... selfseeking...needle...keep score...payback...lie... play games... leave you to sweat it out... distrust...giveup..' get the idea?

them yet I've done better.

Thanks Lord for these comforts and encouragements.

May 8. Dreamt last night that Luke left me because I was not meeting his needs and he was sick and tired of my behaviour. I had to find somewhere else to live. Huge feelings of failure which included thinking of kids and relationship with parents (only right thing I did was get them married). I told Luke. He replied, 'only one person never failed and I am not Him.' No, I am not. How can He understand then?

In the shower and feeling worse, I drew a cross in the moisture on the screen and studied it. You, Christ did 'fail' and worse than I. You 'failed' the expectations of Your family, friends, church <u>and</u> Nation. You just did not 'fail' Your Father. You know how it feels. Oh Lord let me not fail You.

Luke underlines a part of our reading today, '...when a man finds a virtuous wife her worth cannot be measured, indeed he has obtained favour from God.' I don't deserve him, thank You.

June 16. Not in a good place AGAIN!! Not good when you end up screaming out in the shower after work, that you've had enough of men – men ruling your life, encircling me, controlling me – even my 'help' -- counsellor, minister, Luke and God are men!! I'm trapped, bound, choiceless! What started all this? Not sure. What is (not) happening between Luke and I, Dad, Tyler going past in car again, having to see the Dr. (male!) about my 'troubles' and Luke going with me, but I know what ended it – Len! Len, my male coworker who is becoming 'weird', not wanting me to leave work even if I'm finished my area, wanting me to stay behind and wait till he is finished so we can walk out together as it is dark. He gets upset if I don't and makes job difficult for me.

June 20. To doctor, I start taking antidepressants, what a relief! I feel heard! He seemed to have seriously considered what we told him of Martin's ideas including his diagnosis that I am still struggling to overcome Post Traumatic Stress Disorder that possibly includes traces of Stockholm syndrome which is where the victim strongly identifies with the captor. Luke has been really worried as I've been getting up around 0200hrs till about

0500hrs every night for ages now, cleaning, cooking or reading, till I could bring myself to face going back to sleep again, to face my racing terrifying thoughts.

July 7. Psalm 55 was tonight's reading. I remember the first time I read this Lord. You understood my desire to escape and find peace and stillness. You understood the hurt and confusion pain of what the smooth talking, covenant (marriage) breaking Joe did and caused me. You were not distant uncaring, You were real, You are real, You knew, You were and are trustworthy. Thank You for the stillness despite the craziness.

July 10. Tyler, the past is like an unhealed festering sore whose scab pulls off and the guilt, pain, despair and confusion, the what-ifs, what could I have done differently, the terrible black sadness and emptiness oozes like pus out till it seals off again, till the next time. Will this wound ever be cleaned out properly and healed form the bottom up instead of having a false top covering it like the wounds I used to dress once Lord?

I watched Your Sea today and sat in Your warmth and waited to scab over again.

July 17. Three lessons?

1. I watched a little girl in pink with a mop of brown curls, around two years of age, bounce and run onto the beach, stopping to check out something then continue with her family to the waves where she played 'chasey' with them. So full of life, fun and wonder. Why do we, I, lose this? Surely if I trusted You my Father, knew You as I should I would run into life like this. This after all is Your world and I am Your child.

2. Walked to a section of coast where there is ocean for as far as you can see to the left and right. All this, plus all I cannot see, You hold easily in Your hand. How much water – just water – can I hold in mine?! The power of the incoming tide smashing against the rocks You still with a glance. How big, how powerful are You? Can You not handle anything, everything that comes my way?

3. I wrote a version of John 3:16 in the sand putting 'you' instead of 'world' and adding 'repent.' It was interesting to watch the responses. Some glanced, one looked, most walked over or

past without seemingly noticing these eternally life changing words of Yours – but did our ancestors not do the same and not just to words but The Word?!

July 21. Tonight's reading was 1Corinthians 15:51-57. About one day when there will be no more pain, and Revelation 19:11, 22:6. And a statement -- 'Pain will either turn us against God or draw us to Him.' I don't know where Tyler is now, Alyssa found her excuse to turn with Jean's death – 'How could God kill her?', but I because of You keep turning, burrowing closer, deeper with pain. Lord I don't know, but it seems as though with You or not the pain would still there. Pain with the hope of something good at the end is just bearable in my experience. But away from You – and I do remember still how that was – you have pain and no hope. It is the no hope that destroys not the presence of pain, and You are the giver of hope. So pain with You is better than pain without You, may the ones I love come to know this too.

August 5. Tonight as Luke was backing out from our supermarket car parking spot Ty drove in very fast and very close, so close to Luke's side of the car that Ty's mate really struggled to get out of the passenger seat. We thought he was going to hit us. He strode into the shop without a backward glance. This cold, distant scary male is a stranger.

August 11. I have a fear problem – you don't say! But Martin does. I need to teach my brain new and right ways of thinking and not connect the wrong dots that have been programmed. I'm to talk to Luke about feelings, especially about sexual stuff. Why do I turn on my side in a foetal, protective position, withdrawing? I need a cuddle when I do this even though I'm not wanting one.

Tyler is now driving past in the daylight as well as at night, ducking down trying not to be seen at dangerous speeds, neighbours are telling us of seeing him as well and voicing safety concerns for others walking or reversing out on to road.

September 1. Martin getting me to talk, memories of hating, but having to sit between Mum's sweaty legs in the car and not wanting her to touch me, the fire and believing Dad to be dead, Murray trying to run me over with the tractor, moving out into the sleepout and falling out of bed often – 'no wonder I'm having problems, wants to probe deeper.' I want to run.

September 7. Discussing getting into heaven at Bible Study, some ladies are 'hoping they will 'hopefully' be in Heaven'. I need to be more than hopeful Lord! Hopeful that what I've done is good enough gives me no hope at all! I spoke up and said 'It's what we are IN Christ that gets us into Heaven NOT what we DO in Christ'. They did not seem to understand what I was trying to explain as they prayed about what they <u>must do</u>, as in read their bible more, go to church more, tithe better, give more, serve more....

Lisa feels that her first attempt at filling in for Marie was not appreciated as she was never asked to do so again.

September 15. Martin is digging into family relationships – basically aggressive and hostile. Those red lines did not help to diminish my fear to sleep; I do not want to dream.

And so my dear Reader we have arrived at the beginning. Martin was to retire not long after this visit, after he had taught me to stop, breath and consider where the feeling or desire for a certain action was coming from and to discern if it actually was right for the now, to question it. I was to allow myself the freedom to enjoy Luke without fear, God was watching.

God had used Martin to bring me to a place where I could write – A lot of past years entries were groaning of 'will it ever end' in regards to the cyclic stresses mostly because of Tyler's' actions. Thank You Lord for I feel in part it is not just because Ty has withdrawn but I have been able to 'jump off the roundabout' by Your using of Martin to grow me. Thank You that again my life does feel like a prize.

September 18. I heard a sermon over the radio – 'true acceptance is never based on performance. A relationship built on what you do is not a relationship built on love'.

I asked Luke what true acceptance is built on then, he replied, 'the person.' So, me being me should be acceptable. Interesting thought Lord. I know this is right for You and Luke, but my family? 'Just as I am I come' –You accepted me, dirty, imperfect, out of control but loved me enough to guide me into improvement instead of leaving me as You found me. Luke is doing a similar work, Martin also (though he is paid too!). Good true friends are like iron sharpening iron as I've heard said..

October 28. I am reading Psalm 131 where a weaned child that no longer frets for what it once demanded is compared to a soul that has learned the same lesson. A call to learn humility, patient endurance and contentment in all of life's circumstances, whatever they are, though I do not understand God's reasons. Can I in my circumstances 'hope in the Lord'? Can I wait in faith and patience without fretting and without wavering, questioning God's wisdom? Can I trust Him while He works in me His good, acceptable and perfect will?

November 6. Thank You also that I am again able to say 'All the way to the end of my race, to let You in, to let Luke in, whatever the cost Lord.

November 27. At 0200hrs Emergency rang, Tyler had been brought in by the police. He'd been assaulted and wanted to see us. We went in. He talked for several hours, confessing and apologetic. He's always acted up to get his father's attention but it never worked, last time he only got a restraining order. I was drained after, over 2 years of not seeing and even longer since had a 'normal' conversation then to see him with his face all beaten up; not easy. Worried that he now knows for sure the mobile number he has is ours. So I warned him if he starts up again I will change it again despite his fear that if he has an accident he won't be able to contact me.

December 25. Luke and I are having Christmas lunch with my parents. Mum is complaining that she 'has not heard from Tyler and how sad it is'. Dad is telling me that Ty 'has a lot of enemies in this town and had better watch his back.'

The following are some of the notes from the messages at Summer Convention – 'There are no second standard people. ALL have the image of God; ALL are on level ground at the foot of the Cross. ALL=ALL All are loved, all are valued in God's world. Romans 14:17. A challenging reminder: 'do not call unclean what God calls clean'. Do not bag yourself, this denies the sufficiency of Christ's death to renew and clean.'

I am a new creation that is impatient to grow!

Deuteronomy 33:25. Isaiah 40:29-31. God gives power to the faint, he increases the strength of those who have none, new strength for each day for as many days you have, not physical strength but grace filled strength to face and get thru challenges.'

Yes have I not experienced this even from the beginning and perhaps even when I did not truly know You. Each time I got up and kept on going, how I got through those early days, the court cases, the lies, the access challenges, then Tyler, then Ally, family, church friends, me, Yes! Thank You Lord, thank You.

January 4. Reading *Abide in Christ*[34] 'Abide You command You provide. I give consent to let You do all for, in and through me, it is a work You do – the fruit and power of Your redeeming love. My part is to simply yield, trust and wait for what You have engaged to perform. Mine is to obey. His is to provide. It is good to go back over what you thought you knew and be reminded, rechallenged.'

Am I resting or striving?

January 6. We attend a wedding. The Minister defined the difference between a marriage and just living together –'The base or foundation of marriage was a promise. The foundation of living together is performance.'

Yes and yet I would say my first marriage was performance based – was this because of having 'tried' beforehand? Because as soon as I did not live up to expectations he looked elsewhere and compared me to others, including his mum, sister-in-law or my mum or others at his work.

February 8. Attend Nan's funeral, my last grandparent. Why are they saying the Lord's Prayer if unconverted? Oh Lord are my family saveable, is there any softness left in their hearts? The uncle that used to call me 'fatty' tells me that I'd 'failed to convert mum, and how they had laughed over my efforts. I would not convert any of them here so not to try.' I had to speak of my memories of her.

February 9. I fail to convert? No! God does not fail and it is

---

34   Andrew Murray. Abide in Christ. The Joy of being in God's presence. Whitaker House. Unsure now if this is a quote or my summary using some of A.M.'s words.

He who does the converting not me! They are the ones that fail, fail to see His mercy. I do not want an unjust God. For those still breathing I have prayer!

February 20. Lord when was I 'saved'? This study, *When Godly People Do Ungodly Things*,[35] makes me wonder if I was, when I knew You existed, and made everything and that I did not want to go to hell, but that I was 'seduced' away for a season. Thank You Lord that life without You was not good overall and that I searched for the 'more' and found You, the One who provides much 'more' than I could have known.

March 3. Midnight. Police knocking at our door looking for Tyler, he'd missed a court appearance and they want me to contact him.

I do but wish I had not. Ty's replies were not nice; I was a 'nothing' who had 'never loved him, only Ally.'

March 18. I have an awareness of – 1. Too many fears. Too little time in my life when I have not been afraid. Help me to trust more.

2. I am still looking to others to meet needs of acceptance and affirmation instead of God. Why rejection from church family was still so painful and needing praise for my comments in studies and why need not met as people cannot; only God can.

3. Too much me. Too much pride, too much wanting to do 'great' things for God, too much need to be 'noticed and commended' by people. This is hard to discern. Is my desire to have people hear my story to show what God has done or to show 'me'?

Help me to do what You set before me to the best of my ability to PLEASE You, not because I'm looking to please people. Help me to be content to be invisible and 'useless' when You want this also.

April 2. Ty's been driving past again late at night, very fast with horn blaring, we call these 'flybys'. He texted today -- when r u going to see ur son Lisa? Dose he have to wat for and other 3yrs again? That's not a very good mum to t at all! I answered that

---

35   Beth Moore When Godly people do ungodly things. Arming yourself in the age of Seduction. LifeWay Press 2003.

I'd be a McDonalds at 1930hrs tonight. No answer, no show. He however texted the next night with several unpleasant comments, basically accusing me of not showing at the time I had said I would.

Notes from the Easter Convention – 'You IN me!' I know this yet sometimes it just blows my mind! If I unzipped myself would I see You? No! It is by faith, feeling very occasionally, that I <u>know</u> Your presence, still pretty amazing though.

Who I am in regards to my relationship to God – not other people or things – IS the most important thing about me. Don't go to the past to define yourself but the future, 'up there'.

God cannot be disillusioned with me as He has no illusions about me.

There are 12 Commandments. The 11th is the one Jesus told the disciples in the New Testament. The 12th is 'Thou shalt bash on as in keep on keeping on'.

So my lessons from Convention: Trust God, Do the right, Remember and Trust God, Just do it!

Ty texted (it was his number that showed) yet again while at convention – 'court it is then! You have got a son in this world Lisa that you don't even see anymore because of Luke. The last time you saw him was 3 yrs ago its a joke. Luke your getting a avo aginst you so he can see him mum! Joe.'

April 26. Reading Psalm 16. Lots to consider. In life I have discovered and known Your care, protection and provision so why do I stress? Why do I lose the focus and priority of You (Your presence) over all else? If I am complaining about 'others dragging' me down, help me to drag them up with the way I pray aloud. Allow me to pray with my experiences of Your faithfulness forming my prayers. If this is what You want and not my pride, allow my 'vision' of You to lift them up to my 'level' not bring me down to theirs – that's if I have the right view of things!

May 6. Tyler has rang Alan asking him for help to contact me as he cannot find me, yet he is texting us with -- when are you going to see yor son again Lisa what another 3 yrs down the track also is Luke a control freak that he wont let your own son see you. Friggin Hell Jesus Christ God dam it.

Where is his mind Lord, what is he trying to achieve? Why bring our minister in to it? I was upset at his deliberate use of words showing contempt for You.

June 2. The 'without excuse' verse Romans 1:20 is buzzing around. I knew enough. I was evading responsibility, excusing, justifying, why I did as I did especially with Joe? I'm sorry Lord. I am guilty of so much, Paul's not the worst, **I** am! Thank You for staying with me, for the still burning candle, for the smoking reed to not have been extinguished.

June 16. I had organised another meeting at McDonalds, Tyler did not show again.

June 17. Evening Sermon, 'Abraham was asked to sacrifice his only son –the cost of wanting to go all the way'. (Gen.22)

I'm sorry I fear the pain Lord, help me for I still want to go all the way. 'Abraham's test, pain came after 30 years of following You'. I worry – yes ahead of time – what You may ask me to go thru that will hurt as much if not more than I have already felt, paid to follow You.

For a while now I'd been struggling with an internal tumult regarding the issue of being or not being 'chosen, elected' yet again and what gifts (and having no idea what mine were do not help either!!) or jobs I was meant to be serving my church by. My ideas were not the same as the leadership's and I was finding no answers.

July 6. Tonight's reading and comment was by Joel Stowell on Psalm 131. 'Jesus knew it wasn't wise to accelerate through life with our gas gauge registering on 'weary' all the time. Mathew 14:13, Mark 6:31. When was the last time you could echo the Psalmist's words, 'I have calmed and quietened my soul'? Put up a stop sign at the intersection of your busy life. Find a place to be alone. Turn off the distractions that keep you from listening to God's voice and let Him speak to you as you read His Word. Let Him refresh your heart and mind with the strength to live life well for His glory.'

Lord help my heart to not be haughty, I fear it has become so or my eyes lofty. Help me to stop concerning myself with great matters, with things too profound for me that will not affect our relationship. I once could calm and quieten my soul and rest in You – help me to do that again and not be so fretful, searching for answers and jobs that You do not wish for me.

July 19. Thoughts after tonight's reading – I've hidden myself for so long Lord, made a 'person' who was expected. I'm still not sure who 'me' actually is but I am still <u>relieved</u> not to have to play 'games' to keep safe from You, that You see 'me' and still are here with me. I still think I 'project an image' of myself that I think they want, more than I should. Help me to be me regardless of where I am and who is watching. I only want to have one face and that one is to reflect You.

July 29. Mixed feelings about being back from holidays, stress increases. But Lord is it because I am too concerned about what others think or what I think they think! Help me to lose this please it's not good for me physically, emotionally or spiritually, Sunday's workload has increased, evening meals every Sunday now as well as morning teas, Lord I cannot do as some, I am me and I should not feel guilty that I can't. They can do as they want, I should be able to decide for myself what suits me, what I can manage.

July 31. When the 'F' word was on my tongue at work tonight, because I was putting myself down, calling myself names and hearing past voices doing the same, I was able to sing 'Blessed, blessed, blessed, blessed child of God' over and over again. The 'voices' went silent.

August 1. Tonight's comment by David Roper on Psalm 59, says it so well, tells it all '...David was thinking of Saul's army that was closing in on him. I think, however of the thoughts that return to menace us. They come back at nightfall, snapping and snarling: 'You're stupid.' 'You're a failure.' 'You're useless.' 'Who needs you?' When we have such thoughts, we can revel in God's unconditional, unending love. His steady devotion is our refuge in the dark night of selfdoubt and fear. Dear Lord, I am so thankful that You love me unconditionally. Please chase away destructive thoughts that keep returning to take away my confidence in You and Your work in me. I want to rest in You and Your love.'

August 12. Convicting Sermon. Oh Lord I'm sorry about my complaining to self, mostly about feeling 'overlooked', missing out on leading studies, not asked to sing or teach Sunday School, even today not being in charge of the catering anymore as Marie is – as it should be! I had 'forgotten' yet again that this was complaining against You and the position You have or have not put me in. Help me to see me clearly and not to think highly of me and what I think I can do and to rest in what I have and am doing and be happy that there are others called to do things. Help me to rest; that it is okay if never happens for I should not be up front talking of You if I get notice or attention and not You.

Tyler keeps texting over the next several days. What follows is only a sample and again the obscenities are changed to *'s – at all start acting like your his mum to him!

Go **** ya self fatty! You didn't give a **** when th son turn 21 theirs no excuse for it . By th looks of it starting to think that your not hes real birth mother at all over the years Got a D+A test!

Ty had never said anything to us about what he had planned or wanted for his 21st. We did not even know where he was. I had texted him with our love for this day, and said I'd be at McDonalds. I sat in Mc. Donald's alone, as he did not show, and ate cake and remembered

wish th years would go faster so you can rote in your grave. The world would be a better place without you! Your not th real mother at all just a slut instead and sleeping with random men over the years!

so go and roat in your grave so it can get ****** and ******* and go to Hell.

be geting a phone call from lawyer and takeing to court to get this D+A test done to prove your not th real mother hear!

How can th son be a part of Lis and Luks life when you KICK HIM OUT OF HOME at age 13! Because son would of still e in life if you didn't kick out in 1st place! So thats you own ******* flout and you to blame

August 19. Lord what should I do now he is threatening us? Would he really actually do something like this? Is he just trying to scare? Can I really believe that, I wish I could but I'm not sure. Earlier in the day I had wondered how much more God should need to show me for me to trust Him more. Answer: Nothing. He has shown me enough as he had Israel in only 1year in the dessert, yet they did not trust Him to win the next war for them – Oh I'm sorry, Help!

August 21. I have a poster from a friend 'trusting I'm where God wants me to be' – Oh my Lord Abba help me, I struggle so with this at times.

August 22. 'HaHa! Done the track again Lisa so suck ****! I'm even happy to die up hear its a dream came true like hearven up hear at th race track!...You had you time to see me but you lost it fot good!'

Help me to trust and rest in You Lord in this. So hard, each time wondering if this is the last. Please help him.

August 27. Study on *Daniel*.[36] Again there's a lot to think about with application and understanding of my past. 'Daniel 6:17-28, Psalm 55. Ransomed unharmed from battle (I'd already previously marked v.18), living in a lion's den =Satan's world we have opportunities to emerge from hurtful situations unhurt or not ruined as the Aramaic can mean. Jeremiah 10:19 = you made your bed, lie in it accept it (just as Mum said all those years ago!!) but see God's response Jeremiah 30:12, 17. Come to a situation where you get incurable wounds, call out to God for he can heal wounds. You will not haemorrhage for the rest of your days from wounds of sin's consequences though you could face battles like Daniel because of your own innocence, not related to your sin, instead'.

My story or what! Of You in my life, Your working. Help me trust with everything else for You <u>have</u> done the biggest. One day the bleeding will stop – it has slowed. My flame, smouldering reed is burning bright, thank You.

August 30. A sample of texts from Ty today and my reply -- You know Joe's dad he still have his guns down in the gun shed and dose hs shooting still. Even the grandson knows how to shot

---

36    Beth Moore Daniel. Lives of integrity Words of Prophecy. LifeWay Press 2006 Probably notes taken during Session 6.

a gun now haha.

Both have gun licences now!

Hille Hitlar

Tyler because I do love u I have found ur messages hurtful and disrespectful. As u show no desire to change ur tone I am changing the phone number so I will not have to receive and read such hurtful stuff from the son I love. Mum.

Are you going to be a brick wall and push your son away for good? What is Cas needs to ring you again with th hospl if son got into trouble again.

September 2. Sermon based on Numbers 16. 'Do not overestimate your own importance and contributions.'

Okay Lord I think I have got it – have I? Be happy, content with what I'm doing, don't push to do what I think I should be, just cook and clean toilets. I took Ann home, during our conversation she said that she 'had been watching me since the first time I'd come to St. David's, seen some big changes in me, some fast, with my history, gifts including my desire to accumulate knowledge and study feels I will either speak or write one day'. I told Luke, he 'does not see me ever doing either of these' – back to earth Lisa! I see pride as a problem, so don't let this happen if it worsens this Lord.

September 11. I rang Mum; she tells me they 'are having some not so nice calls from Tyler but once he has vented it is all good.' So it's acceptable as he is just venting!

September 14. I find myself missing Ty's messages; at least I knew he was somewhere and okay enough to be mad at me.

September 23. Message on the home phone from Tyler, He's interstate and won't be back. Then a text 'had ur chance to see... good luck with that *******....'

Throughout October we were plagued with phone calls and messages on the home phone that involved weird noises or singsong accusations broken by long silences or background music. Then at the end of the month we got an interstate phone call from a lady he had been staying with. She told us that he owed her money and had stolen stuff including her house keys. Ty had lied to people, leading them to believe he was homeless, jobless and that I was a real baddie, side swiping his side swiping his car. As he had been ringing this number a lot she had presumed I was a close friend, not the 'bad Mum'. She is now getting rude texts accusing her of stealing from him.

November 3. Thinking. Comment on 1 Corinthians 3:1-15 in the book *World Aflame*[37] 'Any work done by a follower of Christ to the glory of God is gold, silver, precious stone. But if any follower works with any self-interest or personal ambition involved it will be wood, hay and stubble and will be burnt.'

Okay Lord, You know that I know and question all my motives and feel that none are pure, all things I do or say have something in them for me – so I will have no works left to be rewarded for. I so much want to be the best, with the most because You have given me the most – I want to 'pay back' out of gratitude by being Your best – Ha! How much pride is in that!! See what I mean! Yet Lord I feel as though there is none, especially in St. David's who owes You as much as I, as none have been given as much.

Psalm 139:23-24. Search me and make sure I work because of You and wanting Your smile not because of me. Lord help me not to stress about motives too much, question but not stress and let You sort it out and to trust Your leading and limiting of wrong stuff.

November 24. Mum rang, 'has heard from Tyler several times, and seems to be going good.' I replied 'great at least I know now he's alive.'

November 27. Letter in our mail today, an insurance letter stating we owe over $2000 for damaging Tyler's car. I was able to prove by the wrong addresses, the dates given and where we actually were, that we had not been responsible.

During December the phone calls and messages on our home phone from Tyler continue. I get a 'tortured' voiced 'm...u...m....' Luke gets one with the 'angry it-is-all-your-fault' voice. The police keep calling and leaving their cards looking for Tyler, this will continue till he hands himself in or is caught. He has an outstanding warrant for a traffic incident over a year back for

---

37    Billy Graham World Aflame The World's Work (1913) Ltd. 1965. Pg. 223

travelling at 130kms in a 60km area!

December 15. I'm struggling with changes at church, no kitchen to 'hide' in and work as open and visible. I'm told to keep out, causing me to struggle with feelings of rejection. I do not feel good when I can't do stuff.

December 25. We spent the afternoon with my family. Ironic and sad how my brother and his sons used as a swear word, sometimes in its entirety, the Name of the One who gave us the reason to have this day of festivity and family gathering! Their use felt deliberate, it was loud forceful and frequent. I felt as if Murray was saying 'do you hear me Lisa?' Oh Lord sometimes I wish You were not as respectful of the free will You gave us – just bash us over our thick heads and make us follow You before we have to bow the knee, before we enter hell.

Thoughts over Convention time – Thank You for the 'reminders' of my need and dependence on You. For the thorn(s) that drive me from me to You again. That reminds me of my weakness and inability and teaches me again of Your strength and ever presence. For I know without You I can do nothing and nothing for me includes living, being, coping.

Lord let me praise You.

Let my life praise You for as long as You lend me breath. *(If ever I love You tis now Jesus)*[38] L. ................

Abide with me from morn till eve, for without You I cannot live; abide with me when night is nigh, for without You I dare not die. *Sun of my Soul*[39] by J. Kemble 1792-1866.

January and the phone calls from Tyler continue. Occasionally he leaves the message – I'm available -- so I text a time and date to meet at McDonald's. He never shows.

January 11. Is it time to just completely let go and give Tyler over to God till he can contact me like any other person asking to meet and see, then consider what to do?

---

38   My Jesus, I Love Thee. (1Pt. 1:8) Words by Jas. Duffill. Music by A. J. Gordon.  No.69 in Alexander's Hymns No.3. Marshall, Morgan & Scott Ltd.

39   Sun of my Soul. Words by John Keble. Music by Paul Ritter. No. 263 in Alexander's hymns No.3.

January 12. Luke is trying to adjust the driver's door on our car before I go out 'as it is catching.' No wonder there is a huge dint in that side! My first thought was Ty; Luke says 'No.' Someone must have backed into it when he'd parked it outside Alan's place the other night. But when I came back home Luke had found a message on the home phone from last night – a faint crackly voice said 'I just ran into back of Mum's car...I'm sorry.' Was it a teary voice or a peg-on-the-nose voice? We went and looked at the road where Luke had parked our car. Thick skid marks down the street, looked pretty deliberate. We contacted the police. To have found the car he would have to have been looking for it. The police agreed and strongly advised an intervention order. We are to go to court tomorrow and follow through with this.

Despite several other scary close calls involving Ty over the last year on the road Lisa still needed 'more' before she could do this to her son. Though the unknowing of would Ty have done this if the car had been occupied was troubling. So was the realisation that Tyler was now carrying out his threats, it was no longer just words.

Okay Lord, give one more 'sign' that this is needed.

Home from church, and there is another garbled and unpleasant message on our home phone. Okay Lord that's the sign, no remorse just the same old same. Alan and his wife visit to counsel and pray. Marie is now fearful, wondering if they could be in danger and asking how I can cope! I reply my bare truth –'he could not touch me without Your okay.'

January 14. To go to court again at the end of the month, what happens then will depend on if the police have been able to find Tyler to serve him and if he contests. If he breaks it he could face a two year jail term – Oh Lord for a phone call? Applying for a twelve month order, I'm not sure I can bare this, are You sure Lord, is this what You really want of me Lord, to 'hand' him over? Reject him again?

There are 7 messages that had been left on the home phone while we were out including garbled noise. Music? Ally recognises the sounds as words of a song and writes down the ones she hears –'...this place about to blow..haahaa..' She also writes out all the words of this song called Blow -- scary stuff, my legs go wobbly.

Later there is a text from Ally – You did the right thing mum. Your baby boy went years ago, he's never going to be that person again, this is who he is and he didn't turn out this way because of you. He chose to be this person. You may feel as if you're hurting him by doing this but think of all the people you are helping. He has to learn that he needs to pay for his mistakes and be made accountable. You're a 50 year old Mama and still get paranoid and scared and I'm a 19 year old mum and still need to have someone walk me to the toilet. I love you, don't forget that and I'm proud of you, and so thank you for finally doing this xxx. You were a good mum, you were just conflicted on what to do, we all understand the pain – hurt for you but we also know if he takes out on his threats and hurts one of us that'd hurt you more.

January 15. 11 phone calls in 10 minutes. We turned the phone off.

January 16. Minister from the other church where Tyler had gone to Youth Group rang; Ty had rung and just left our number and his name. We talked, and he prayed.

January 17. Phone calls began at 0800hrs. Luke answered and said that if he kept this up the police would be notified. From then on for the next 15 min till we turned the phone off it rang continuously only stopping to start again. A couple of hours later, after turning the phone back on there was a message in a high pitch squeak sing song like little kid voice – 'Lisa's car gonna to get ****** up again permanently its gonna to be a right off if gonna to ignore me your cars gonna to get ****** up permanently (voice now almost normal but still singsong like) no more c..a...r...r..r...hahaha say good bye to your c..a...a....r...r..r... no more car hahaha'.

The police believe he has gone interstate again. The calls kept coming during the day but infrequently. God I don't understand – what happened, why? Where's the 'good'?

January 20. What follows are some of the calls and messages we received today – <u>1057hrs.</u> Slow laboured speech – 'been 10yrs since you talked to your son and when are you going to talk to

# THE MAKING OF A JEWEL

your son again. It's been 10years since he got kicked out of home, do we have to take legal action and take Luke to court and take out an AVO against him so he can see his mum again and if Luke breaks AVO 2years imprisonment or $26000 fine on the spot. Get into contact with your son.'

1059hrs. 'and how dare you (speech faster) that you forget about him that not exist in your life anymore so payback is a ***** all those years you done to him you deserve what got coming for you as year coming.'

Alan rings, Tyler has left messages along the lines of me not contacting him for 10 years now and for him 'to do something about this, thank you'.

1440hrs. Hung up as I said hello.

1700hrs. As I lifted handset he hung up.

1715hrs. Teary voice gave a mobile number and repeated it.

2023hrs. Angry and aggressive voice 'Do I have to call Irene or Bill or Mark and Jo to get in contact this is a ******* joke a complete ******* joke(pause) if not will be Rev. Alan if not will be church if not be Don if I have to get in contact by that way THANK you VERY much!'

2040hrs. Mark (Luke's son) had left a message 'wanting to get hold of you guys give us a buzz when get this'. Luke did. Ty had rang them looking for us. I rang Dad, as worried that Ty may have been ringing them. Dad curtly told me they had not heard from him and hung up. I then rang the police; the order had still not been served. Why would he not talk to me when I answered the phone if so desperate to talk to me?

2210hrs. I answered the phone, there's music playing. I spoke 'Ty if you want contact, want to talk why don't you talk now? This is absolutely ridiculous!' He hung up, I turned the phone off.

January 21. Phone calls started at 1624hrs, sometimes I picked up, and sometimes I did not. They just hang up if I speak.

2103hrs a message is left in fast angry speech, 'if you're not gonna to get in contact with me LISA I've got Pastor Dick **** mum from St. David's Church(gives mobile number) that is (repeats number and pauses) I'm on to you ******* make contact with me!' I rang the number, a muffled sound, then a giggle then a professional sounding female voice asks me to leave a message, my turn to hang up.

January 22. Our breakfast reading was by F. E. Graeff on 1Peter 5:7. – 'Cast all cares and worries on Him. That is hard to do. If we believe the last part of the verse it makes it easier – God is far ahead of us in our problems. 'Oh yes, he cares, I know he cares, His heart is touched with my grief; when the days are weary the long night dreary, I know my Saviour cares.'

Alan rings at 1045hrs. He seems a bit rattled. Ty had rang 7 times last night last time at 2150hrs, leaving a verbal message instead of music 'Lisa please get in contact ASAP won't say it again Pastor Dick *****'

We organise our home number to be a silent number. I ring Mum – now she tells the truth (I think)! They have been having a lot of trouble with Tyler, so has Murray, who was there at this moment telling her that Joe has fixed everything. Joe has been in contact with them both, Tyler has been threatening them with murder but the police will be picking him up shortly in a couple of hours, Joe assured them. They have a court case in the next month and anyone with history with Ty can go and talk so all will be settled at one time, once for all.

The more I considered what I'd heard the sicker I felt, shaky and chest pain. I rang Mum back later after talking to Luke and told her they can say what they want to Joe about their problems but I do not want anything about me discussed with Joe. This idea terrifies me more than Tyler does! Mum 'cannot see why this is a problem as he is being so helpful. Murray was crying as he could not understand why I want nothing to do with him' – it was he who refused to speak directly to me just before but was telling her what to say! The police had encouraged her to take out an Order in the past but she 'cannot as she's the grandmother and loves him.' So what does that say about me Lord?! Why tell me all this now? I've asked several times in the past, but was always told they had no problems. I'm tired of secrets Lord. She said they did not want to worry me as I had enough worries. Great so just lie and tell me everything is great between them and Tyler when I'm trying to explain to them it is not between me and him and being made to feel that there is something wrong with me! I ring the police, still have not served Tyler. They advised me 'not to do the group thing, it is not the way it is done anyway.'

1719hrs. Message 'Ohh Pastor Alan (mobile number given) that is (and repeated number). It was Ty but in an accent trying to sound like Alan, it would have been hilarious if not so sad.

1725hrs. I answered the phone, music, I spoke 'why not speak Ty? You are ringing around getting people to make me contact you well I'm talking, why aren't you? I'm tired of this, I don't understand why, what game you are playing, you are just turning people against you. If you continue I will have to involve the police' and I hung up after giving time for him to talk. The music had become softer as I talked. The phone started ringing as soon as I'd hung up. Luke turned it off.

1958hrs. A Police Sergeant rang my mobile; Tyler had been located interstate and served with the order.

January 24. I listened to Ty's last message several times just to hear his voice, the 'accent' still made me smile – will I ever hear it again, will it be a voice of hate or...?

January 25. David rang. Ally is meeting with Joe but is worried how I will react. Joe is offering to pay to move them closer to where he is living so he can protect them. Oh Help! I'm sorry but I feel as if my 'dream' life with You and Luke is coming to a close, Joe is moving in to take over, to control and destroy all joy, happiness, peace and hope I have, those I love, to finish what he started. Help! Am I going mad? Am I the 'baddie' after all? Inventing this bad stuff about him, imagining it in my craziness?

January 26. Struggling this morning as Joe and the past filling my mind and heart. Had to deliberately remind myself (and praise You that I could!) that You see all, provide all, know all, are all powerful and love unchanging, my Strength, Salvation. This is why I am not to fear or fret.

January 27. Thoughts I'm sorry that Jesus had to die as He did and yet I am glad. I am sorry that I had to go through what I did yet I'm glad as the result is Life. I fear for Ally and what family may go thru and yet please do whatever Lord to give them Life also. You are trustworthy – only what is for our 'good' happens.

January 28. Ally told me 'they all spent the day at Joe's family home and that it was very good, very nice all was lovely.' Oh Lord have I been so terribly wrong? It was Ally who begged me not to make her spend time with him. Have I been the 'baddie'? Thinking, and remembering access and that time. I mostly felt that I was competing, struggling to have, to get Tyler and Alyssa's respect and love for me. I expected them to love Joe he was, is their Father. I did not expect them to hate me, to name call, to compare and find me waiting as unable, unwilling to do as their Dad told me to. It was my fault he had no home, could not provide them with clothes or take away on holidays. I lived in his shadow, he could do no wrong, I could do no right. I am feeling as though with Ally I am back under his shadow, I never left it with Ty and I fear I will be found lacking again. Oh Lord, help me to be **free**, to feel worthy.

January 29. Beginning to realize I am probably more fearful of what people, especially the ones I care about or respect think of me as a person than my Lord and this **should not** be so. I owe my very being to Him. They can hurt me terribly but they do not destroy me and they are very fickle. Oh Lord I'm sorry, please help me, and redirect me. Psalm 4:8 – 'I will both lie down in peace, and sleep; for You alone O LORD, make me dwell in safety.' I do not often live the truth of this but I do know and trust this – how contradictory is that!

January 31. The police serve Luke with an Apprehended Domestic Violence Order from Tyler, the court hearing is in 4 days' time, interstate. I don't understand Lord – what are You up to, what do You want us to do? So many lies as fact, so hurtful. All that Ty has done towards us he has turned around and said that Luke has done it to him and me – though I am not aware of him chasing us down the street with a gun. It will go on police records that Luke is armed, violent and dangerous.

February 1. Tonight's reading and comment was on Psalm 55:22. 'Cast your burden on the LORD and He shall sustain you; He shall never permit the righteous to be moved.' Thy burden is uniquely yours; no person has exactly the same weight of responsibility and care as you...Jesus promises not the total removal of the burden, but His unfailing strength and support.'

Jane prayed, holding my hand, in tears. Lord it was the most meaningful, real, personal prayer experience with another I've ever had; again she reminded me that she will always love me. We have to write a letter explaining why we are okay with having no contact with Tyler in any form but totally disagree with his reasons and why we cannot make that first hearing.

February 4. Lord as I floated on my bit of Sea I thought and wondered – I 'should' be stressed and anxious; I 'should' feel this about what Tyler is doing. I am sad for him but I feel peaceful? When I examine this it seems foreign and yet so right if trusting You. You already know the next court date. You already know if Alan is going to be served next (he had asked me if he may be!). In some ways Luke and I have to go thru the needed motions but all is in Your hands I don't see how it can be 'good' but then I don't have too because **You tell me** it is!

February 10. Have been reading the commentary, *Mathew*[40] 'Fear is the emotion we express when faced with something stronger than we are and more threatening than our resources... anything which threatens to be over our head is under HIS feet.'

Fear is what I have felt again with Joe back telling Murray that Ty will be in police custody in a couple of hours, back in Ally's life and nice. I know because the past has taught me well that I have no power strong enough to protect myself from Joe, he almost destroyed me once and I gave him permission to treat me that way so I know, so I fear. BUT I am forgetting what God did then and can, will again. If I but thank Him and trust Him and His promises to keep me and live in light of this nothing that is not 'good' will touch me.

February 22. Reading Deuteronomy 7:78, and thinking on the phrase – '...but because the LORD loved you....' And a quote from J.E.Hall – 'The love that Jesus had for me, to suffer on the cruel tree, that I a ransomed soul might be, is more than tongue

---

40   Charles Price. Matthew. Can anything good come out of Nazareth? Focus on the Bible Commentary Series. Christian Focus Publications 1998. Pg.193-194.

can tell'.

Who am I, what am I that You the great LORD, the I AM should gaze at and consider? That You who only have to speak to make worlds and universes, chose to stoop to surround me with all Your passion and power that is far beyond anything else? That You would forsake everything that is Yours to be spat upon and jeered at to be made a mockery of by me and my kin to become the eternal One who died. Who am I, what am I? I am me.

March 1. I am so small and insignificant compared to the world and yet I am so important that God wanted me for His daughter, His Jewel. Amazing Love – not understandable fully even this side of the 'fence' so how can an unbeliever understand? Remember I thought Lil talked nonsense, was a bit weird!

March 2. Ally tells us that 'Joe told her Tyler had served orders against everyone who had done so to him.' Luke pointed out later I 'was not in the 'everyone'. Not sure what to make of this, or how to feel.

March 6. Court. The 'group' were there, Joe, his mum, brother and wife – who I'd once been very close to, and my brother and his wife. I sat apart with Luke till he had to go and put more money in the parking meter. I was invisible to my brother, he and Joe were as Joe's mum and Murray's wife, in one another's laps almost.

I felt a violating betrayal, my body began to tremble and I 'hid' on the steps. I wanted to run. A Salvo, a male came and sat with me. Hoping for the comfort of him speaking scripture I told him I was a Christian; disappointingly I only got very lame worldly jokes. I was relieved when Luke came back; his shoulder was warm and safe.

My parent's names were on the list. Mum had told me they'd decided not to put an order against Ty, not to be in the 'group'. I was glad they were not there. I felt devastated for Ty to see all his family standing together against him, I was glad he did not show. Luke and I were called in after the others. The 'group' had come out with their legal representative, arms waving and heads together in heated discussions. We sat and listened after giving our names. The Judge ruled 'granted till further orders'. I had to ask the lady at the desk what this meant as we had no legal representative. 'Forever, unless I decide to reapply to the Courts to change it.' Not the 12 months I was looking for -- forever Lord? Tyler cannot contact me ever again**, never**? How will I ever know if he has changed, if it would be safe for us to apply to change the order? Never Lord...not what I wanted him to be served with, Oh Lord why?

March 8. I feel as if I get one more rock, weight of sadness in my heart I will **drown.** I cannot think too much. I talk as though it's not happening to the 'real' me; it's too much Lord at present. Just have to 'wait' on You. Never Lord? And what of my parents, of mum saying they were not and yet their names were there – I'm tired of the games, I'm tired of my bloody family, not supporting, being there for me. I want nothing ever to do with them again Lord. So, my last memory of seeing my son is him roaring past our house, finger up yelling obscenities. Forever....

March 16. Local paper had a piece on Domestic violence, defining this sort of abuse as 'broad but includes behaviour that is physical or sexually abusive, emotionally and psychologically abusive, economically abusive, threatening or coercive or in any way controls or dominates a family member that makes them fear for their wellbeing.....' Oh, well that's pretty clear and conclusively damming.

March 25. Interstate Lawyer rang; Tyler did not show so the order against Luke was thrown out. Luke 'felt a bit sorry for Ty, he felt that Ty needed to have had this. '

We gave thanks for God's visible hand in all of this. We were away from home so dependent on a neighbour opening and reading over the phone any 'important' looking mail; on 'picking' from the Yellow Pages an interstate Lawyer that would 'hear' us. We did not want Tyler in any more trouble but we did not want Luke described that way. He seemed to be familiar with this matter, as Tyler's name had come up in the court lists there. We did not ask why. We had also prayed for one who would not rip us off financially. He actually charged us less than quoted as he had not needed all the work he'd done when Ty did not show. We had not wanted to have to travel that distance as it would have taken several days by car. He had also been able to make our absence accepted by the courts there.

March 26. Reading *'Living on the Ragged Edge'*.[41] 'Ecclesiastes 6:10. Isaiah 45:9-12. Daniel 4:35. God's Sovereignty. God what have You done? (Or my question, what are You doing?) 'I have done My Will'...So long as I fight the hand of God I do not learn the lessons He is attempting to place before me. Everything that touches me comes through the hand of my Heavenly Father who <u>continues to love me,</u> who <u>continues to maintain control</u> of my life, who <u>continues to be totally responsible</u> for my life as He does with all His created things...That's why he is God!...When I find myself getting anxious again it is usually because the size of mankind has gotten greater than the size of my God. The horizontal has overshadowed the vertical...and I have momentarily lost sight of who is still on the throne!' (Underlining by me)

I needed the reminder, Thank You. Help me to give You Ty and all my pain and worry about him to You and to Thank You for peace and contentment about this 'relationship,' this part of my life, heart without guilt. – I do not have to understand God's will (why God?). I just have to trust Him because I **know** His love and care of me.

The Easter Convention at Tree Tops this year, for the first time ever, created a huge conflict within me, causing upset and confusion and questioning my relationship with God. I write of remembering coming away with the following 'lesson' – 'I'm not a mature Christian as not educated in how to read and understand biblically, so I am not worshiping the true God of the Bible, not reading the Word rightly, not understanding His electing' -- so a speaker, a Principal of a Bible College, told me when I spoke to him, questioning what I had heard, wanting clarification, hoping he had not said what I thought I'd heard. But he had.

So who have I been worshiping? Do I want to worship this God this speaker talked about? No! But do I have a choice? Probably not. Trapped. No joy or comfort in my skin being saved but having no hope for loved ones. Do I love more than God?

---

41 Charles R. Swindoll Living on the ragged edge. Coming to terms with reality. Word Publishing 1985. Pgs. 182-183.

April 11. Thinking on and off about what I heard over Easter and about God and denominations and the people who have it 'all' worked out and are 'safe' regardless. Who am I Lord to question those who are so educated? What does the quote 'heresy is truth taken to its logical conclusion' in the context of an article on Predestination and Calvinism say about me? Am I a heretic because my 'logical' conclusion is that those not 'elected' must be hell bound? Why does this keep coming up Lord, what do You want me to do?

April 29. Mathew 18:34. '...unless you are converted and become as little children ... humbles ...as ...child......' (Underlining etc. by me) '<u>become **as**</u>'...Lord help me to do so, to rely more fully on Your desire as my Father to provide, protect, take worries, burdens, to trust without thinking, to 'do' for, to depend on as a child unthinkingly does of their Father. Later on I got thinking – do consequences really matter, should I really fear them for Ty and Ally and self? No, they are not eternal, You are bigger. As with the story I read yesterday, the murderer was still executed for his crimes but went to heaven as he'd become a believer – so did his consequences <u>really</u> matter? And what of the thief being crucified who Christ told He would be seeing in Paradise?

May 1. After a person in general conversation at my work said 'thank God' in regards to a loved one recovering well from surgery they looked directly at me and asked, 'Is there really a God?' 'Yes, there really is a God', I answered. This is the first time I can remember ever being asked so directly, Thanks Lord.

One day during work in June I became involved in a discussion with a very 'Aussie' looking Australian who had become a Buddhist, and planned to travel overseas to deepen his knowledge and ability to 'empty himself', to be instructed by a master. I discovered I did not have answers for his counter replies to my statements. His God was mine, as both believed in resurrection which is the same as reincarnation, both were for peace and holiness and both demanded 'works'. In my head I knew he was not right, yet my inability to speak that and show his erroneous thinking rattled me; this and the messages from the speaker at convention that were still rolling around in my head deeply unsettled me. The following entries for this month may show you my dear Reader a little of the struggle within –

June 23. John 7:1-24. Settle and remain unmoved, accept nothing less but realize all that Jesus faced as a result will be yours. All the way no matter what – remember Lisa!

June 25. Thoughts – The same temptation comes in many 'costumes' For example – 'the cost is too high; do you really need to pay it? The whole thing is a huge con! Look at how you are 'threatened' if don't do as commanded! Who says it is for real? Others are just as passionate and convinced that what they believe is right, are you trying to say they are wrong? You're not educated properly to correctly understand the Bible and so know the God of the Bible, who He really is, what He really asks.....'

Okay, so who is my God? Has God really said? (Gen.3:1!) Which God? Does it matter? Enter DOUBT! Enter questions of your ability. Yours without the Spirit or yours with the Spirit, to rightly judge, discern, understand, your logic. Enter Satan. Again. Shift focus. 'Noise', is louder than Spirit's whisper. John 9:30-33 REMEMBER!

June 27. REMEMBER! Last year's speaker at Summer Convention had said, 'you can be doing the motions of being 'alive' yet be spiritually dead. 'Proof' of spiritual life is the hunger or appetite.' Remember the shopping bags full of Mills and Boon books swapped for bags of Christian literature, none of which was fictional or romance! 'Can have all the education for your doctrine to be right but no presence of the Spirit within.' was something else he said. Oh God let me see You and hear You, feel You anew. Wake me up. I am fearful of where I've been going.

June 28. Hebrews 13:9. – 'Do not be concerned about various and strange doctrines. For it is good that the heart be established by grace, not with foods which have not profited those who have been occupied with them.'

I wonder how wrong I would be but the desire to replace the word 'foods' with the word 'doctrines' is there. If right then this verse is speaking of what I've been doing! How I've insulted and hurt God and Christ, my Companion and Helper by calling God and His Word a 'con'. What dangerous ground I've been treading, playing with ideas and words is not good, STOP! Lord help after You forgive me yet again. Mercy vast and free – Oh how wonderful, how amazing!

June 30. Interstate on holiday, at church. One reading was 2Thess.3:3. –'But the Lord's faithful. He will strengthen you and protect you from the evil one.'

Sermon was from Genesis 21:1-21. 'Is walking with God good or best?' I was listening but not much as knew this 'story' or so I thought till the Minister started applying – then I heard, listened and considered. Oh boy LORD when You want my attention You do grab it!

'Verses 1-2 – 25years of trusting for promise (kids), doubt of goodness and faithfulness. Shame and frustration. Wrestled till believed. Don't let go, be a Jacob. Choices. Good vs. bad, easy. What about good vs. best? Which is best? We learn this thru what we choose.

Verse 9. Mocking is equal to expressing hatred. Verse 11 Abraham is caught in the middle, they are both his sons. Last time God said they were to stay, this time they are to go. There are ongoing effects of choices. Galatians shows there are two ways of relating to God; our strength/self vs. God's/faith, slave vs. free.

The good way is okay, logically achievable but is also the one we can do without God.

The best way is often scary, crazy, or illogical as it is the way of faith, God promises to take care of, protect and provide.

Which choice forces me to trust God more? Individual choice as another person facing the same can choose differently, no two people have the same faith struggle.'

Thoughts – leave marriage (first one that is!), put Tyler into care, get involved with and marry Luke, ask Ally to leave, intervention order against Ty, stay faithful to my God.....All forced me to trust God.

July 1. Tonight's reading – '1Cor.10:13 – 'No temptation has overtaken you except such as is common to man: but God is faithful, who will not allow you to be tempted beyond what you are able, but with the temptation will also make the way of escape, that you may be able to bear it.' Many of us go through trials and testings and some have sorrowful feelings unknown to even those dearest to us. At times the problems appear 'one step too far'. Being on the edge leaves you with a feeling (as the apostle Paul had) that to be with Christ would be far better! Be patient, wait on God, and the reality of the 'escape route' will be shown you.'

Thinking about the '<u>way</u> of escape' interesting. Sometimes nothing changes, no new direction or change in the clouds or weight and yet everything is different deep inside, though outwardly still heavily cloaked. Accept this without questioning and analysing, this is your escape route!

July 28. Reading an article in a Church magazine – 'Martin Luther, critic of the Church around 1521 – earnestly, persistently taught justification by faith alone and the supremacy of Scripture's authority said – 'unless therefore I am convinced by the testimony of Scripture or by the clearest reasoning – unless I am persuaded by means of the passages I have quoted – and unless they thus render my conscience bound by the Word of God I cannot and I will not retract, for it is unsafe for a Christian to speak against his conscience...there I stand I can do no other: May God help me! Amen.'

My thoughts – I believe that teaching a Christian who is prayerfully relying on the Holy Spirit's guidance and instruction, not to trust their feelings or conscience may not be a good thing. I had taken this on from 'educated' men and lost my direction to the extent I was questioning the importance of scripture as compared with anything else out there taught by man.

Go back. Remember with the emotions of the time what you were before you called out to God and what happened after calling out and never let anyone take from you as 'not real and authentic' what you <u>know</u> of God that <u>He</u> has shown you in your 'closet'. He is real. His word is truth. It works. It is relevant. It happens. Go against what he has shown you, what you know and you have nothing, for there is nothing. Choices. Choose. I choose what I have been taught of Him by God, His Spirit and His Word.

THE MAKING OF A JEWEL

What I know by experiences that He has given and taken me through and how He has opened up His Words to me.

## Epilogue

It now seems a lifetime ago since these events occurred.

Ally's relationship with David ended. There was another confused and sad child who could not understand why Mummy and Daddy were no longer bestfriends. Both moved on to new partners and more children. Years later Ally talked of how she would go into the bedroom to find him trying to hang himself because they'd had a fight or inject himself with an overdose of insulin as she watched because she disagreed with him. Domestic violence comes in a lot of colours.

Tyler? Well forever is a long time, an unbearable long time for a mother. If I allow myself to wonder the heaviness of the load is too much to live with alone. And there are friends of Ally's saying that he may have a child....

In some ways a story of one's life journey here does not end till death ushers us into our eternity, so there is always additions, more to say.

While editing this book I became aware that there seemed to be an error of thought within some entries you my dear Reader have waded through. And so I felt it was only right to share this new thought with you so you could ponder with me what it teaches and how this could change one's view of God.....

I had been reading Hebrews 12 and considering the word 'chastening', see verses 5 – 11. Punishment was a word I thought I was familiar with, and I thought chastisement was sort of the same thing, having often felt that God was punishing me for my past sins by all that was going 'wrong'. But today for some reason my thinking did not sit right, so out came the Oxford Dictionary.....

<u>Punish.</u> Cause (offender) to suffer (by or with a penalty, for offence), inflict penalty on (offender); inflict penalty for (offence)......

<u>Penalty</u>. Punishment, esp. Payment of sum of money, for breach of law, rule, or contract....

BUT this is what Jesus the Christ has already done for me on the Cross. In Him, I have no penalty to pay, God cannot punish me further.

<u>Chastisement</u>. Discipline, punish by inflicting suffering; moderate; restrain, subdue.....

<u>Discipline</u>. Branch of instruction or learning; mental and moral training, adversity as effecting this......bring under control, train to obedience and order....

Check out Proverbs 3:11-12 – ' Do not despise the chastening of the LORD' nor detest His correction: for whom the LORD loves He corrects, just as a father the son in whom he delights.'

So, punishment to discipline from Abba was not to leave me feeling more selfrottenness and uselessness but to aid in building me, lifting me up higher. I, myself, by allowing Satan a foot hold was punishing me, keeping me wallowing in all that was not good and edifying. When God disciplines you *will* know why and grow better for it.

As well as this I also realised that I had almost crossed a line so busy was I with comparing self with others that I was in danger of pushing my LORD out of my centre, of not finding full satisfaction and contentment in Him alone. Of being in danger of being more desperate, more thirsty, for a glimpse of my son than His!

All proving I am still a work in progress. Still in need of Your refining; of repentance and forgiveness; of Your mercies which are new every morning that You give me.

Oh, for the day when all my facets are fully cut and radiantly shining. Maybe one does occasionally now and then but there is still a long way to go till this Jewel is perfected so I press onwards and upwards – All the way no matter what, my Yahweh. Just bring me home please.

For the LORD is faithful. He has 'set my feet upon a rock and established my steps' (Ps.40:2). I feel as though I'm living proof of Peter's words, that the God of all grace after I'd suffered a while, (and though He was still perfecting me, meaning I'd still face troubles and suffering), He has established, strengthened and settled me.(1Pt.5:10)

By His sufficient forever grace I can with trembling (for as J. I. Packer writes -- 'only those who 'walk in the light', seeking to be like God in holiness and righteousness of life, and eschewing everything inconsistent with this, enjoy fellowship with the Father and the Son; those who 'walk in darkness', whatever they may claim for themselves, are strangers to this relationship...... 'God is love' is the complete truth about God so far as the Christian is concerned') declare the truth of Romans 8:28, as expounded by J. I. Packer but personalised by me – 'that all things work together for good to them that love God and are called according to His purpose (Rom.8:28). Not just some things, note but all things! Every single thing that happens to (me) expresses God's love to (me), and comes to (me) for the furthering of God's purpose for (me). Thus, so far as (I am) concerned, God is love to (me) – holy, omnipotent love – at every moment and in every event of every day's life. Even when (I) cannot see the why and the wherefore of God's dealings, (I know) that there is love in and behind them, and so (I) can rejoice always, even when, humanly speaking, things are going wrong (very, terribly wrong!), (I know) that the true story of (my) life, when known, will prove to be, as the hymn says, 'mercy from first to last' – and (I am) content.' [42]

How about you my dear Reader? Are you content? How's your soul?

I'm going to make a cuppa.....Bye.

---

42    J. I. Packer Knowing God. Hodder and Stoughton 1973. Pgs. 134-135

# THE MAKING OF A JEWEL

## *Additional bits and pieces*

Ponder the following quote from an unknown source – 'What people fail to understand is that significance is measured by an eternal value. Significance given to us on earth will never do. People can be so fickle. Popularity can come and go. Relationships can fail. Jobs can be won and lost. Money, health are fleeting. Sport only lasts for a time. But – if we are significant to the Creator and Ruler of the universe who has given us a certain amount of honour and who unconditionally loves, accepts, cares for me now and forever having seen me at my worst and still loved me to the point of giving His life for me – then that kind of significance is something the world can never offer. It is that kind of significance you find in the Lord Jesus who for your sake and mine was made a little lower than the angels but who is now crowned with honour and glory because He tasted death for you that you might live forever and ever with Him!

Now my dear Reader, I would like to share with you some rather lengthy – sorry! -- segments from a couple of books that I read after most of the diary entries you've read, which I found to be very challenging yet affirmingly encouraging --

'Develop the picture of your worth and value from God, not from the false reflections that come out of your past....

What right have you to belittle or despise someone whom God *loves* so deeply?.... "Well, I know God loves me, but I just can't stand myself." That's a travesty of faith, an insult to God and His love It is the expression of a subtly hidden resentment against your Creator...

What right have you to belittle or despise someone whom God has *honoured* so highly?.... (1Jn.3:12)...Do you think that when you consider God's son or daughter worthless or inferior, He is pleased by your socalled humility?

What right have you to belittle or despise someone whom God *values* so highly? .... (Rom.5:78)...God has declared your value. You are someone whom God values so highly as to give the life of His own Son to redeem you.

What right have you to belittle or despise someone whom God *provided* for so fully? .... (Matt.7:11.Phil.4:19) This doesn't sound as if He wants you to be selfloathing or to feel inadequate.

What right have you to belittle or despise someone whom God has *planned* for so carefully? ..... (Eph.1:35)

What right have you to belittle or despise someone in whom God? ... (Eph.1:6...Matt.3:17)......

Let God love you and let Him teach you how to love yourself and how to love others. You want love. You want God to affirm and accept you and that's what He does. But because of wretched programming from the other sources, it is difficult to accept love. In fact, it is so hard that you may think it is more comfortable to go on the way you are.[43]

If I have no right, has anyone else other than God?

The following extracts are from *Healing the Scars of Emotional Abuse*[44] –

Emotional abuse is harder to spot and easier to deny....
.....Emotional abuse is the consistent pattern of being treated unfairly and unjustly over a period of time, usually by the same person or people. It can also be a onetime traumatic event that is left unresolved. Emotional abuse is an intentional assault by one person on another to so distort the victim's view of self that the victim allows the abuser to control him or her.....

....it is vital not to measure abuse on a scale of 'bad' to 'worse'. (Woops! I did this in the Preface, pg.2) Rather, it is important to acknowledge its presence, whether in the past or the present. Emotional abuse always accompanies physical or sexual

---

43    David A. Seamands. Healing for Damaged Emotions. Recovering from the Memories that cause our Pain. Chariot Victor Publishing. 1991. Taken from Part 2 Healing our low selfesteem. Pgs. 73-75.
44    Gregory L. Jantz, PhD with Ann McMurray Healing the scars of emotional abuse. Revell 2009 Pages as listed following quotes.

abuse but stands fully on its own as damaging and destructive to an individual.....

Attempting to minimise their abuse is one of the chief denial techniques developed to survive emotionally through the abuse.....

....I have found that when people suspect they were abused, in most cases they were. If the relationship you had in the past or the one you have now is with a person or people who consistently make you feel worthless you are being abused....

Of course, not all relationships are perfect, and people say or do things in anger that they regret later. But if those things are a pattern, and if they are used to degrade and control, no matter how subtle they may seem or how much the other person tells you they are really for 'your own good' in truth they are abuse......

.....Many of the types of abuse identified in this book will take the form of a message – the spoken and unspoken messages passed on to you as a child that constitute the basic structure of your selfidentity and selfesteem.... .....Whether you were emotionally abused as a child or an adult, the messages were meant to belittle, devalue, shame and ultimately control. Additionally, if these messages were given by the very people you looked to for love and guidance, the very ones whose opinions you trusted, they have been given the appearance of validity and have added weight.....the ultimate goal of emotional abuse is control.........

...Kindness, compassion, empathy and affection may not have been characteristics you grew up observing, and therefore you did not have the chance to model them fully in your adult life. If you were raised in an abusive environment and realize you are perpetuating that environment, it is possible to intentionally alter the way you relate to yourself and others. The first step is knowledge – knowing how harmful your behaviours are to those you love and to yourself, can provide you with the motivation to make positive changes. (Pgs.12 – 15)

Signs of emotional abuse – Making the person feel worthless; Putting the blame for one's mistakes on the other person; Minimizing the other person's point of view; Threatening or hinting of physical or sexual abuse; Going into fits of rage or anger;

Failing to fulfil commitments or promises made or implied; Lying to avoid responsibility for the truth; Refusing to acknowledged the other person's feelings; Verbally or physically humiliating the other person through inappropriate gestures, comments, or 'jokes'; Using shame or guilt to manipulate the actions of the other person; Not allowing the person to articulate his or her feelings; Denying the person access to his or her personal possessions or pets; Withholding financial resources; Refusing to communicate with the other person – the silent treatment; Displaying extreme ranges of mood; Making conditional agreements in which the conditions keep changing to avoid fulfilling the agreement; Using a hostile or sarcastic tone of voice with the other person; Being critical of each action, thought, or remark of the other person; Viewing others as a part of that person's own personality as opposed to individuals with their own thoughts, feelings, and opinions; Belittling, humiliating, marginalizing, and/or ignoring the other person.

God can rebuild.

At the most basic level Emotional Abuse robs you of your sense of security and value this leads to an ever present feeling of anxiety or fear.

The oppressive anxiety and fear you feel must have a reason… (this) varies: you are bad, stupid, ugly or unwanted or you are the wrong sex, age or whatever. No matter what reason is provided, you are to blame…You are guilty of causing the abuse.

False guilt is an oppressive burden that is not based on reality but on the warped views, ideas and attitudes of others. Emotional abuse transfers those warped views onto you…. produce mindnumbing, actionparalysing shame….

Hand in hand with false guilt is false hope – hope that if they are just good enough, thin enough, bright enough or hardworking enough the abuse will stop and the people who are supposed to love them will finally start acting in a loving way. (Pgs. 38 – 41)

When security is gone, when fear must be dealt with on a daily basis, when the oppressive weight of guilt and shame crushes the spirit, when hope is extinguished in the rush of despair, often the only way to respond is with anger…. Often in the abused person this anger is directed inward. Presented daily with 'proof' of total unworthiness the emotionally abused can turn the frustration on themselves.... Having no other outlet it is released on their own bodies. The physical pain they feel becomes a way of purging their allconsuming anger and emotional pain. (pg.43)

It is said depression is only anger turned inward. It takes a great deal of energy to deal with Emotional Abuse and stay buoyant. Some people simply run out of strength to climb the mound of abuse heaped upon them, they slip into the pit of depression. Unable to escape from anger, fear, shame and guilt they attempt to shut down all of their emotions, with no visible way out they curl into themselves, isolating themselves from others and imploding their world. (Pgs.43-44)

A tremendous feeling of rage is characteristic of those who are abused. For the most part it is kept tightly locked away out of sight. To let it escape would mean to face the rancid reality of failed hope, so it stays tightly controlled year after year, bound and hidden while the rest of the personality makes the transition from child to adult. (Pg.45)

<u>Emotional abuse through words</u>
Through their words and tone of voice, they imprint messages on the minds of those who hear. These messages, repeated often and forcefully, infiltrate to the inner being of their victims, shaping the way they view themselves....there are several distinct methods the emotional abuser can use to dispense his or her abuse....

The Overbearing Opinion.... Restricts the flow of free expression, treating his or her opinions and feelings as if they were as incontrovertible as facts. The personality of the abuser is superimposed onto the abused, stifling the abused's ability to bloom on his or her own...

The Person Who Is Always Right... Events are constantly being turned around in his or her favour....you may also begin to believe that your abuses has been right all along...you begin to second guess your ability to make decisions, for they never seem to be the right ones.

The Judge and Jury...not only make the decisions, they also

make the laws. What might be a reason for doing something on Monday may cease to be a reason on Tuesday....the judgeandjury abusers use the obedience of others not for good or safety but for their own comfort or control.

The PutDown Artist ...Some of the most destructive abusers are people who habitually put down another person through their words...If you are a victim... you learn to suspect all relationships... this form... is the verbal equivalent of a physical beating...

The StandUp Comic...the butt of his jokes is always you...if you are the only one who isn't laughing, there must be something wrong with you...this type of abuse can leave a deep sense of outrage at being used for another person's pleasure...Often the only defence against this type of abuse is to become a clown yourself, beating your abuser to the punch by beating up on yourself...

The Great Guilt Giver...the weight of the guiltgiver comes on a brick at a time, just long enough for you to adjust to the weight before another one is added....year after year, message after message, remark after remark. Usually not delivered in haste or loudly, but with a sigh, with a sad, disappointed look that communicates that you are the cause of all his or her problems. If it weren't for you, life would be so much better.

If you were emotionally abused in this way, you may feel as if you have no importance to your abuser. In fact, you may feel as if the abuser's life would be so much better if you weren't around to mess it up. Nothing could be further from the truth.

For guiltgivers, the most important person in the world is the one on whom they heap their guilt. Without you, they would be responsible for their own failures....they have chosen to shift responsibility from themselves onto you....With you feeling guilty and at fault, there is always away for you to 'make it up' to the person you have 'harmed'........

The Preacher...They don't so much communicate with other people as preach at them...They use these 'sermons' as a way to pontificate on the faults of the person specifically and the world in general....

The Historian ... view of the past is decidedly onesided... dangerous because seem to be presenting facts. They back up those facts with details...But often the 'facts being presented are actually the abuser's opinion of what you said and why....Their manipulation of the past helps them to control people in their present and future.

The Silent Treatment Abuser....The silence, the loss of verbal relationship, is meant to exact an emotional toll on the other person, who often will go to great lengths to attempt to restore communication with the abuser. This level of control is precisely what the abuser is looking for, as well as a way to vent his or her anger at the other person. By not verbally expressing that anger, by 'avoiding' showing anger, the abuser is allowed to feel as if the victim is the only person at fault for whatever wrong is perceived by the abuser...

Turn Up the Tape. Verbal abuse is like a tape recorder that never stops playing....You hear the words in your head whether you want to or not.... Really listen to what those messages are saying to you, find out when they were recorded and by whom, and begin to erase them by taping over them with positive, uplifting, encouraging messages of selfesteem and selfworth that come through healthy relationships. (Pgs.61-79)

<u>Emotional Abuse through actions</u>

...through actions that accompany those words, such as physical intimidation, manipulation and physical threats.....They attempt to control not only behaviour but circumstances as well.... The abuser may lash out at objects or smash possessions out of rage...may withhold needed items or resources dispassionately out of cold calculation. In every incident of physical or sexual abuse, emotional abuse is present. Emotional abuse, however, can be present without overt physical harm. Yet danger lies in the escalating nature of emotional abuse. If someone is accustomed to abusing you emotionally, physical abuse is never far away.

The Commander in Chief .... consistency and order, but laughter and spontaneity.. rare... physical discipline but physical affection rare. Life is not something to be enjoyed but something to be controlled....When ideas and opinions are supressed, emotional avenues are stopped up...

The Ventaholic ...is like a volcano that erupts in violent fits whenever the pressures of life get to be too much... robs those around them of any sense of peace...., produces an overwhelming fear of imminent disaster. Never safe, never secure always on guard....better to shut up and take it, better to stuff your own anger that add it to the mix.

The Intimidator ... "If you....then I" the classic words of intimidators. Their control over your behaviour is always issued in the form of a threat. Sometimes ..delivered at the top of their lungs. Other times slipped into conversation on the wings of a whisper. However it is given, the threat is understood....can be of two types: the ones who are all talk with no real consequences behind their words or the ones who mean every word and back it up with action....

The Rollercoaster ....The types of abuse talked about so far have been ones of consistency...Roller coasters are just the opposite....The only thing constant about them is their inconsistency....it is a rollercoaster ride in the dark. You just hang on for dear life and shift whenever you can. The upanddown mood swings of the roller coaster rob those around him or her of any sense of peace. The house is not a haven; booby traps are everywhere. Safety and security can be found only outside the home....

The Dr. Jekyll and Mr. Hyde ...Concealment, deception, gentleness in public but harshness in private... When we deny certain aspects of our personality, we experience fragmentation. When...taken to the extreme, it leads to the compartmentalizing of all life's activities... when I'm in public I can only act and feel this way, but when I'm in private I can do whatever I want.... When I'm in public I'll show that I love you, but in private I'll prove it's a lie..... Living with a Jekyll and Hyde means living a life of secrets. No one must know what your private life is really like...

The Illusionist... are generally highly intelligent, charismatic people who thrive on being seen well by others. As long as there is an audience they are 'on'…Because it takes a great deal of energy to be 'on', their 'off' persona may be the exact opposite.... Being in relationship with an illusionist can cause you to doubt your own judgement. Because illusionists are generally highly intelligent, they are able to convince you, even in the face of contrary evidence, that the concerns you have are invalid. If there is a problem you are always portrayed as the source. Feigning confusion they appear shocked that you find their behaviour unusual. If you ask other people, people who have seen only the carefully constructed illusion you may not get validation of your concerns. Instead you may hear a reiteration of how wonderful the illusionist is. Your reality of events and circumstances is constantly denied, down played, explained away or rejected....

This is a pernicious form of emotional abuse in that it causes the abused to second guess his or her own assessment of the relationship and the circumstances surrounding the relationship. As such, many will stay in the relationship for an extended period of time until their ability to help their abuser maintain the illusion demands too greater an emotional toll. At this point the abused person will leave but with her sense of self seriously tattered. After all how could anyone leave such a great person? Because others have not seen through this illusion the abused person who leaves can appear to be in the wrong....

The Person Who Plays Favourites.... Few things are as devastating to a child as the realization that her parents love a sibling more than her.... Children are not stupid. They can sense it even when the parent does not. Desperately they attempt to figure out what is wrong with them. The reasons they come up with can cause lifelong damage to selfesteem.....

The Role Reverser....Often the most familiar use of the role reverser is in sexual situations, in which the parent, often the father, will put onto his daughter the role of lover…daughter takes on the role of the wife....When this abuse take an emotional form, it is often very subtle. Parent and child may appear to the outsider as having a very loving relationship. People may comment on how close the two of them are....emotional incest.....needs are unmet. A child needs to be a child, to have a parent to look to for guidance and example...

The Empty Promiser...Even if the other person fulfils some sort of imposed condition on their compliance, they find a way to renege at the last minute...teaches children the lie that word's don't really mean anything, that words can be used to manipulate other people to do what we want, and that we don't have to live up to our promises..... When we fail to live up to our promises we teach those around us that we don't value them enough to follow thru.

The Wrath-of-God Abuser.....(has) to stop shouting long enough to listen...stop feeling sorry and start feling forgiven...stop viewing his heavenly Father as an awesome representation of his earthly one – full of righteous anger with no healing grace.... God should never be used to diminish your sense of self. Religion should not strip away your selfworth; at best it should contribute to your selfidentity. (Pgs.83-105)

<u>Emotional Abuse through neglect</u>

As damaging as the other types of emotional abuse ate, it is the *absence* of the expected, of the needed, that wounds. .... 'the silent treatment'. It was as total a withdrawal as possible of one person from another. For whatever reason, the abuser withholds relationship from the other person......According to Dr. Bruce D. Perry, an internationally recognised authority on brain development, 'During the first three years of life, the human brain develops to 90percent of adult size and puts in place the majority of systems and structures that will be responsible for all future emotional, behavioural, social, and psychological functioning during the rest of life.'...The tragedy..is that it can take place in homes where physical needs are met, even extravagantly met. Children need more than food on the table and a roof over their heads....When emotional needs are not met, children have difficulty progressing developmentally....

The MIA Parent

...most often in fathers...marginal contact if any...No matter what other relationships are formed afterward, the one with an absent father never has a resolution....Worst of all is the suspicion that....you weren't special enough to him.....You cannot continue to make yourself responsible for his actions, to blame yourself for his leaving. Once you rid yourself of that guilt, you can begin to rebuild your sense of selfworth.

The Distant Caregiver

...aren't missing...aren't gone forever...just show up in spurts....It is dangerous to think that because a child is physically able to be away from the parent, he or she is well equipped to be emotionally apart as well. In distantcaregiver abuse, parents prematurely withdraw themselves emotionally from their child..... such action is abusive, for it denies children the emotional anchor from which they can explore their own identity....

The Emotionally Detached Parent

....(the child may) never been allowed to be a child...never been allowed to expect or even demand attention, affection and validation from ..toobusy parents. pgs. 110-119)

There comes a time...when our physical bodies say. 'Enough.' This is especially true of the stresses produced through constantly undergoing feelings of anger, fear, shame, and guilt, for these emotions exact a physical toll.....Our bodies are God's gift to us to enjoy and use to accomplish his purpose for our lives. Taking cae of yourself isn't a luxury. It isn't indulgent or selfish. It's necessary. And you are worth living a life of good health and joy. (Pgs. 184 & 186)

If your most fundamental relationships include emotional abuse, that abuse will hinder your attempts to build healthy, positive relationships with yourself, with others, and with God. It is possible, though, to rebuild intimacy in your key relationships through understanding and accepting your true self. (Pg. 189)

A time to Heal

An understanding of who you truly are comes from the One who created you in the first place.

Emotional abuse steals away your identity. It sucks up all of the wonderful, positive characteristics of your true nature and seeks to replace them with false truths and negative images....It is wrong.....It may have taken society a while to appreciate and speak out against how wrong emotional abuse is, but God has always known.

As your creator, God knows who you are. God loves you for who you are, even if you were not loved by others in the past and even if you have difficulty loving yourself now. While others were abusing your fragile sense of self, your secret self has always been safe with God....Psalm 139:118...... 'Wherewas God when I was being abused?' The answer is found in Psalm 139 – even in the midst of the abuse, God was there to guide them and hold them fast....Who you are is safe in Him.. It doesn't matter how far your abuse has taken you, it is always possible for God to find you and bring you back to yourself....You are wonderful God says so! Therefore, it's time to evaluate your relationships through God's filter and seek to strengthen and maintain those that agree with God that you are 'fearfully and wonderfully made'....step by step, day by day...Remember, God already knows everything there is to know about you. In fact, he knows you better than you know yourself And yet He sent His Son to die for such as I – amazing Love! ....You can relax in his love and be yourself.... find time...whatever your other relationships, you must protect this time to grow with God, because it is vital for your recovery and healing....My prayer is that you will continue to heal from the scars of emotional abuse.

May you become a strong, resilient person who, through your experiences, develops an extra measure of compassion and empathy for the tremendous amount of pain in this world.

May you come to know yourself as God knows you, and to follow His love to greater love for yourself and others.

May you hold hope close to your heart as a promise and a gift from God. (Pgs. 277-284)

THE MAKING OF A JEWEL

www.ingramcontent.com/pod-product-compliance
Lightning Source LLC
Chambersburg PA
CBHW021138080526
44588CB00008B/115